The National Interest in International Relations Theory

Also by Scott Burchill

AUSTRALIA IN THE WORLD (*with Gary Smith and Dave Cox*)

THEORIES OF INTERNATIONAL RELATIONS, third edition (*with Andrew Linklater, Richard Devetak, Jack Donnelly, Matthew Paterson, Christian Reus-Smit and Jacqui True*)

The National Interest in International Relations Theory

Scott Burchill

Senior Lecturer in International Relations
Deakin University

First published 2005 by
PALGRAVE MACMILLAN
Houndmills, Basingstoke, Hampshire RG21 6XS and
175 Fifth Avenue, New York, N.Y. 10010
Companies and representatives throughout the world

PALGRAVE MACMILLAN is the global academic imprint of the Palgrave Macmillan division of St. Martin's Press, LLC and of Palgrave Macmillan Ltd. Macmillan® is a registered trademark in the United States, United Kingdom and other countries. Palgrave is a registered trademark in the European Union and other countries.

ISBN-13: 978–1–4039–4979–0
ISBN-10: 1–4039–4979–4

This book is printed on paper suitable for recycling and made from fully managed and sustained forest sources.

A catalogue record for this book is available from the British Library.

Library of Congress Cataloging-in-Publication Data
Burchill, Scott, 1961–
    The national interest in international relations theory / Scott Burchill.
        p.   cm.
    Includes bibliographical references and index.
    ISBN 1–4039–4979–4 (cloth)
    1. National interest.   I. Title.

JZ1320.3.B87 2005
327.1′01—dc22

2004065751

10   9   8   7   6   5   4   3   2
14   13   12   11   10   09   08   07   06

Printed and bound in Great Britain by
Antony Rowe Ltd, Chippenham and Eastbourne

This book is dedicated with love to my wife, Robyn Colegrave, and our two children Zoë and Callum.

Contents

Acknowledgements

I wish to acknowledge the intellectual support of Gary Smith, Andrew Linklater, Noam Chomsky and Gabriel Kolko. The word processing and editing skills of Daniel Flitton and Faris Mallouhi made the preparation of this manuscript considerably smoother than it otherwise would have been. I am also grateful to Alison Howson, Guy Edwards and Steven Kennedy at Palgrave Macmillan (UK) for their encouragement and professionalism. I was very fortunate to have Christine Ranft as the copy-editor for this book.

Matthew Mangan, the Managing Director of Australia Asia Centre for Education Exchange (AACE) has been a generous sponsor of my research. His philanthropy, encouragement and enthusiasm were essential ingredients in this publication and I remain very thankful for them.

Introduction

> Providence never intended to make the Management of publick Affairs a Mystery, to be comprehended only by a few Persons of sublime Genius, of which there seldom are three born in an Age.
>
> (Jonathan Swift, *Gulliver's Travels*)

> If citizens are to support the government which prosecutes it, soldiers are to die for it, and foreign policies are to conform to it, what could be more appropriate than to ask: What is national interest?
>
> (Charles A. Beard, *The Idea of National Interest*)

There have been two seminal analyses of the term 'the national interest' as it is used and understood in both the conduct of diplomacy and in the study of international politics.

The first, *The Idea of National Interest* by Charles A. Beard, was an historiographical inquiry into the use of the term in modern United States history and foreign policy up to the period of Roosevelt's New Deal in the 1930s (Beard 1934; 1966). In his investigation Beard traces the earliest claims made on behalf of the national interest back to sixteenth-century Italy and seventeenth-century England when 'reasons of state' (*raison d'état*), 'dynastic interests' and the 'will of the sovereign' began to lose their efficacy and were replaced by a term which more accurately reflected changes that were occurring in contemporary forms of political diplomacy (Beard 1934; 1966, pp. 21–6).

Beard's study is important because it explains how 'the national interest' as an idea and the rise of the nation-state as a modern form of political association were coterminous. Beard's detailed examination of US

1

diplomatic records reveals that the term gained currency in the very debates which ultimately framed the United States Constitution towards the end of the eighteenth century.

More controversially and with remarkable prescience for the future direction of research in International Relations, Beard examined the role played by national interest arguments in defending US commercial and territorial expansion in the nineteenth and early twentieth century. Anticipating discussions which would occur later between conservatives and radicals, realists and Marxists, Beard's account emphasised the extent to which the economic interests of certain groups within US society have, over time, been presented as those of the national interest of the United States. This is a critically important claim and one that is supported with extensive documentation and relevant case studies of US regional diplomacy.

Surprisingly, Beard's magisterial analysis has been largely forgotten and has been out of print for over four decades, a fact which belies its importance in the field but which might be explained by his personal experience of political hostility from Establishment quarters. Beard is perhaps best known for highlighting the economic self-interest of the 'founding fathers' as a factor in the drafting of the US Constitution: in the early twentieth century this was, at the very least, a controversial perspective. His approach to political analysis, which can be described as a non-Marxist materialist approach, was also used to explain the basis of US foreign policy during its early imperialist phase.

Beard described his book as 'an inquiry into the things and patterns of conduct covered by the formula "national interest"' in the modern historical experience of US diplomacy (Beard 1934; 1966, p. 28). From an International Relations viewpoint,[1] what is missing from Beard's analysis is a broader theoretical outline which can be applied to ways the national interest is constructed generally by nation-states, as well as an engagement with contending approaches which stress the autonomy of the state from the constituent groups which comprise it. Beard's account fails to acknowledge the existence of international theory which reflects directly on the subject matter of his analysis; his account is strictly historical and empirical. This book, in part, seeks to rectify this deficiency.

---

[1] The capitalisation of International Relations is used throughout to refer to the academic discipline. Lower case is used when the general domain of international politics is indicated.

In his seminal analysis *National Interest*, Joseph Frankel was conscious of just what an elusive concept 'the national interest' is (Frankel 1970). Much of his account comprises a range of definitional and category distinctions which remind us how ambiguous and contested the formula has been ever since its entry into the lexicon of foreign policy analysis and the study of international politics.

Arguably the most important division Frankel draws in his study is between those who use the national interest to explain and analyse the foreign policy of nation-states and those who employ the term to justify or rationalise state behaviour in the international realm. This cleavage is characterised as a split between *objectivists* who believe there are permanent objective criteria against which foreign policies can be evaluated, compared and contrasted, and *subjectivists* who emphasise the changing priorities and preferences of decision makers as well as the public defences and explanations of their actions (Frankel 1970, pp. 15–17).

According to Frankel, *objective* national interests are those which relate to a nation-state's ultimate foreign policy goals, independent of but discoverable by policy makers through systematic enquiry. These are permanent interests, comprising factors such as geography, history, neighbours, resources, population size and ethnicity. *Subjective* national interests are those which depend on the preferences of a specific government or policy elite, and include ideology, religion and class identity. These interests are based on interpretation and are subject to change as governments themselves alter.

Given that Frankel's account focuses primarily on the ingredients of decision-making in foreign policy and has a self-consciously behavioural slant rather than a philosophical or normative method (Frankel 1970, p. 27), this sort of distinction is important and meaningful. It is also a distinction preserved in more recent studies (George & Keohane 1980). From a constructivist perspective, for example, Jutta Weldes argues that 'the national interest' is important to international politics in two ways.

> First, it is through the concept of the national interest that policymakers understand the goals to be pursued by a state's foreign policy. It thus in practice forms the basis for state action. Second, it functions as a rhetorical device through which the legitimacy of and political support for state action is generated. The 'national interest' thus has considerable power in that it helps to constitute as important and to legitimise the actions taken by states. (Weldes 1996, p. 276)

The distinction enables Frankel to examine the aspirational and operational aspects of the term, to establish permanent criteria for comparison and to assess the human motivations behind international diplomacy. As an account of the geopolitical, cultural and psychological dimensions which come together to form 'the national interest' as an expression of foreign policy, Frankel's account has few if any peers.

In outlining the problems of methodology for such a project and his preference for behaviouralism, Frankel claims that 'unfortunately the theories of international relations supply no clues for our search of the meaning of national interest as a whole' (Frankel 1970, p. 27). This is an important remark in at least two respects. First, in contradiction to an earlier suggestion that the national interest is used in a variety of ways to achieve a range of purposes, Frankel seems to be implying here that there is a single meaning of the national interest which can be ultimately revealed. And secondly, Frankel argues that theories of international relations will shed little if any light on this task.

The primary purpose of this analysis is to challenge Frankel's claim by showing how the term 'the national interest' is variously understood within the major theoretical currents of the discipline of International Relations (IR). By examining how conventional (realism, liberalism), progressive (English School, constructivism) and critical (Marxism, anarchism) theories of international politics understand the concept of the national interest, it is possible to move beyond Frankel's primary concern with decision-making in foreign policy for the purpose of comparing and contrasting the foreign policies of nation-states.

The objective/subjective dichotomy which underlines Frankel's approach remains an important taxonomy and must be considered in any treatment of the subject. However, contextualising the concept with the well-established theoretical schools which constitute contemporary IR theory is a more sophisticated method of examining the national interest as an organising concept in international politics. It is an approach which refutes Frankel's claim that a study of the national interest cannot be theoretically and philosophically informed.

Within each theory of international politics, the national interest is a significant point of intellectual orientation: sometimes it is the very foundation of a theoretical approach (traditional realism) while in other cases it is a means to rationalise and mask decisions taken for a variety of other reasons (Marxism). It will be argued here that a survey of how the term is understood across the theoretical spectrum within International Relations reveals much that Frankel's methodology cannot. Even if the national interest has become a debased currency in recent years it remains in wide circulation, both in political and academic domains. It deserves a further examination, this time from the perspectives offered by leading contemporary theories of international politics.

One early attempt to do this was made by Martin Wight in his renowned lectures on international theory delivered at the London School of Economics in the 1950s when the discipline of International Relations was still in its adolescence. Despite the impact they had on students who attended them, these lectures were only published posthumously in 1991 (Wight 1991). One of them, devoted to 'theory of national interest', compares and contrasts the approaches of three groups – realists, revolutionists and rationalists – to the idea of the national interest. Although concise, limited in scope and underdeveloped, Wight's analysis constitutes an important beginning to any theoretical consideration of the concept. He uses both historical writings and current events (for the 1950s) to show the very different understandings of the national interest across the ideological and philosophical spectrum. His remarks will be used here as a useful starting point and an indicator of the direction needed for a broader and more detailed contemporary analysis of the discipline, particularly in the important distinction he makes between realist and rationalist perspectives.

How can we account for Joseph Frankel's pessimistic conclusion that 'theories of international relations supply no clues for our search of the meaning of national interest as a whole?' One answer is that at the time Frankel wrote his account, international theory remained comparatively impoverished. At the time, debates within the area were dominated by two approaches: realism and liberal-utopianism. Since the late 1960s, however, there has been enormous growth and development in the field which, in turn, provides new contexts for intellectual consideration of the national interest. A primary task of this analysis is to assess the extent to which contemporary international theory provides new insights into the political functions of the term.

A more specific explanation of Frankel's pessimism, however, springs from his definition of international relations theory in narrowly positivist terms.

We have grown accustomed to the idea of theories within the 'natural sciences', but for many like Frankel, the suggestion that the political and social worlds also lend themselves to theoretical inquiry is problematic. As one sceptic has noted, in the analysis of international relations, 'historical conditions are too varied and complex for anything that might plausibly be called "a theory" to apply uniformly' (Chomsky 1994, p. 120). If by theory the sceptic is referring to the levels of certainty and exactness, standards of proof and 'scientific rigour' normally associated with the 'physical' sciences, then he has a point when he claims that 'if there is a body of theory, well tested and verified, that applies to the conduct of foreign affairs or the resolution of domestic or international conflict, its existence has been kept a well guarded secret' (Chomsky 1969, p. 271).

There is a world of difference between the 'physical' and the 'social' sciences, and it is difficult to argue that the methodology of the former, with its emphasis on testable propositions and the production of falsifiable hypotheses, can be automatically applied to theoretical endeavours in the latter without serious problems arising (see Burchill 2001). Thus for Frankel, little of any scientific worth is likely to be revealed about the national interest by conventional, non-scientific theories of international politics. It may still be a 'social science' but only a behaviouralist approach which focuses tightly on foreign policy decision-making is likely to reveal anything meaningful about what is generally held to be the prime consideration of modern diplomacy.

Frankel's seminal account of the national interest was a product of the scientific turn in International Relations which occurred most notably in the US during the 1960s: the so-called 'behavioural revolution'. Scholars such as Frankel, Morton Kaplan, and nuclear deterrence theorists such as Albert Wohlstetter, Thomas Schelling and Herman Kahn, believed that the historical and empirical claims of classical realists such as Hans Morgenthau were too vague and impressionistic. For them, the study of international politics required greater precision and scientific rigour in order to uncover its underlying patterns and laws. Inductive methodology, applied to either prove or refute empirical claims and to predict human behaviour, was their preferred approach.

The value of such methods in the study of international politics was soon challenged by traditional or 'classical' IR scholars such as Hedley Bull who believed that important dimensions of international politics were neglected by the advocates of social science and were unlikely to be explained by this method (Bull 1966). According to Linklater,

> the search for patterns ignored the life-blood of international relations which is to be found, for example, in the beliefs states have about the rights and wrongs of using force or intervening in one another's internal affairs. It is to be found in their attitudes to international law and in the moral problems and tensions which have manifested themselves in many different ways throughout recorded international history, specifically in debates about the morality of war. Bull did

concede that the social-scientific method had forced the analysts of international relations to aim for greater conceptual clarity and precision. But he argued that social-scientific approaches failed to match traditionalism in understanding unique historical events and in reflecting on the moral and cultural framework which is specific to the society of states. (Linklater 2000, p. 4)

Consistent with Bull's critique of the scientific turn in International Relations, this book will argue that the term 'theory' in the study of international politics should not be limited to a narrow 'scientific' or positivist formulation which is implied in Frankel's analysis. Contemporary explanatory and constitutive theories of international politics – few if any of which could be described as 'social science' – consider the national interest in a much broader, less restrictive sense. Instead of focusing on decision makers and the various 'inputs' into decision-making, this book will be concerned with locating the national interest within the internal theoretical debates of International Relations, and thus with questions largely ignored by both Beard and Frankel.

For example, does the national interest remain a substantive concept in an era of economic globalisation? If it is still considered the guiding motive of state diplomacy, can it be properly defined and can IR theory assist in this challenge? Does it perform domestic ideological functions for political elites? Is it inseparable from considerations of contemporary nationalism or should it be understood as a socially constructed international norm?

These and other related questions will be considered in three broad sections. The first will examine the national interest within the framework of *conventional* IR theory, in particular realist and neo-realist perspectives. This is where the term has been traditionally defined, developed and posited as the very basis of diplomatic practice.

The second section will examine *critical* perspectives of the national interest by looking at Marxist and anarchist approaches. These two traditions pose major challenges to claims that the nation remains an active agent in international affairs with collective, common interests, instead focusing on the particular interests of special groups within it.

The third section will examine how *progressive* theoretical approaches understand the term, focusing on liberal, English-School and constructivist theories. Liberalism has historically been anti-statist and looked forward to the triumph of market forces over nationalism: globalisation is the ultimate realisation of liberal economic philosophy. The English School, on the other hand, has substantially qualified the stark pessimism of contemporary realist assumptions about international life and the never ending struggle for power and security. The English School argues that only enlightened self-interest is a morally defensible approach to foreign policy for states. Constructivists have recently revived debate about the normative foundations of diplomacy and how norms shape current understandings of the national interest. They argue that the national interest is inseparable from conceptions of national identity.

This book does not focus on the national interest as a tool for the assessment of foreign policy, although by implication it will raise a number of issues and questions which bear on that task. The extent to which individual governments invoke the national interest for domestic political advantage is an important and worthy study because the concept is assumed but rarely explained or defined. It is also used as a political lowest common denominator – to de-legitimate arguments for diplomatic action based on wider obligations to the species as a whole. However, that is a separate empirical enquiry which ranges well beyond the parameters of this theoretical study which is confined to what the discipline of International Relations understands by the national interest.

The book endeavours to demonstrate that despite its continuing relevance for conventional IR theory and the revival of the term in constructivist theory, in an era of economic globalisation 'the national interest' cannot fully withstand the critique mounted by neo-liberal perspectives and critical approaches such as Marxism and anarchism. Despite its wide currency in political circles as a legitimation tool, and a residual relevance in the domain of security policy, a theoretical investigation reveals it to be a term largely devoid of substantive meaning and content.

1
Origins and Antecedents

Before the 'formula' of the national interest, to use Charles Beard's perceptive expression, can be placed in a range of theoretical contexts within the discipline of International Relations, it is important to recognise and understand its evolution as a term of political discourse. The intellectual origins and history of the idea of 'the national interest' are virtually inseparable from how rulers came to define their justifications for state policy.

This chapter will trace its development from Rousseau's conception of the 'general will' and the earlier doctrine of *'raison d'état'* most closely associated with Machiavelli, to its use as a term of modern diplomacy. The key components of the national interest will also be outlined. The chapter begins with a brief etymological analysis.

Etymology and epistemology

In the discourse of politics, the concept of *interest* is a contested and problematic idea (Connolly 1974). Though it has a range of meanings, '*interest* is a significant example of a word with specialised legal and economic senses which, within a particular social and economic history, has been extended to a very general meaning' (Williams 1983, pp. 171–3). Although its etymology is complex and difficult to trace, it is possible to use the word 'interest' in both its *objective* sense (a general or natural concern, having an objective right, claim or stake in something) and its *subjective* sense (a general curiosity or having the power to attract curiosity or attention). This is a distinction now preserved in the negatives *disinterested* (not affected by objective involvement in a matter – impartial) and *uninterested* (not being attracted to something or having no power to attract – a subjective judgement).

From a political perspective, it is significant that 'our most general words for attraction or involvement should have developed from a formal objective term in property and finance [the Latin derivation is *interesse*, meaning (i) compensation for loss, and (ii) an investment with a right or share]', so that conflicts of interests can be seen as contests which stem from the very structure of our society and, specifically, matters of property (Williams 1983, pp. 171–3). The state of 'having an interest' can therefore mean holding an objective and/or subjective stake in something, but also, crucially, *being affected either positively or negatively by that stake*. Both usages of 'interest' are relevant to this analysis (see Hirschman 1986, ch. 2).

According to Beard, when secularism and political economy displaced theology as the principal concern of intellectual elites in the late fifteenth century, 'interest shrank to an economic conception in writings and negotiations involving policy, statecraft, and social affairs generally' (Beard 1935, p. 155). A key moment, therefore, is the word's etymological shift from a spiritual to an objective material conception, now meaning 'a gain in wealth as measured by the prevailing economic standards – a gain in land, houses, material capital, money, credits, and exchangeable commodities' (Beard 1935, p. 155). Beard also noted a residual subjective dimension to the term, given that interest also involves human perception and interpretation. The question, 'how can I maximise my interests?' may not always be successfully answered by those who pose it, but it remains an aspiration, a conscious thought process.

As has been noted, the materialist conception of interest in its plural form – *interests* – can be divided into two related senses, property and property owners. Beard argues that this often leads to definitions of *the national interest* which amount to either the sum total (or cumulative aggregation) of particular property interests or the most important and significant interests amongst many.

> It is used to describe outward realities such as material plant and equipment, or aggregations of plants and equipments. . . . The term is also applied to the *owners* of such tangibles, as for example, when we speak of utility interests, railroad interests, shipping interests, and aviation interests . . . . There is a tendency in practice to regard the national interest as a mere aggregation of particular interests, or to interpret it in terms of the most active and dominant interests, even though they may be in the minority – considered either as the proportion of persons or corporations involved or as the proportion of capital measured by pecuniary standards. (Beard 1935, p. 156)

In policy discussion where *the national interest* is central to decision-making, it is the owners of property – *property interests* – who are actually being considered. According to Beard, this can never be an objective or quantifiable process because interests cannot be separated from human motive and concern. There is no such thing as an objective reality called *the national interest*. Considerations of *the national interest* is an ineluctably subjective assessment:

> As far as policy is concerned, interest inheres in human beings as motive or force of attention, affection and action. As motive or force it cannot be defined absolutely, or isolated, or fully comprehended by the human mind . . . . Those who merely discuss policy likewise bring their interests to bear, consciously or unconsciously, and their interests, both intellectual and economic (salary, wages, or income), are affiliated with some form of ownership or opposition to the present relations or operations of ownership ... The intellectual impossibility of isolating and defining interests in absolute terms is responsible for a large part of the confusion that reigns today in discussion of policy. (Beard 1935, pp. 156–7)

Nor, according to Beard, can ideas and material interests be separated. They are inextricably bound to one another.

> Interest, subjectively considered, may take the form of an idea, and every idea pertaining to earthly affairs is attached to some interest considered as material thing and is affiliated with social relationships. Neither can be separated from the other in operations called 'understanding,' 'appraisal' or 'measurement.' . . . There are, to repeat again and again, no ideas without interests, and no interests without ideas . . . . (Beard 1935, pp. 157–8)

This claim has important implications for all analyses of *the national interest* which attempt to disaggregate its component parts. In particular it represents a challenge to claims (by classical realists) that permanent, fixed national interests can be identified as objectives which should determine the conduct of the foreign policy of states. It also means that *the national interest* cannot be reduced to its component parts for scientific measurement and assessment.

> But men are not endowed with the power to isolate ideas from interests, to assign mathematically measured values to them, and to discover

which is more potent than the other in the stream of occurrences called history . . . . So we return again – ideas and interests are known to exist, if anything is known; they cannot be isolated in fact; they cannot be measured; they cannot be separately appraised, for appraisal is a form of mathematical valuation; but a realistic view of the world must include both. (Beard 1935, pp. 158–9)

Here, Beard's remarks echo Marx and Engels in a famous passage from *The Communist Manifesto*, and in a less well-known extract from *The German Ideology*, where it is claimed that all ideas have a material reality as interest, and each can only be understood in the context of the other. For Marx and Engels, the material reality of ideas are expressed as class interests.

Does it require deep intuition to comprehend that man's ideas, views and conceptions, in one word, man's consciousness, changes with every change in the conditions of his material existence, in his social relations and in his social life? What else does the history of ideas prove, than that intellectual production changes its character in proportion as material production is changed? The ruling ideas of each age have ever been the ideas of its ruling class. (Marx & Engels 1998, pp. 58–9)

The production of ideas, of conceptions, of consciousness, is at first directly interwoven with the material activity and the material intercourse of men, the language of real life. Conceiving, thinking, the mental intercourse of men, appear at this stage as the direct efflux of their material behaviour. The same applies to mental production as expressed in the language of politics, laws, morality, religion, metaphysics, of a people. (Marx 1974, vol. 1, 1A).

In a remarkably prescient observation, Beard is led to conclude that any analysis of the national interest must entail an inquiry into the ideas which express and represent the interests to be considered. It will be subsequently argued that these are the key questions behind critical perspectives of *the national interest* contained in Marxist and anarchist theory.

The only operation that seems appropriate when 'interest' is mentioned is to inquire: what ideas are associated with it? And when an 'idea' is mentioned, to inquire: what interests are associated with it? (Beard 1935, pp. 157–8)

How, then, does Beard proceed with his account of the national interest if a scientific and quantitative analysis will not reveal anything very meaningful? If ideas and interests are inseparable phenomena and the whole process of articulating and determining *the national interest* is unavoidably subjective, on what basis can an examination of the 'formula' go forward? Beard's answer is that any serious inquiry must focus on the documentary history within a particular national setting. As we might expect from a historian, the national interest can only be truly revealed in retrospect.

> The question – what is the national interest? – can be answered, if at all, only by exploring the use of the formula by responsible statesmen and publicists and by discovering the things and patterns of conduct – public and private – embraced within the scope of the formula. (Beard 1934; 1966, p. 26)

The general will

At the very basis of claims for the national interest is an assumption that a political community can speak with a common voice. This is only possible, however, if the various expressions of particular individual interests which comprise all complex societies are suspended when those societies need to take collective decisions which are binding on all members.

Rousseau was one of the first people to think systematically about the common expressions of a political community, and in particular what happens when the common and particular interests within a society cannot be easily reconciled. The term he gave to the legitimate basis of common political expression was 'the general will':

> only the general will can direct the powers of the State in such a way that the purpose for which it has been instituted, which is the good of all, will be achieved. For if the establishment of societies had been made necessary by the antagonism that exists between particular interests, it has been made possible by the conformity that exists between these same interests. The bond of society is what there is in common between these different interests, and if there were not some point in which all interests were identical, no society could exist. The bond of society is that identity of interests which all feel who compose it. In the absence of such an identity no society would be possible. Now, it is solely on the basis of this common interest that society must be governed. (Rousseau, Book II, I, 1960 p. 190)

It is common within political philosophy to regard Rousseau's idea of the general will as constituting the outlines of early democratic theory and government by legitimate consensus or majority view. This is not in dispute here. However, it also possible to view Rousseau's notion as forming the basis upon which later ideas about the national interest have been constructed. For Rousseau, societies have common interests which should form the basis of decision-making and policy. In fact they are the binding forces which keep society from disintegrating into antagonistic groups and individuals.

Rousseau claims that 'sovereignty ... [is] no more than the exercise of the general will' (Rousseau, Book II, I, 1960 p. 190) and that the general will 'is concerned only with the common interest' (Rousseau, Book II, II, 1960 p. 193). Here, as we shall observe later, Rousseau's words are almost indistinguishable from claims made by contemporary realists in the discipline of International Relations. Although he doesn't elaborate on the forms which these common interests take, he has no doubt that they exist and that they form the very basis of legitimate behaviour by political communities. Once the French Revolution effectively redefines the state as the instrument of the nation, a key moment in the definition of the nation's interests has been reached.

Just as importantly for the subject under analysis here, Rousseau is fully aware of the dangers of allowing particular interests to dominate the common interests of society:

> the general will, if it be deserving of its name, must be general, not in its origins only but in its objects, applicable to all as well as operated by all, and that it loses its natural validity as soon as it is concerned to achieve a merely individual and limited end, since, in that case, we, pronouncing judgement on something outside ourselves, cease to be possessed of that true principle of equity which is our guide. (Rousseau, Book II, IV, 1960 p. 196)

Rousseau's warnings about the dangers of private interests capturing the apparatus of state anticipate the basis of critical objections to the national interest. As we shall see later in the study, critical conceptions of the national interest argue that dominant private interests within society will direct state policy to advance their particular circumstances. For critical perspectives of the national interest, the claim that a complex society can have common interests is largely a myth which serves the interests of dominant groups. In the following passage, Rousseau is not conceding that the triumph of particular interests is

likely, but is nonetheless clear about the implications of elite dominance for the welfare of the community and the very survival of the
state.

> So long as a number of men assembled together regard themselves
> as forming a single body, they have but one will, which is concerned
> with their common preservation and with the well-being of all.
> When this is so, the springs of the State are vigorous and simple, its
> principles plain and clear-cut. It is not encumbered with confused or
> conflicting interests. The common good is everywhere plainly in
> evidence and needs only good sense to be perceived. Peace, unity
> and equality are the foes of political subtlety.
>
> But when the social bond begins to grow slack, and the State to
> become weaker; when the interests of individuals begin to make
> themselves felt, and lesser groups within the State to influence the
> State as a whole, then the common interest suffers a change for the
> worse and breeds opposition. No longer do men speak with a single
> voice, no longer is the general will the will of all. Contradictions
> appear, discussions arise, and even the best advice is not allowed to
> pass unchallenged.
>
> Last stage of all, when the State, now near its ruin, lives only in a vain
> and deceptive form, when the bond of society is broken in all men's
> hearts, when the vilest self-interest bears insolently the sacred name
> of Common-Weal, then does the general will fall dumb. All, moved
> by motives unavowed, express their views as though such a thing
> as the State had never existed, and they were not citizens at all. In
> such circumstances, unjust decrees, aiming only at the satisfaction
> of private interests, can be passed under the guise of laws. (Rousseau,
> Book IV, I, 1960 pp. 269–70)

In the space of a few words, Rousseau not only provides a philosophical
basis for what will become a key term in the study of international
politics, he also identifies the principal objections which will arise to
the integrity of such an view – an idea which in the context of eighteenth-
century thought was on the radical fringes of legitimate expressible
philosophy.

Perhaps Rousseau had in mind Thucydides' remark that an 'identity
of interest is the surest of bonds whether between states or individuals'
(Thucydides 1954; 1972, p. 107)? Though it is not spelled out in detail
by Rousseau in the context of the general will, that which 'men assembled
together regard ... as forming a single body' – the binding force which

enables them to express a common interest or general will – is what he called 'civic religion'. Civic religion or loyalty was necessary to generate social cohesion and patriotism, to inculcate the idea that citizens had special ties and held a shared commitment to a common political association. Though it is misleading to claim that by 'civic religion' Rousseau was actually referring to nationalism in its modern form, there can be little doubt that he had unwittingly anticipated nationalist sentiment emerging to fill the binding role that he had outlined. This is a key moment in the history of modern state formation and International Relations theory.

In more contemporary parlance, Rousseau was emphasising the importance of the process by which people come to see themselves as members of an imagined community, with a common language, cultural mores and practices, as well as a shared historical experience (Hobsbawm 1990, p. 85). The development of national consciousness and the subject of nationalism generally is a vast topic which has been widely and thoroughly examined (see for example, Carr 1945; Gellner 1983; Hobsbawm 1990; Anderson 1991; Gellner 1997). Each study wrestles with the definition of nationalism as much as it debates its causes and origins. Some emphasise the importance of nationalism in defining a people's political identity. Others stress peoples' collective imagination and solidarity, their shared feelings of a common fate, their sense of place, belonging and attachment to a homeland, and the process of bonding together by the exclusion of outsiders. Nationalism has also been studied as a process of industrial modernisation, a product of recently invented mythical traditions and as a political movement which articulates the aspirations of a group who wish to be governed in common.

This study will confine its focus to the political expression of Rousseau's 'general will' which, in the modern era, has been appropriated by nationalism. It will be argued here that growing nationalist sentiment, the redefinition of the state as the instrument of the nation, combined with the idea of the general will, forms a very powerful force in the discourse of contemporary international politics – the idea of the national interest.

Raison d'état

Beard's investigation was stimulated by Meinecke's study of the origins and transformation of the interests of princes and estates into *raison d'état* up until the rise of the modern nation-state (Meinecke 1998).

Meinecke's examination began with Machiavelli and from there went to Richelieu, Grotius, Frederick the Great, Hegel and to Treitschke. Beard sought to extend Meinecke's investigation of the continental European experience in the Age of Absolutism by tracing the transformation of *raison d'état* into *the national interest* within the Anglo-Saxon world (Vagts 1966, pp. xiv–xv).

According to Meinecke, the origins of *raison d'état* lie with the beginnings of the social contract, and can be traced back to two sources, 'firstly, to the personal power-drive of the rulers, and secondly to the need of the subject people, which allows itself to be governed because it receives compensations in return' (Meinecke 1998, p. 10). In return for surrendering some of their freedom to the state, individuals receive an undertaking from the state that it will act in the common interest of the society.

The core doctrine of *raison d'état* is conventionally associated with Machiavelli's reflections on sixteenth-century statecraft. In *The Prince* and elsewhere, Machiavelli argues that the survival of the state was the paramount political consideration for rulers – an end in itself. Overcoming threats to the state by whatever means are necessary, both moral and immoral, is the first duty of the prince who is charged with a special responsibility for its preservation. In other words, the means necessary to achieve this goal are less important than the end itself:

> if a prince wants to maintain his rule he must be prepared not to be virtuous, and to make use of this or not according to need .... he must not flinch from being blamed for vices which are necessary for safeguarding the state ... a prince, and especially a new prince, cannot observe all those things which give men a reputation for virtue, because in order to maintain his state he is often forced to act in defiance of good faith, of charity, of kindness, of religion. And so he should have a flexible disposition, varying as fortune and circumstance dictate. As I said above, he should not deviate from what is good, if that is possible, but he should know how to do evil, if that is necessary. (Machiavelli 1961; 1999, pp. 50 & 57)

As a formula and guide for rulers, *raison d'état* is strikingly simple: 'Thus *must* you act, if you wish to preserve the power of the State whose care is in your hands; and you *may* act thus because no other means exists which would lead to that end' (emphasis added, Meinecke 1998, p. 10). According to Wight, the doctrine of *raison d'état* implied 'that statesmen cannot be bound in public affairs by the morality they would respect in private life [and] that there is a "reason of state" justifying unscrupulous action in defence of the public interest' (Wight 1986, p. 29). According to Craig and George, *raison d'état* was,

> the idea that the state was more than its ruler and more than the expression of his wishes; that it transcended crown and land, prince and people; that it had its particular set of interests and a particular set of necessities based upon them; and that the art of government lay in recognising those interests and necessities and acting in accordance with them, even if this might violate ordinary religious or ethical standards. (Craig & George 1983, p. 5)

If the self-preservation and well-being of the state is the ultimate value and goal, and the maintenance and extension of power the means, *raison d'état* requires a high degree of rationality and expediency in political conduct (Meinecke 1998, p. 6). In fact it represents a direct challenge to claims that there is a universal moral law governing human behaviour, especially in politics and diplomacy. The doctrine of *raison d'état* invariably invokes a separation of power and ethics and, therefore, commensurate conflict between them. Much of the debate surrounding Machiavelli and the doctrine of *raison d'état* centres on this very controversy, the struggle between political necessity and ethical virtue.

At the basis of *raison d'état*, and subsequently the 'national interest', are a defence of the state as both a moral good and a unit of political organisation. According to Treitschke, 'the State is in itself an ethical force and a high moral good'. 'Moralists must ... recognise that the State is not to be judged by the standards which apply to individuals, but by those which are set for it by its own nature and ultimate aims' (Treitschke 1916, pp. 106 & 99). According to *raison d'état*, the preservation of the state is a moral imperative and it cannot be judged against the criteria used to assess individual conduct.

At a time when the state is under pressure from various directions, including economic globalisation and the rise of humanitarian intervention as a challenge to traditional notions of sovereignty, it is worth recalling what contemporary International Relations scholars have offered in its defence. According to pre-eminent neo-realist Kenneth Waltz,

> States perform essential political, social and economic functions, and no other organisation rivals them in these respects. They foster the institutions that make internal peace and prosperity possible. In the state of nature, as Kant put it, there is 'no mine and thine.' States

turn possession into property and thus make saving, production and prosperity possible. The sovereign state with fixed borders has proved to be the best organisation for keeping peace internally and fostering the conditions for economic well-being. (Waltz 2000, p. 51)

Leading English School theorist Hedley Bull has also offered a lengthy and powerful defence of the 'state's positive role in world affairs'. According to Bull, the state plays an essential role in the promotion of international order and remains the preferred and pre-eminent form of political community, even for secessionists, nationalists and aspiring revolutionaries. It is, says Bull, the 'common political form experienced by the whole of mankind'.

According to Bull, the growing number of states and the expansion of their economic, social and political functions has been overlooked by those who regard the state as the principal obstacle to higher levels of international justice, peace and progress. Against charges and claims that the state is in terminal decline, Bull makes the following points:

- war, economic injustice and environmental damage have deeper causes than a particular form of political organisation and would not be eradicated by the replacement of the state;
- the modern state – as a government supreme over a particular territory and population – has provided order on a local scale;
- the sovereignty of states and their reciprocal recognition is the basis of international order – the states-system 'holds anarchy at bay';
- states have formed an international society of common interests for the purpose of peaceful co-existence, thus limiting and constraining their conflict and rivalry;
- states maintain important monopoly powers which limit conflict and advance co-operation (the legitimate use of violence, the capacity to adjudicate in disputes between citizens, a monopoly of taxation, the command of a citizen's loyalty, the authority to represent and bind citizens in international negotiations, etc.);
- no viable alternative forms of political community have been produced, no higher political authority than the state exists, and the states system has shown that it can be reformed (Bull 1977, 1979, pp. 139–56).

The preservation of the state, of which the doctrine of *raison d'état* is the ultimate expression, therefore remains a foundation principle for conventional theories of International Relations. The state is not just a principal actor in international politics, it is an essential one if peace and order are to be found in political life. Its external behaviour, now often characterised in national interest terms, is based on an assumption that its preservation is not just obligatory but positively desirable.

On the other hand, the opposition to *raison d'état* and the pacifying influence of the state can be found in a variety of quarters. For example, in his seminal study of European state formation Charles Tilly observed that over the last millennium, 'war has been the dominant activity of European states', for an obvious reason: 'The central tragic fact is simple: coercion *works*; those who apply substantial force to their fellows get compliance, and from that compliance draw the multiple advantages of money, goods, deference, access to pleasures denied to less powerful people' (Tilly 1992, p. 70). For Tilly, states and coercion are inseparable.

The anti-state argument has long been led by the anarchist tradition which regards the artificial barriers imposed by the establishment of nation-states as a principal cause of moral estrangement within the species. Anarchists believe that wars are largely a consequence of the imposition of the states system, which they regard as an unnatural social formation that is normally instituted by violence. So, for example, European and North American attempts to impose states systems in conquered territories after the collapse of the colonial system are seen by some anarchists as the principal source of most violent conflicts in the modern world, especially in the Middle East, Southern Europe, Central Asia and East Asia.

Michael Bakunin was not a particularly systematic thinker, however his critique of the state from an anarchist perspective and, in particular, his attack on the doctrine of *raison d'état* represents an important counterpoise to arguments in support of the state by realist and English-School thinkers.

According to Bakunin, freedom and peace could only be achieved through the dissolution of all states and the creation of a universal federation of free associations. States are oppressive, illegitimate, imposed systems of autonomous power – by nature they are evil. Their authority negates liberty and exploits the species by denying human beings the capacity to realise their true potential. In a withering critique of the state and the doctrine of *raison d'état* subtitled 'A Critique of Rousseau's Theory of the State', Bakunin warns against claims that the state has interests which enhance human freedom and should therefore be maintained and strengthened. It is worth quoting him at length to fully demonstrate the extent and dimensions of anarchist hostility to the state and the interests that are invoked in its name.

On the amorality of pursuing state interests:

> whatever conduces to the preservation, the grandeur and the power of the State, no matter how sacreligious or morally revolting it may seem, *that is the good.* And conversely, whatever opposes the State's interests, no matter how holy or just otherwise, *that is evil.* Such is the secular morality and practice of every State. (Dolgoff 2002, p. 132)

On the dangers of exclusionary political communities and the endemic conflict inherent in state formation:

> The existence of one sovereign, exclusionary State necessarily supposes the existence and, if need be, provokes the formation of other such States ... We thus have humanity divided into an indefinite number of foreign states, all hostile and threatened by each other. (Dolgoff 2002, p. 132)

On the division between insider and outsiders, the included and the excluded, and the ways in which state (and later national) interests shortsight each community, discouraging them from pursuing obligations to the whole of humanity:

> *The State, therefore, is the most flagrant, the most cynical, and the most complete negation of humanity.* It shatters the universal solidarity of all men on the earth, and brings some of them into association only for the purpose of destroying, conquering, and enslaving all the rest. It protects its own citizens only; it recognizes human rights, humanity, civilization within its own confines alone. Since it recognizes no rights outside itself, it logically arrogates to itself the right to exercise the most ferocious inhumanity toward all foreign populations, which it can plunder, exterminate, or enslave at will. ... the State can have no duties toward foreign populations. (Dolgoff 2002, p. 133)

On the immorality of *raison d'état* and the dangers of patriotism:

> This explains why, since the birth of the State, the world of politics has always been and continues to be the stage for unlimited rascality and brigandage, brigandage and rascality which, by the way, are held in high esteem, since they are sanctified by patriotism, by the transcendent morality and the supreme interest of the State. This explains why the entire history of ancient and modern states is

merely a series of revolting crimes; why kings and ministers, past and present, of all times and all countries – statesmen, diplomats, bureaucrats, and warriors – if judged from the standpoint of simple morality and human justice, have a hundred, a thousand times over earned their sentence to hard labor or to the gallows. There is no horror, no cruelty, sacrilege, or perjury, no imposture, no infamous transaction, no cynical robbery, no bold plunder or shabby betrayal that has not been or is not daily being perpetrated by the representatives of the states, under no other pretext than those elastic words, so convenient and yet so terrible: 'for reasons of state'. (Dolgoff 2002, p. 134)

On the criminal nature and logic of Machiavellian statecraft:

The great Italian political philosopher Machiavelli was the first to use these words, or at least the first to give them their true meaning and the immense popularity they still enjoy among our rulers today. A realistic and positive thinker if there ever was one, he was the first to understand that the great and powerful states could be founded and maintained by crime alone – by many great crimes, and by a radical contempt for all that goes under the name of honesty. ... Machiavelli concluded from these facts, with a good deal of logic, that the State was the supreme goal of all human existence, that it must be served at any cost and that, since the interest of the State prevailed over everything else, a good patriot should not recoil from any crime in order to serve it. He advocates crime, he exhorts to crime, and makes it the sine qua non of political intelligence as well as of true patriotism. Whether the State bear the name of a monarchy or of a republic, crime will always be necessary for its preservation and its triumph. (Dolgoff 2002, p. 135)

The purpose of these extracts is twofold: 1) to highlight the division between those on the one hand who promote the state as a structure which, amongst other benefits, pacifies human society and remains a vital, albeit imperfect form of political organisation and those on the other who view it as existentially evil; and 2) to demonstrate that many of the arguments for and against the national interest prefigure the concept itself, and can be found in debates surrounding Rousseau's idea of the social contract and Machiavelli's doctrine of *raison d'état*. Importantly, these arguments extend beyond what are said to be the pernicious domestic consequences of state formation. They reach to the consequences of forming bounded exclusive political communities for international order and peace.

Since Rousseau claimed sovereignty for the 'general will' and the French Revolution displaced absolutist with popular sovereignty, the 'people's sovereignty' embedded in the concept of the nation has dominated sovereignty theory and practice. With the French Revolution the modern world entered an era that naturalised and universalised the nation-state. In so doing, the idea of the national interest was born.

The interests of nations

In the discourse of international politics, the concept of 'the national interest' is commonly employed in two separate, though related ways. It is used to *shape political behaviour*, by serving as a means of defending, opposing or proposing policy. And it is employed by students of international relations as an *analytical tool* for describing, explaining and assessing the adequacy of a nation's foreign policy. Underlying both usages are implied assumptions about what is best for a national community, in both domestic and foreign domains (Rosenau 1964).

Until the French Revolution the term 'nation' referred to a racial or a linguistic group and, according to E.H. Carr, had no political significance. The nation was identified with the person of the sovereign, so that international relations were essentially relations between royal families (Carr 1945, pp. 2–4). This conception of the nation was illustrated by the policy of mercantilism, which was designed, not to promote the welfare of the community and its members, but to augment the power and wealth of the state, of which the sovereign was the embodiment. Because export markets were thought to be fixed in size, the only way for a nation (defined in terms of the ruling elite) to expand its wealth was to capture it from other nations, if necessary by waging trade or colonial wars. According to Carr, 'mercantilism was the economic policy of a period which identifies the interest of the nation with the interest of its rulers' (Carr 1945, pp. 5–6).

The doctrine of *raison d'état*, which is usually traced back to the writings of Machiavelli, referred to the interests of the monarch and the royal court. Thus Louis XIV's famous remark, 'L'état, c'est moi' ('The state – it's me'), had both symbolic and substantive meaning when it came to defining the state and its interests. However, in the eighteenth century, Rousseau rejected the idea that the embodiment of the nation could be found in the person of the sovereign or the ruling group. In what was to become a fundamental principle of both the French and American revolutions, Rousseau identified the 'nation' with 'the people' (Carr 1945, p. 6). Henceforth, it came to be accepted that nations or national groups, rather than individual rulers, had a right to political independence and statehood. The 'democratisation of nationalism' in the nineteenth century, a process largely driven by the middle classes of Europe, led to the idea, and subsequently the stated right, of national self-determination. The principle of self-determination became defined in terms of the rights of national groups to be governed in common and to comprise an independent political community: sovereignty, previously understood as the power and interests of the monarch, would be vested in the nation. International relations would now 'be governed not by the personal interests, ambitions and emotions of the monarch, but by the collective interests, ambitions and emotions of the nation' (Carr 1945, p. 8). The citizens of the state claimed a right to be consulted about the affairs of the political community to which they belonged. This change was driven by the rising power of the emerging middle classes of Europe after the industrial revolution.

In needs to be said that in the wake of the French Revolution the 'nation' comprised the most powerful groups or classes in society. It was only in the twentieth century with the extension of universal suffrage that the 'nation' was again redefined to include those sectors of society whose interests had earlier been excluded: women, the working class and ethnic or racial minorities, for example. To the extent that the assertion of national interests is therefore an authentic expression of the welfare of the entire community, it is a consequence of political democratisation and therefore a relatively modern claim.

According to Beard, this is the period when claims made in the name of 'the will of the prince', 'dynastic interests' and '*raison d'état*' lost their efficacy. New political allegiances to new political entities were soon reflected in the language of politics. Political actors had made claims on behalf of the national interest as early as the sixteenth century in Italy and the seventeenth century in England; however it became commonplace from the time the US Constitution was drafted (Beard 1966, pp. 22–6). With the exercise of sovereignty shifting from the personal control of the sovereign to eventually that of a popular representative body, the emergence of the nation-state system, and the expansion of international economic relations, the stage was set for the birth of the modern conception of 'the national interest'.

As the twentieth century unfolded and political participation spread to all classes, the objectives of national policy in the newly industrialised societies became defined as advancing the economic and social welfare of all members of the nation. By the early decades of the century, wages, conditions of employment and the question of unemployment, became the concerns of national government policy. These were the interests of both the middle and working classes, 'and must be asserted, if necessary, against the national policies of other countries; ... this in turn gives the worker an intimate practical interest in the policy and power of the nation' (Carr 1945, p. 19). Thus the projection of national policy outwards to the rest of the world became broader than simply the question of national security. The economic welfare of the whole nation became an integral focus of the nation's foreign policy. In the democratic era, national policy was founded on the support of the whole population. The quid pro quo was 'the loyalty of the masses to a nation which had become the instrument of their collective interests and ambitions' (Carr 1945, pp. 20–1).

To some extent, understanding how nations came to assert common political interests presupposes the idea of the nation as both an independent political community and as the sole legitimate agent in international affairs. In earlier periods, political communities had been based on empire, colony, city-states and theocracies. However, since the French Revolution the principle of self-determination has entitled a group of people to constitute themselves as an independent political unit, with a number of attendant rights and obligations. Invariably, the form and extent of this political unit has coincided with a national community: the nation has come to be seen as the *natural* basis of the state, although there have always been exceptions such as the multi-national state.

Although widely conflated, 'nation' and 'state' are nevertheless quite different agents.

> The state, whether we think of it as the apparatus of government or as the field in which the apparatus works, is the unit of political power. The nation is a community of men; and though modern usage restricts it to communities of a political character or having political aspirations, the nation is still a community of human beings, not a territory or an administrative machine. Hence the state may, in a loose way, be described as 'artificial' or 'conventional', the nation as 'natural' or 'organic'. (Carr 1945, p. 39)

The concept of the 'nation-state' is therefore a marriage of two quite separate concepts which are now routinely conjoined in political discourse.

The principle of self-determination forms part of the process of democratisation, in particular the right of self-government. It is an expression of political freedom and implies that individuals have a right to be consulted about the affairs of the political unit to which they belong as well as the form of that political unit (Carr 1945, p. 37). Since the end of the eighteenth century, the principle of self-determination has been almost universally interpreted as meaning that '"states" and "nations" ought to coincide, that states should be constituted on a national basis, and that nations ought to form states' (Carr 1945, p. 39). However, as Carr argues, 'self-determination is not a right of certain recognised and pre-determined nations, but a right of individual men and women, which includes the right within certain limitations to form national groups' (Carr 1945, p. 47). This is often forgotten by students of international relations. Debates within International Relations have become accustom to thinking of nation-states as the only viable expression of political association at a global level when the forms of political community which express people's political aspirations have changed, and continue to change, over time.

By customarily accepting the nation-state as the only legitimate form of political association in the international realm it is possible to ignore or dismiss the suggestion that special groups within it are in fact key agents in the conduct of international relations. As will be seen, this argument is the departure point for critical conceptions of the national interest.

It is important, however, to recall that the emergence of what might be called interest-governed behaviour in diplomacy was a progressive development from the period of unconstrained violence and competition. As Hirschman says, 'genuine hope arose that, with princely or national interest as a guide, statecraft would be able to produce a more stable political order and a more peaceful world'. Hence Bismarck's famous distinction between legitimate *interessenpolitik* and more malignant *Machpolitik* (Hirschman 1986, p. 38).

'The national interest': essential ingredients

At the beginning of the previous section it was noted that 'the national interest' is commonly employed in two related ways, first to describe, justify or oppose foreign policy and secondly, as an analytical tool for assessing and explaining the external behaviour of nation-states. This book will primarily assess the adequacy of the national interest as a conceptual tool by examining it from a range of theoretical perspectives.

Underwriting this assessment are a number of assumptions about what the national interest is thought to be, which are generally accepted by supporters and critics alike: that is to say, the claims are acknowledged even if their validity is challenged. It is important that these be noted before separate theoretical assessments are made.

First, at the very basis of the doctrine is the claim made by states that, however major their differences, the members of society have a number of crucial interests in common. For example, they have the same interest in protecting their national sovereignty and territorial integrity from external attack. Or more broadly, they have a common interest in ensuring that their capacity to administer their own affairs is not infringed upon by those outside the community. States normally give the highest priority to survival, or what is technically described as national security. This is defined as the capacity for deterring a military attack and military defence in the event that an attack from outside materialises.

The national interest therefore presupposes a process of bonding by exclusion. It works by dividing the world into insiders and outsiders: those whose interests are attended to (the nation) and those whose interests can be ignored (aliens, the rest). This assumption remains a powerful obstacle to cosmopolitan and universalist approaches to international politics.

Secondly, states argue that certain national interests are permanent and do not change with transient governments. For example, they may argue that specific national assets, either strategic (maritime routes, port access) or economic (resources), are always likely to be coveted by external powers and that the state therefore has a permanent national interest in securing them for 'insiders'.

States whose security has been threatened via traditional invasion routes, for example, factor this into their strategic doctrine and defence force structure. Even the neutralisation of proximate threats – maintaining good relations with neighbours in crucial geo-strategic locations – is an assumption that is not open to political reinterpretation. This is simply a fact of diplomatic life and does not alter with a change of government. The national interest in this sense demands political bipartisanship. Few governments or politicians allow themselves to be characterised as being a threat or in contradiction to the national interest, which in contemporary political discourse is the ultimate measure of patriotism. Bipartisanship on foreign policy in democratic states is a good indication that there are national interests above the cut and thrust of partisan politics.

The perceived permanency of national interests is also enhanced by the high levels of secrecy and confidentiality surrounding military and security matters. The special trust that is granted to intelligence agencies in liberal democracies, for example, presupposes their unshakeable commitment to the pursuit of agreed national interests. This is the only basis upon which their activities – frequently extra-judicial – can be legitimately shielded from media scrutiny and parliamentary oversight.

Thirdly, governments are the agents which interpret and articulate the national interest. As they do, they assert a sovereign right and a monopoly power. But they also muster enormous persuasive influence which attempts to exclude alternative claims made on behalf of the citizens of the state. Whether or not the interests of a national community are always maximised through their promotion as a national unit is a matter of debate which is only occasionally permitted to enter the national political dialogue. It cannot be assumed, for example, that whatever policy or decision is said to be 'in the national interest' is axiomatically true or that addressing an issue from a national perspective is always best for a particular group of nationals. If it was, regular claims for secession by ethnic, religious and cultural minorities across the world would not be made.

After all, why should 'our' interests be privileged when the group is a state but not when it is either a smaller or a larger group? Do *our* interests always count for more than the interests of others, providing we can conclusively define who *we* are (Donnelly 2000, p. 165)?

It cannot always be certain that the national interest has primacy in international diplomacy. Although states are reluctant to grant outsiders rights to 'interfere' in their 'domestic sovereign affairs' or concede that they have obligations to humanity which override their national concerns, states must now wrestle with competing rights asserted by the international community which may be, overall, in the best interests of the national community. As we shall see in subsequent chapters, the obligation to provide permanent settlement to political refugees and the emerging norm of intervention to relieve a humanitarian crisis are contemporary illustrations of this challenge. The national interest as a formula on which to base diplomacy is under threat on a number of fronts.

The national interest: means or ends?

According to Rosenau it was the Second World War and the implications of 'total war' for the masses that clearly demonstrated the public's vital stake in foreign affairs and the conduct of diplomacy. From this moment, analysts of international relations began to focus on the national interest 'as a concept which could be used to describe, explain, and assess the foreign policies of nations' (Rosenau 1964, p. 35). In other words, the national interest came to be seen as an explanatory and evaluative tool.

Rosenau describes the first group of scholars to elevate the concept of the national interest to the forefront of their concerns as 'objectivists' because they believed that 'the best interest of a nation is a matter of objective reality and that by describing this reality one is able to use the concept of the national interest as a basis for evaluating the appropriateness of the policies which a nation pursues' (Rosenau 1964, p. 35). The objectivists were not especially concerned with explaining the methodological or philosophical basis of their approach because 'the correspondence between their descriptions and the objective situation is self-evident' (Rosenau 1964, p. 35). This argument was uncritically adopted by Frankel in his major study (Frankel 1970).

But is it? According to Rosenau, the national interest is 'a standard that is just as misleading and unempirical a means of explanation as any moral principle or legal precept'. It is 'merely a label that may denote the entire spectrum of human wants and needs and thus in no way differentiates the circumstances that are likely to lead a nation to define its wants and needs' (Rosenau 1969, p. 157). Thus for Rosenau, the national interest is merely a way of describing the ends to which foreign policy should be directed.

Other theorists make a crucial distinction between means and ends. In any political community, says Bull, individuals have common interests in the primary goals of social life which are sustained by order. These include common interests in 'restricting violence' (to maximise personal security), 'respect for agreements' (because of their interdependence for material needs), and 'the stabilisation of possession' (as a consequence of scarce resources and limits to human altruism). These common interests might be driven by fear or enlightened and rational self-interest, but they emphasise the difference between process and outcome or means and ends (Bull 1977, pp. 53–4). According to Bull,

> the criterion of 'national interest', or 'interest of state', in itself provides us with no specific guidance either in interpreting the behaviour of states or in prescribing how they should behave – unless we are told what concrete ends or objectives states do or should pursue: security, prosperity, ideological objectives or whatever. Still less does it provide us with a criterion that is objective, in the sense of being independent

of the way state ends or purposes are perceived by particular decision-makers. It does not even provide a basis for distinguishing moral or ideological considerations in a country's foreign policy from non-moral or non-ideological ones. (Bull 1977, p. 66)

Bull argues that to say that something is in someone's interest is merely to say that it 'serves as a means to some end that he is pursuing', a matter of objective fact. But whether or not something actually is in someone's interest will depend on the ends that he is pursuing. Thus the idea of interest 'is an empty or vacuous guide, both as to what a person does do and as to what he should do. To provide such a guide we need to know what ends he does or should pursue, and the conception of interest in itself tells us nothing about either' (Bull 1977, p. 66).

Once the ends of state policy are agreed and defined, however, the conception of national interests becomes more meaningful. It then represents the political means most likely to realise the policy ends. The national interest comprises a 'rational plan of action' to achieve agreed ends, which can be contrasted with policies based on sectional interests, the interests of alliances and international organisations, or the ad hoc and uncritical pursuit of established policy (Bull 1977, p. 66–7).

The various ways in which the national interest has been understood and used as an explanatory and evaluative tool in international politics can be best illustrated by examining it from a range of theoretical perspectives, both conventional and critical. The first of these theories, the realist tradition, has done more to define and promote the term than any other approach.

2
Conventional Perspectives: Realist Approaches

> He who would do good to another must do it in Minute Particulars. General Good is the plea of the scoundral, hypocrite and flatterer.
>
> (William Blake, *Jerusalem*)

> To say that a policy or practice is in the interests of an individual or group is to assert both that the recipient would somehow benefit from it and that there is therefore a reason in support of enacting that policy ... as it is used in our society, 'interest' is one of those concepts that connects descriptive and explanatory statements to normative judgement.
>
> (William Connolly, *The Terms of Political Discourse*)

Realism is widely regarded as the most influential theoretical tradition in International Relations, even by its harshest critics. Its ancient philosophical heritage, its powerful and original critique of liberal internationalism, together with its influence on the practice of international diplomacy have secured it an important, if no longer dominant position in the discipline. No other theory has given as much form and structure to the study of international politics, especially to the sub-fields of Security Studies and International Political Economy (see Donnelly 2000).

As its name implies, realism seeks to describe and explain the world of international politics *as it is*, rather than how we might like it to be. Accordingly, the world is revealed to realists as a dangerous and insecure place, where violence is regrettable but endemic. In their accounts of the conflictual nature of international politics, realists give high priority to the nation-state in their considerations, acknowledging it as the supreme political authority in the world. Explaining the frequent violent behaviour of nation-states can only be done, however, by focusing on the role of power and the importance of the most powerful – the Great Powers. The relevance of an approach which accords priority to military power, perceptions of vulnerability, superpowers, wars and the perpetuation of a system which seems chronically troubled by conflict, was obvious to all in the most violent of all centuries – the twentieth.

Realists are unified in their pessimism about the extent to which the global political system can be made more peaceful and just. The international realm is characterised by conflict, suspicion and competition between nation-states, a logic which thwarts the realisation of alternative world orders. Realism is a pessimistic theoretical tradition. Fundamental changes to the structure of the international politics are unlikely, even if they are needed. The apparent immutability of the international system means that it will not come to resemble domestic liberal orders, however desirable the analogue may be. For realists, international relations is a world of recurrence and repetition, not reform or radical change.

As realism evolved after the Great War as a critique of liberal internationalism, or what E.H. Carr called liberal utopianism, its focus was firmly on explaining the behaviour of nation-states in the international realm. Although the immediate motivation was to uncover the causes of war, which liberal approaches in the 1920s had conspicuously failed to achieve by the end of the 1930s, realism was also concerned to explain diplomatic behaviour more generally, though in a systematic and theoretical way. One of its most powerful and influential explanatory tools was the idea of 'the national interest'.

This chapter will examine the idea of the national interest as it has been articulated by two groups within the broad realist tradition: classical realism, closely associated with the work of Hans Morgenthau, and neo-realism most closely connected with the ideas of Kenneth Waltz. It will then assess the status of the national interest within the realist tradition generally, as well as the problems which arise in its modern conventional usage. The chapter concludes with an assessment of the relevance of national interest as a tool of realist thought in the era of economic globalisation.

Morgenthau: the national interest as a tool of analysis and a guide for action

According to Rosenau, the impact and implications of 'total war' in the Second World War for the mass of ordinary citizens clearly established the public's direct stake in foreign affairs and the conduct of diplomacy. From this moment, analysts of international politics began to focus on the national interest 'as a concept which could be used to describe, explain, and assess the foreign policies of nations' (Rosenau 1964, p. 35). As has been noted, Rosenau describes the first group of scholars to elevate the concept of the national interest to the forefront of their diplomatic concerns as 'objectivists' because they believed that the best interests of a nation were actually a matter of objective reality, so that by describing this reality it was possible to use the concept of the national interest as a basis for evaluating the appropriateness of foreign policy (Rosenau 1964, p. 35). The objectivists were not especially concerned with explaining the methodological or philosophical basis of their approaches because the connection between their descriptions and objective reality was self-evident (Rosenau 1964, p. 35).

Arguably the best-known exemplar of such an approach is Hans Morgenthau, one of the founding fathers of the realist school of International Relations and the author of the seminal text, *Politics Among Nations*. Morgenthau's book was written in the aftermath of the Second World War as the United States was emerging as the world's major economic and strategic power. It was not only an attempt to consolidate the principles of realism, which had seemingly been vindicated by the war. It was also designed to provide intellectual support for the role the United States was to play in the post-war world. Morgenthau's most important work straddled two worlds: it was an intellectual statement destined to influence generations of students in the academy and a series of guidelines for US foreign policy makers confronted by the uncertainties of the unfolding Cold War.

From the tone and style of the book it is possible to sense the extent to which the US academic community was influenced, if not enthralled by developments in the natural sciences during this period. Morgenthau took up E.H Carr's challenge to create a science of international politics by applying the positivist methodology of the 'hard' or natural sciences to the study of international relations. The intellectual rigour of this approach would reveal the underlying 'reality' of world politics, from which certainties and predictions could be deduced. Not surprisingly, Morgenthau's writings are scattered with references to laws and principles, objectivity and science.

His definition of theory, for example, is explicitly borrowed from the natural sciences. Theories, according to Morgenthau, should be judged 'not by some pre-conceived abstract principle or concept unrelated to reality', but by their purpose which is 'to bring order and meaning to a mass of phenomena which without it would remain disconnected and unintelligible'. They must be 'consistent with the facts and within itself'. In other words, theories must be factual, independent and retrospective. Theories must also satisfy strict empirical and logical criteria: 'do the facts as they actually are lend themselves to the interpretation the theory has put on them, and do the conclusions at which the theory arrives follow with logical necessity from its premises?' (Morgenthau 1948; 1985, p. 3). Morgenthau clearly believes there is a knowable reality or 'rational essence' of foreign policy which theories can reveal (Morgenthau 1985, p. 7). This is similar to the methodological approach of positivism. Its application to the study to international politics has tried to provide the field with greater coherence, rigour and intellectual respect. It later inspired the discipline's epistemological debates which erupted in the 1980s.

Morgenthau's account of world politics is underpinned by the contrast he draws between two schools of modern political thought and their conceptions of the nature of humanity, society and politics. The first, which closely resembles liberal-utopianism, 'believes that a rational and moral political order, derived from universally valid abstract principles' can be achieved by conscious political action. It 'assumes the essential goodness and infinite malleability of human nature, and blames the failure of the social order to measure up to the rational standards on [a] lack of knowledge and understanding, obsolescent social institutions, or the depravity of certain isolated individuals or groups. It trusts in education, reform, and the sporadic use of force to remedy these defects' (Morgenthau 1985, pp. 3–4). This school believes in the perfectibility of the human condition.

By contrast the second school, with which Morgenthau identifies and that he calls realism, believes the world's imperfections are 'the result of forces inherent in human nature'. According to this approach, 'to improve the world one must work with those forces, not against them'. In a world where conflicts of interest are endemic, moral principles can never be fully realised, only approximated through a temporary balancing of interests. Absolute good cannot be achieved, but a system of checks and balances can help to produce acceptable outcomes. Principles of universal relevance can be deduced from historical experience rather than abstract moral or ethical codes (Morgenthau 1985, pp. 3–4).

Morgenthau wrote with a sense of certainty about international politics because he believed it was governed by immutable laws, 'deriving either from human nature itself, or from the dynamics of inter-state competition'

(Clark 1989, p. 87). He believed it was possible to create a science of international politics by applying the methodology of the natural sciences to the social and political worlds. The systematic rigour of this approach would reveal the underlying 'reality' of world politics – the true 'rational essence' of foreign policy – from which certainties and predictions could be deduced (Morgenthau 1985, p. 7).

Morgenthau's definition and understanding of 'the national interest' is outlined in what he lists as the 'six principles of political realism' which, taken together summarise his general approach to international politics.

> The main signpost that helps political realism to find its way through the landscape of international politics is the concept of interest defined in terms of power. This concept provides the link between reason trying to understand international politics and the facts to be understood. It sets politics as an autonomous sphere of action and understanding apart from other spheres, such as economics (understood in terms of interest defined as wealth), ethics, aesthetics, or religion. Without such a concept ... we could not distinguish between political and nonpolitical facts, nor could we bring at least a measure of systemic order to the political sphere .... We assume that statesmen think and act in terms of interest defined as power, and the evidence of history bears that assumption out .... A realist theory of international politics, then, will guard against two popular fallacies [for understanding foreign policy]: the concern with motives and the concern with ideological preferences. (Morgenthau 1985, p. 5)

> Realism assumes that its key concept of interest defined as power is an objective category which is universally valid, but it does not endow that concept with a meaning that is fixed once and for all. The idea of interest is indeed of the essence of politics and is unaffected by the circumstances of time and place .... the kind of interest determining political action in a particular period of history depends upon the political and cultural context within which foreign policy is formulated. (Morgenthau 1985, pp. 10–11)

For Morgenthau, the 'concept of interest [is] defined in terms of power'. It 'imposes discipline upon the observer' of international politics, and 'infuses rational order into the subject matter of politics, and thus makes the theoretical understanding of politics possible' (Morgenthau

1985, p. 5). National interests are permanent conditions which provide policy makers with a rational guide to their tasks: they are fixed, politically bipartisan and always transcend changes in government. The 'national interest ... is not defined by the whim of a man or the partisanship of party but imposes itself as an objective datum upon all men applying their rational faculties to the conduct of foreign policy' (Morgenthau 1977, p. 9). They are 'a fact to be discovered rather than a matter of contingent and constructed preferences' (Donnelly 2000, p. 45).

Morgenthau argues that 'interest is the perennial standard by which political action must be judged and directed' because the 'objectives of foreign policy must be defined in terms of the national interest' (Morgenthau 1985, pp. 9 & 528). Although he recognised that at any particular point in time the interests of a nation should be informed by the 'political and cultural context within which foreign policy is formulated', defining interest in terms of power would largely overcome the problem of subjectivity (Morgenthau 1985, pp. 8 & 5). The relative power of nation-states can be assessed and measured, and is therefore an important objective reality. The national interest is normally defined in terms of strategic and economic capability because international politics is seen primarily as a struggle for power between states. However, Morgenthau concedes that the definition of power will change over time: on some occasions economic power will be crucial, at other times military or cultural power will be decisive.

According to Morgenthau, the desire for power, which he regards as the principal driving force behind state behaviour, is an internal or endogenous characteristic of states. States are led by human beings who have an innate 'will to power'. This means states have what Morgenthau called 'a limitless lust for power' and are always on the lookout for opportunities to dominate their rivals: a commitment to absolute rather than relative power, which is both insatiable and an end in itself (Morgenthau 1946, p. 194; Morgenthau 1985, p. 208). Although Morgenthau is conscious of the structural constraints of an anarchical system, the driving force in international politics is the desire for strategic supremacy which is ultimately rooted in human nature.

Although morality cannot be the basis of forming national interests, Morgenthau refers to the 'moral dignity of the national interest', implying that at the very least the term is a morally defensible guide to foreign policy formulation (Morgenthau 1951, p. 33). However he emphasises over and over, the detachment of the national interest from political and ethical perspectives: 'The national interest of great powers and in good measure the methods by which it is to be secured are impervious to ideological and institutional changes' (Morgenthau 1962, p. 199).

Claims by critics such as Tucker that the term he privileged in understanding international politics was open to subjective interpretation which rendered it analytically useless, seem to have prompted Morgenthau to define the national interest more specifically and concede that his critics had a point (see Tucker 1952). In an article written after the publication of *Politics Among Nations*, Morgenthau argues that that the national interest

> contains a residual meaning which is inherent in the concept itself, but beyond these minimum requirements its content can run the whole gamut of meanings which are logically compatible with it. That content is determined by the political traditions and the total cultural context within which a nation formulates its foreign policy. The concept of the national interest, then, contains two elements, one that is logically required and in that sense necessary, and one that is variable and determined by circumstances. (Morgenthau 1952, p. 287)

In other words, there is an invariable component of the concept which refers to the protection and security of the physical, political and cultural entity called the nation. These minimum features – territorial integrity, political institutions and cultural mores – are 'unaffected by the circumstances of time and place', and therefore enjoy bipartisan political support (Morgenthau 1952, p. 288). Thus Morgenthau can claim that the fundamental national interest of every state is to 'protect [its] physical, political and cultural identity against encroachments by other nations' (Morgenthau 1951, p. 172). However, there is also a variable component which is historically and circumstantially contingent, that varies from nation to nation and time to time. This component includes personalities, sectional interests and public opinion.

It is not clear that this distinction entirely takes care of the objective–subjective charge made against Morgenthau's concept of the national interest. After all, even objective facts need to be subjectively identified: the selection of certain objective facts to highlight is a subjective choice. The elevation of 'interest defined in terms of power' is clearly a subjective judgement and few analysts in the field would confidently argue that the elements of power in international politics can be easily and objectively delineated or quantified.

Morgenthau concedes that the national interest will only remain 'the last word in world politics' as long as the planet is politically organised into nations (Morgenthau 1952, p. 288). He also appears to backtrack on his earlier quest to develop a science of international relations and emphasise the constraints on behavioural science in this area. Subsequently in 1952 he argued that

the contribution which science can make to this field, as to all fields of policy formation, is limited. It can identify the different agencies of the government which contribute to the determination of the variable elements of the national interest and assess their relative weight. It can separate the long-range objectives of foreign policy from the short-term ones which are the means for the achievement of the former and can tentatively establish their rational relations. Finally, it can analyse the variable elements of the national interest in terms of their legitimacy and their compatibility with other national values and with the national interests of other nations. (Morgenthau 1952, p. 289)

This is quite a shift from 1948. Science, it now seems, can uncover the invariables but say little or nothing about the variable components of the national interest. This is a significant concession to the limits of his own methodology. The relationship between variable and invariable components of the national interest is not extensively explained by Morgenthau.

Morgenthau also responds to the claims made in critical circles that the national interest is merely the clothing which dominant economic interests wear in order to disguise their particular interests and the extent to which those interests are furthered by the state. As we shall see, this is the very basis of Marxist and anarchist claims.

Group interests exert, of course, constant pressure upon the conduct of our foreign policy, claiming their identity with the national interest. It is, however, doubtful that, with the exception of a few spectacular cases, they have been successful in determining the course of American foreign policy. It is much more likely, given the nature of American domestic politics, that American foreign policy, insofar as it is the object of pressures by sectional interests, will normally be a compromise between divergent sectional interests. The concept of the national interest, as it emerges from this contest as the actual guide for foreign policy, may well fall short of what would be rationally required by the overall interests of the United States. Yet the concept of the national interest which emerges from this contest of conflicting sectional interests is also more than any particular sectional interest or their sum total. It is, as it were, the lowest common denominator where sectional interests and the national interest meet in an uneasy compromise which may leave much to be desired in view of all the interests concerned. (Morgenthau 1952, p. 289)

This is an interesting remark for three reasons. First, it exposes Morgenthau's definition of power as being relational rather than structural (see Strange 1988, pp. 24–9). Expressions of sectional power can be measured in individual success stories and case studies where domestic actors profit, rather than the ability of dominant interests to determine the overall structure and context of foreign policy which best serves their interests. This appears to be a very narrow understanding of power in the world economy and international relations generally, which ignores the capacity for hegemonic states to set the rules and structures in which diplomacy is conducted.

Secondly, Morgenthau seems to equate the policy-making process which forms the national interest and foreign policy with a marketplace where interest groups compete on an equal footing for influence over government. Again, this does not seem a particularly realistic view of the policy-making process in complex societies such as the United States, where the level-playing field of influence is difficult to perceive.

And thirdly, the idea that despite competing sectional claims the national interest is somehow more than the sum of its parts, remains a vague and unsupported assertion. The result, described as 'the lowest common denominator', an 'uneasy compromise', leaving 'much to be desired' is hardly an inspiring or explicit defence of the concept. Nor does it leave the national interest as a clear and unambiguous principle of international politics which would be obvious to statesmen and academics alike.

As we shall see in a subsequent chapter, Morgenthau's notion of fixed, objective national interests which are not subject to sectional pressures or control, has been widely challenged. To foreshadow one critique it is worth quoting Ernst Haas who argues from a critical perspective that

there is no unified, immutable, and stable conception of national interest. Different groups entertain different policy motivations at any one time and tend to change their motivations over a period of time ... The conception of national interest which prevails at any one time is no more than an amalgam of varying policy motivations which tend to pass for a 'national' interest as long as the groups holding these opinions continue to rule. These motivations may be homogeneous or conflicting, depending on the nature of the ruling group. (Haas 1953, p. 382)

Another group of analysts who also want broadly to explain foreign policy behaviour sought to preserve the utility of the concept of the national interest by avoiding judgements of the *worth* of foreign policies, and instead used it as an analytical tool for explaining diplomatic behaviour. This group, which Rosenau calls the 'subjectivists', denied the existence of an objective reality which is discernible through systematic inquiry. For them, the national interest is not a singular objective truth which prevails regardless of whether or not it is perceived and understood by the members of a nation, but is in fact a set of subjective preferences which change whenever the needs and objectives of the citizenry change. For the 'subjectivists', the national interest can be disclosed by studying the decision-making policy process in each government. And because this involves a consideration of values, it is not susceptible to objective measurement. The national interest is whatever the policy elite is seeking to preserve and enhance (Rosenau 1964, pp. 35–6). This is clearly not an approach which Morgenthau could accept.

Morgenthau's realism is based on a priori assumptions about human nature (the rational pursuit of self-interest, will to power, utility maximisation, etc.) which by definition cannot be tested or verified to any meaningful extent. He makes a number of claims about the biological basis of the human drive for power and domination, without explaining other aspects of the human condition which are not as egoistic. What if these assumptions are flawed or do not conform in any actual sense to a shared reality? How can altruism beyond the interests of the nation be explained in national interest terms? (Donnelly 2000, pp. 44–9).

What are the implications for Morgenthau's book if there are no laws of politics at all, only subjective impressions? What happens to Morgenthau's argument if, as some post-modernists claim, there is no 'objective truth' or if there is no simple division between 'truth and rationality' on one hand and 'prejudice and subjective preference' on the other? Morgenthau sees strengths in a dispassionate and amoral approach to international relations when others might regard this as little more than a cover for, and rationalisation of, immoral and unethical behaviour.

Morgenthau's formulation of the national interest raises a number of other questions which, according to those who have rejected the salience of classical realism from a range of perspectives, he never convincingly addressed. For example, to say that states pursue their own interests does not tell us very much that is specific about their behaviour. To claim, as he does, that states ought to or even must define their interests in terms of power, rules out the identification of interest with ethical priorities such as justice, religious beliefs, human rights, altruism, the welfare and prosperity of its citizens and any obligations to humanity beyond the narrow concerns of the state. In fact he explicitly rules out any factors which are independent of considerations of power. And yet although states may try to accumulate power, that is not the only thing they seek to acquire or pursue. They also want prosperity, a sustainable environment and influence for their citizens on a global level, to name only three additional concerns.

According to Donnelly, 'Morgenthau's theory simply cannot tell us whether a state will seek safety or gain, prefer to attack or to defend, accept or eschew the risks of expansion. This indeterminacy is theoretically fatal because these objectives separately may imply radically different policies and together cover an immense range of possible behaviours.' His definition of the national interest amounts to little more than a 'typology for categorising a wide array of divergent, even contradictory, behaviours' (Donnelly 2000, pp. 46–7). This may not prove to be a very helpful set of guidelines for policy makers.

Morgenthau's concept of the national interest also betrays its normative aspects despite his claims of strict objectivity and rugged realism. A normative theory is one that is concerned with what ought to be rather than merely diagnosing what is. In its prescriptive nature, especially his exposition of rules which statesmen must follow and the privileged status of state security above all other considerations, the national interest for Morgenthau appears as much more than a simple neutral description of what is. It contains significant normative intent (Kratochwil 1982; Clinton 1986).

To be fair, Morgenthau maintained a subtle understanding of international politics. He acknowledged that in informing their own national interests, each state must take account of the fact that other states also have legitimate national interests formed in similar ways. When inevitable clashes of interests therefore took place, it was the function of diplomacy to find a peaceful and mutually acceptable resolution.

Waltz: national interests and anarchy

Kenneth Waltz parts company with what he calls the 'traditional realism' of Morgenthau by arguing that international politics can be thought of as a system with a precisely defined structure. Traditional or classical realism, in his view, is unable to conceptualise the international system in this way because it is limited by its behavioural methodology which 'explains political outcomes through examining the constituent parts of political systems'. According to this approach, 'the characteristics and the interactions of behavioural units are taken to be the direct cause of political events' (Waltz 1990, p. 33).

Morgenthau explains international outcomes by focusing on the actions and interactions of the units – the principles of human nature, the idea of interest defined in terms of power, the behaviour of statesmen – rather than highlighting the systemic constraints of international politics. He infers political outcomes from 'the salient attributes of the actors producing them' and ignores the effects of structure on state behaviour. According to Waltz, traditional realists could not explain behaviour at a level above the nation-state – theirs is an endogenous account (Waltz 1990, p. 34). Whereas Morgenthau argued that power is rooted in the nature of humankind, Waltz points to the anarchical condition of the international realm which he claims imposes the accumulation of power as a systemic requirement on states. The former explanation relies on a particular understanding of human nature and the interactions of units (e.g. the idea of interest defined in terms of power, the behaviour of statesmen, etc.) to explain conflict in international politics. The latter abandons such reliance, preferring to treat the international system as a separate domain which conditions the behaviour of all states within it. The distinction, in Waltz's vocabulary, is between reductionist (traditional realism) and systemic (neo-realism) accounts.

The key question which Waltz poses is: why do states exhibit similar foreign policy behaviour despite their different political systems and contrasting ideologies? Waltz cites the example of superpower behaviour during the Cold War to refute the argument that it is possible to infer the condition of international politics from the internal composition of states. The Soviet Union and the United States comprised quite different, if not antithetical political and social orders. And yet as Waltz points out, their behaviour during the period of East–West tension is remarkably similar. Their pursuit of military power and influence, their competition for strategic advantage and the exploitation of their respective spheres of influence were strikingly parallel. The explanation, says

Waltz, can be found in the systemic constraints on each state rather than their internal political, economic or social complexion. These systemic forces homogenise foreign policy behaviour by interposing themselves between states and their diplomatic conduct.

According to Waltz, the anarchic nature of the international system has the effect of socialising states, even non-conformist states with revolutionary regimes dedicated to systemic change, into the game of power politics. In Waltz's terms, states are functionally similar though their capabilities vary enormously. Their influence over and success in this game will depend upon their relative power, but they are all faced with the same primary dilemma: how to find security in an inherently insecure, volatile, dangerous and endemically violent world? The accumulation of military power, either directly or through membership of a military alliance, is the only available strategy for states.

Waltz has a different conception of the national interest to Morgenthau. Like most foreign policy, he regards the national interest as a product of the structure of the international system rather than something which is the personal responsibility and management of political leaders. According to Jackson and Sorensen:

> For classical realists the national interest is the basic guide of respon-
> sible foreign policy: it is a moral idea that must be defended and
> promoted by state leaders. For Waltz, however, the national interest
> seems to operate like an automatic signal commanding state leaders
> when and where to move. The difference here is: Morgenthau believes
> that state leaders are duty bound to conduct their foreign policies by
> reference to the guidelines laid down by the national interest, and
> they may be condemned for failing to do that. Waltz's neorealist
> theory hypothesizes that they will always do that more or less auto-
> matically. Morgenthau thus sees states as organizations guided by
> leaders whose foreign policies are successful or unsuccessful, depending
> on the astuteness and wisdom of their decisions. Waltz sees states as
> structures that respond to the impersonal constraints and dictates of
> the international system. (Jackson & Sorensen 2003, pp. 87–8)

The implication here is that neo-realists believe political leaders have limited discretion in defining the national interest because it is a systemic given. There is little apparent room for debate or argument about its content. Presumably neo-realists are somewhat bemused by the academic and diplomatic discussion which the national interest invariably invokes. It should be obvious to all.

Waltz places much less emphasis upon the national interest as a guide to state behaviour in the international realm. For Waltz, the national interest appears as an incontrovertible given, with the only interesting issue being the means adopted by states to achieve it.

> From an assumed interest, no useful inferences can be made unless we can figure out what actions are required for its successful pursuit ... to say that a state seeks its own preservation or pursues its national interest becomes interesting only if we can figure out what the national interest requires a country to do. (Waltz 1979, p. 134)

As we shall see in the discussion of the English School, Waltz has effectively reversed Hedley Bull's understanding of means and ends. The ends of diplomacy are, for Waltz, uncontroversial. They simply amount to the survival of the state. This is what the national interest comprises – 'each state plots the course it thinks will best serve its interests' (Waltz 1979, p. 113). To illustrate his argument, Waltz finds an analogue for the position of states in a self-help world in the form of a company in a competitive commercial environment.

> States, especially the big ones, are like major corporations. They are at once limited by their situations and able to act to affect them. They have to react to the actions of others whose actions may be changed by the reaction. As in an oligopolistic market, the outcome is indeterminate. Both the situation and the actors exercise influence, but neither controls. By comparing nations and corporations, the elusive notion of the national interest is made clear. By assumption, economic actors seek to maximise expected returns, and states strive to secure their survival. Major firms are in a self-help situation, with their survival depending on their own efforts within limits established by law. Insofar as they are in a self-help situation, survival outranks profit as a goal, since survival is a prerequisite to the achievement of other ends. This corollary attaches to the economists' basic assumption whenever the situation of firms enables them to influence both the market and one another. Relative gains may be more important than absolute ones because one's gain measured against that of others affects the ability to shift for oneself. (Waltz 1979, p. 134)

A number of points are raised here. The first is that states must accept that they can influence but not control the anarchic environment they find themselves in. This supports Waltz's belief in the relative immutability of the structure of the international system. Nevertheless, the comparison with firms in a competitive market may be misleading, given the capacity for companies with monopoly power or even dominant market shares to reshape the actual market to their commercial advantage. The experience of oligopolistic markets is not always 'indeterminate' when sufficient market power accrues to one player.

Secondly, the survival of the state must come before any other policy objective, such as economic prosperity or a higher ethical commitment. At base the national interest comprises the security of the state in an environment which it can do little to alter. This is not widely contested, but given the security of a particular state is not always at risk, it may be free to consider other priorities – i.e. obligations to humanity – without feeling any priority constraints which require it to address security concerns.

Thirdly, the capacity of a state to achieve its security will be determined by its relative rather than its absolute power – that is vis-à-vis other states. According to Waltz,

> to say that a country acts according to its national interest means that, having examined its security requirements, it tries to meet them. That is simple; it is also important. Entailed in the concept of national interest is the notion that diplomatic and military moves must at times be carefully planned lest the survival of the state be in jeopardy. The appropriate state action is calculated according to the situation in which the state finds itself. Great powers, like large firms, have always had to allow for the reactions of others. Each state chooses its own policies. To choose effectively requires considering the ends of the state in relation to its situation. (Waltz 1979, p. 134)

This argument is persuasive but it essentially rules out the notion of co-operative security between states which may eschew zero-sum considerations. Relative power is arguably only a consideration for states with a competitive foreign policy approach. There may be a national interest for states to pool their strategic power in a security community, rather than Waltz's assumption that states will always view themselves in an atomised rather than a collective sense.

Where Morgenthau claimed states were seeking absolute power, Waltz claims they are seeking security which can be gained with relative power. States cannot be anthropomorphised: they don't have aggressive personalities or an innate need to dominate others, as Morgenthau claims, but are driven to maximise their relative power because it is the best way they can secure their survival in an anarchical world.

Some of the differences between realism and neo-realism can therefore be grasped from their respective treatments of the national interest. According to Donnelly, 'Morgenthau saw the national interest as objective and subject to discovery by realist analysis. Neorealists, however, usually see the national interest (beyond the minimal goal of preserving sovereignty and territorial integrity) as subjective and given – "exogenous" to theory – rather than a subject of inquiry or analysis' (Donnelly 2000, p. 31). Exogenous in this sense means 'given or assumed independent of and prior to the interactions being analysed, and thus outside the scope of the theory' (Donnelly 2000, pp. 152–3). From such a central premise of classical realist thought, the national interest is all but ignored by neo-realism's pre-eminent exponent because it is largely assumed. As Donnelly remarks,

> structural realists [such as Waltz] treat interests as shaped by anarchy. Most characteristically, they argue that even states that otherwise would wish to pursue moral objectives are 'forced' by anarchy to define their national interests if not in terms of power, at least in terms of more material interests. The internally generated preferences of states run up against the threats posed by anarchy, leading to a redefinition of the national interest. (Donnelly 2000, p. 153)

For neo-realists, therefore, the national interests of states are broadly identical because the internal or domestic complexion of states is largely irrelevant to their primary diplomatic task – survival. This is a common primary goal of liberal-democratic, totalitarian and theocratic states alike. In other words, for this group the national interest is defined and determined by the anarchical condition of the international system. This is a much less ambitious and problematic claim than the one made by Morgenthau, though it is at times a frustratingly thin account.

Realism and national interests

In the domain of international politics, the term 'national interest' has held special significance for conventional perspectives of the study of international relations. According to both practitioners and academics, the 'national interest' should be the sole objective of a nation-state's foreign policy (Evans 1989, p. 9). For Millar, national interests are 'national concepts, substantially defined in a democracy by public consensus under government leadership' (Millar 1978, p. 40). The role of national leaders, according to this argument, is to take account of the variety of individual, social and sectional interests which exist within a nation, and channel them into a coherent set of policies for presentation to both their domestic constituency and the outside world. By this definition the national interest constitutes the aggregation of individual and group interests, and represents what is in the *common good* or *common interest* of the society.

Recognising these common or national interests is relatively straightforward for both classical realists and neo-realists, who still constitute many of the most influential theorists within the discipline of International Relations. Realists generally highlight the absence of any overarching authority which regulates the behaviour of nation-states towards each other. As has been argued, for neo-realists the world is anarchical and therefore inherently insecure for nation-states: competition and conflict between states is seen as endemic to the system and therefore inevitable. In these circumstances, the primary national interest of nation-states is the pursuit of national security, usually defined as physical survival and territorial integrity. The state has a duty to protect its citizens by accumulating military power, either by acquiring sufficient means to successfully wage war or entering into co-operative defence arrangements with greater strategic powers.

In defining national interests in broadly strategic terms, with the physical protection of the political community regarded as the primary objective of national policy, realists assume that nation-states are unitary actors in world politics. It is presupposed that all members of the community have a common interest in the nation's territorial integrity and physical survival: that in international politics, the whole community speaks with one voice and has a single identity.

The strength of the modern realist approach is that it does not normally go far beyond defining the national interest in terms of strategic power. This enables realism to explain foreign policy in exogenous terms. As has been shown, neo-realists such as Kenneth Waltz claim that there is no necessary link between the internal nature of a nation-state and its external behaviour. They argue that it is possible to abstract the states system (or strategic interaction) as a 'domain apart' from analyses which link foreign policy exclusively with the internal social and economic characteristics of states. Dominant ideologies, religions, modes of production and social organisation are said by neo-realists to have little impact on international behaviour. Even revolutionary leaders cannot escape the anarchical nature of the international system: they are soon 'socialised' into the game of power politics whether they like it or not. Despite the diversity of regimes around the world, neo-realists are able to point to the similarity of foreign policy approaches amongst nation-states.

The crucial conditioning factor, which homogenises the foreign policies of all states regardless of their internal political or social complexion, is the international system itself. According to neo-realists, the anarchical nature of the system – or to put it another way, the absence of a higher political authority than the nation-state – requires states to prioritise their security and survival before any other consideration. Endogenous factors are largely irrelevant because they cannot alter the nature of the system. Giving the highest importance to systemic factors reinforces the long-held realist assumption that nation-states, at least in their external behaviour, can be thought of as unitary actors. This approach to international politics, with its emphasis on exogenous or systemic factors, is not shared by other theoretical accounts.

For neo-realists such as Stephen Krasner, the state is regarded as a unified and autonomous actor with aims 'that are separate and distinct from the interests of any particular societal group'. Because the state is regarded as a neutral power broker between society's various sectional interests, the national interest 'consists of a set of transitively ordered state preferences concerned to promote the general well-being of the society'. It 'cannot be reduced to some summation of private desires' (Krasner 1978, pp. 5–45). According to Krasner's 'empirical-inductive' formulation, the national interest can be deduced from the statements and behaviour of the central decision makers, and must satisfy two criteria. First 'the actions of the leaders must be related to general objectives, not to the preferences of any particular group or class, or to the private power drives of officeholders'. Secondly, 'the ordering of [policy] preferences must persist over time' (Krasner 1978, pp. 35–6). For Krasner, national interests have a transcendent status.

Despite his general adherence to neo-realist principles, this approach puts Krasner squarely in Rosenau's 'subjectivist' group. He wants to focus attention on the statements and actions of decision makers, instead of believing that the national interest has an objective reality. Krasner believes that national interests are indivisible and cannot be reduced to the preferences of particular interests or interest groups. And they must be seen as permanent or at the very least, semi-permanent. There is also a hint in Krasner's perspective that the national interest is more than the sum of its parts, that it is in fact more than the aggregation of individual and group interests. This is not an uncommon idea in realist thought, although there is something of a mystical quality about such a claim. If the national interest comprises more than the sum total of private community interests, what are the additional factors? What additional features are present when the collective interest is formed? Unfortunately, this is rarely explained.

Although self-identified as a realist, Robert Gilpin parts company with Morgenthau, Waltz, Krasner and other realists on this issue. According to Gilpin, who betrays his political economy background in the assertion, 'strictly speaking, states, as such, have no interests, or what economists call "utility functions," nor do bureaucracies, interest groups, or so-called transnational actors, for that matter. Only individuals and individuals joined together into various types or coalitions can be said to have interests' (Gilpin 1981, p. 18). The implication here is that only moral agents can have interests. This is not a claim most realists would be willing to make.

In language more closely associated with both the liberal and Marxist traditions, Gilpin disagrees with many realists on the issue of who or which groups actually drive state policy in the external domain. According to Gilpin, 'the objectives and foreign policies of states are determined primarily by the interests of their dominant members or ruling coalitions' (Gilpin 1981, p. 19). This concession takes the national interest away from a conception of the common good. It represents a direct challenge to Morgenthau's claim that dominant groups are rarely successful in determining the course of US foreign policy and that the national interest is normally a successful compromise between divergent sectional interests. It appears, then, that within the realist tradition there is a broader range of views about the constitution of the national interest, both within classical realism and between classical and neo-realism, than has hitherto been acknowledged. Gilpin seems to accept that the national interest must ultimately be articulated by a dominated group which has the wider interests of the entire community at heart. As we shall see in the chapter on critical approaches to the national interest, he is anticipating some of the objections which have been raised to classical realism's formulation of the national interest.

The national interests: problems as an analytical tool

There has always been a lack of conceptual clarity with the use of the national interest as an explanatory tool. According to Rosenau, there are numerous problems with the use of the national interest as a concept for analytical use.

> One is the ambiguous nature of the nation and the difficulty of speci-fying *whose interests* it encompasses. A second is the elusiveness *of the criteria for determining the existence of interests* and for tracing their presence in substantive policies. Still another confounding factor is the absence of *procedures for cumulating the interests* once they have been identified. This is in turn complicated by uncertainty as to whether the national interest has been fully identified once all the specific interests have been cumulated or whether there are not other, more generalised values which render the national interest *greater than the sum of its parts*. (Rosenau 1964, p. 36, emphasis added)

Although it is routinely asserted that nations act to pursue their national interests, which are assumed to be in the nation's *best* interests, this is never self-evident. As Rosenau says, what is best for the nation 'is not even potentially knowable as a single truth' (Rosenau, 1964, p. 36). Goals and interests are constituted by values and subjective preferences, so there are potentially as many different interpretations of the national interest as there are members of the nation. As Rosenau suggests, 'to explain that a certain policy is in the national interest, or to criticise it for being contrary to the national interest, is to give an imposing label to one's own conception of what is a desirable or undesirable course of action' (Rosenau 1964, pp. 36–7). Subjective interpretations are therefore unavoidable.

Even realists who assert that the survival of the state should be at the very basis of national interests are expressing a subjective preference. Can this judgement be taken for granted? What about secessionist groups or ethnic minorities who wish to leave or reconfigure the nation-state? Or a substantial minority within a state who wish to blend it into a wider regional or global federation? The survival of the (existing) state should be seen as a preference for stasis and the status quo, always a contested idea in international politics. There are realists in the modern world who are all for the preservation and protection of nation-states, though not necessarily as they are presently configured. In fact an argument can be mounted within the realist tradition that until political boundaries are drawn up in a less unrealistic way, the identification of national interests with an emphasis on the common interests of a viable and legitimate bounded community, is fraught with problems. It was E.H. Carr, one of the founders of the realist tradition, who first warned about the dangers of assuming that revisionist states with legitimate grievances about their power, territory and influence, will be forever satisfied with the status quo. There is nothing especially 'realistic' about assuming that the international system as it is currently configured is immutable. Quite the contrary.

Classical realists, in particular Morgenthau, believed they were relieved of the problem of subjectivity because they were dealing with interests defined in terms of power. For them, national power was an objective and quantifiable reality which ultimately determined state policy. However, as much writing in political science has subsequently emphasised, power is neither objective, easy to measure or always clearly defined. How can national power be clearly established? How can the national will or the morale of troops be measured? How much emphasis should be given to economic as opposed to military factors? Or structural as opposed to relational power? And even if all the component parts of the nation's power could be identified, how could they be aggregated? None of these questions can be answered without reference to an expression of individual value preferences. It is difficult, then, to disagree with Rosenau's conclusion that 'a description of the national interest can never be more than a set of conclusions derived from the analytic and evaluative framework of the describer' (Rosenau 1964, p. 37). From this analysis, the idea of 'objective' national interests looks unsustainable.

The question of 'which groups constitute the nation?' may seem an odd one for realists who simply equate the nation with the citizens of the state: those who reside within the existing territorial boundaries of the state. However, this assumption ignores a number of *realities* which do not easily conform to the model. What about stateless nations, such as the Kurds and the Palestinians? What about refugees and exiles from the state; are their interests also represented here? Do national interests extend beyond political communities to moral communities? How should the interests of diasporas be treated? Privileging national interests above all other considerations in the determination of foreign policy leaves many questions like these unanswered. The national interest may be a vital prism for national leaders who want to couch their decisions in terms which will appear to benefit all of their constituents, but they rarely show a preparedness to address these important questions which go the very heart of policy formation.

The other part of the answer to the question – which groups constitute the nation? – deals with the dilemma of aggregating or cumulating the interests of complex heterogeneous societies. How can such a vast array of cultural, ethnic and social groups which expect their specific interests to be represented by the state, be identified and balanced? How are the well organised and articulate with very specific foreign policy interests factored into the wider expression of community opinion? How does the state channel such a wide, and often conflicting clamour of voices into a single, coherent and consensually supported policy? How can the relative weight of so many conflicting interests be determined? These are ultimately challenges for the political process in each community. It may make some sense in a liberal democratic society to rely on the official decision-making process, but what happens in a closed authoritarian state? Because realists eschew endogenous factors such as the nature of the political system within a state in their theoretical considerations, there appears to be a significant gap in their understanding of the national interest. Only a truly democratic government could successfully accomplish the task of cumulation.

How useful can a generalised and even universal conception of the national interest be? The expression of a truly authentic national interest which takes account of these questions is, to put it mildly, a major analytical challenge for realists.

Economic globalisation versus national interests

Contemporary economic and technological developments – grouped under the rubric 'globalisation' – are transforming the nature of international politics, and pose a number of challenges to realist thought, in particular the relevance of traditional definitions of the national interest. Cross-border capital flows, trade liberalisation, the privatisation of government-owned enterprises, deregulation and the need to maintain economies open to foreign investment, are seen as both evidence of the dominance of neo-liberalism since the 1970s and the decline of state power.

Furthermore, the rising importance of non-state actors such as transnational corporations and the foreign investment community are said to not only endanger national economic sovereignty – which is the very basis of national interests – but, according to liberals, are also evidence of the growing interdependence of the world's economies and the commensurate pacification of international relations. To many liberals, globalisation and the promise of a 'borderless world' represents not only a change in the nature of diplomacy but also to the very structure of the international system.

Although some governments have claimed that it is an irresistible force which they are often powerless to influence, the starting point for any discussion of economic globalisation should be an acknowledgment that it is a human creation and not part of the order of nature. As with the establishment of national markets last century, globalisation is in no way the result of the gradual and spontaneous emancipation of the economic sphere from government control. On the contrary, it has been the outcome of conscious and often violent state intervention by advanced capitalist states such as the United States. As Gramsci argued, 'it must be made clear that laissez-faire too is a form of state "regulation", introduced and maintained by legislative and coercive means. It is a deliberate policy, conscious of its own ends, and not the spontaneous, automatic expression of economic facts' (Gramsci 1971, p. 160).

Just as domestically the labour market can only be 'freed' by legislative restrictions placed on trades unions, the creation of the post-war liberal trading regime and the de-regulation of the world's capital markets in the 1970s required deliberate acts by interventionary states. Globalisation should therefore be understood primarily as state policy (see Polanyi 1957; Strange 1996; Hirst & Thompson 1999; Gilpin 2000).

Consistent with neo-liberal economic orthodoxy, during the current phase of globalisation national economic sovereignty has not so much been lost by governments, as enthusiastically given away in certain specific sectors. The state's capacity to direct the national economy has been deliberately and significantly undercut by the globalisation of relations of production and exchange. Significant amounts of sovereign economic power, for example, has been ceded to bond holders, funds managers, currency traders, speculators, transnational banks and insurance companies.

Supporters of globalisation argue that 'economic globalisation is bringing about a "denationalisation" of economies through the establishment of transnational networks of production, trade and finance. In this "borderless" economy, national governments are relegated to little more than transmission belts for global capital or, ultimately, simple intermediate institutions sandwiched between increasingly powerful local, regional and global mechanisms of governance' (Held, McGrew et al. 1999, p. 3).

This is not to suggest that states are simply the losers in a battle with global market forces. The rise of market power and the concomitant decline of state authority are precisely what liberals have always sought. As Strange notes, the impersonal forces of world markets, integrated over the postwar period more by private enterprise in finance, industry and trade than by the cooperative decisions of governments, are now more powerful than states to whom ultimate political authority over society and economy is supposed to belong. Where states were once masters of markets, now it is markets which, on many crucial issues, are the masters over the governments of states. (Strange 1996, p. 4)

Unsurprisingly, these developments, and the ideas which underpin them, represent a major challenge to realist thinking – especially the primacy that is given to national interests. However, it is only very recently that neo-realists such as Waltz, Krasner and Gilpin have responded to the neo-liberal challenge. Their rebuttal has a number of separate components to it, but can be summarised in Krasner's claim that 'there is no evidence that globalisation has systematically under-mined state control or led to the homogenisation of policies and structures. In fact, globalisation and state activity have moved in tandem' (Krasner 1999, p. 223). For realists, national interests remain relevant because the claims made about globalisation's challenge to the autonomy and relevance of states have either been grossly exaggerated or entirely mistaken.

First, neo-realists are sceptical of the extent to which economic globalisation is a truly global phenomenon. They point to Africa, Latin America, Russia and the Middle East as significant regions of the world which have been relatively untouched by the forces of globalisation. Globalisation remains predominantly a Western experience (see Waltz 2000).

Secondly, if trade or capital flows are measured as a percentage of Gross National Product, the level of economic interdependence in the world in 1999 approximately equals that of 1910. The figure is even lower if interdependence is measured by the mobility of labour, and lower still if measured by the mutual military dependence of states. Neo-realists are therefore unimpressed by claims made about the unprecedented levels of contemporary economic interdependence in the world (see Hirst & Thompson 1999). They are willing to concede that money markets specifically, have been truly globalised as a result of the Nixon 'shocks' of the 1970s and advances in information tech-nology. As a consequence there has been a loss of state autonomy and control in this area. However, they also point out that financial markets in 1900 were at least as integrated as they are now (Waltz 2000, p. 2). And capital flows in the nineteenth century as a percentage of global economic product were far greater than current levels (Gilpin 1996, p. 17).

Thirdly, in response to the liberal claim that only the market model will produce sustained levels of prosperity, Waltz reminds liberals that in the 1930s and 1950s, growth rates in the USSR were among the world's highest, as was Japan's in the 1970s and 1980s when a model of corporate mercantilism was practiced. Historically a 'one size fits all' model of political economy, now sometimes called the 'Washington consensus', has not been the only route to economic modernisation or successful growth.

The anti-statism of neo-liberalism is also difficult to justify. Liberals forget or ignore the fact that 'states perform essential political, social and economic functions, and no other organisation rivals them in these respects. ... States turn possession into property and thus make saving, production and prosperity possible. The sovereign state with fixed borders has proved to be the best organisation for keeping peace internally and fostering the conditions for economic well-being' (Waltz 2000, p. 4). According to realists, there is no alternative form of political community which is likely to capture the loyalties of people across the globe. It is important to remember the political underpinnings of globalisation and its management by state officials in any discussion of the virtues of a market economy (see Gilpin 2000). The acquisition and management of state power is at the very basis of contemporary economic globalisation.

Neo-realists remind liberals that as a preferred form of political community, the nation-state has no serious rival. They can cite a number of important powers retained by the state despite globalisation, including monopoly control of the weapons of war and their legitimate use, and the sole right to tax its citizens. Only the nation-state can still command the political allegiances of its citizens or adjudicate in disputes between them. And it is the nation-state which has the exclusive authority to bind the whole community to international law. As Krasner argues, not all the constituent parts of a nation-state's sovereignty are equally vulnerable to globalisation (Krasner 1999). If they were, most public discussion of national interests within liberal democracies, especially in relation to regulation of foreign investment or the negoti-ation of free trade arrangements, would have evaporated some time ago. Clearly that has not occurred. If anything, the awareness and discussion of economic globalisation has raised the profile of national interest considerations. To give a brief example, public concerns about the takeover of national business assets by 'foreigners' – especially iconic brands with high local profiles – is frequently expressed as a contest between economic efficiency and the need for foreign investment in the economy on the one hand, and the national interest on the other.

Fourthly, economic activity is not as global as some liberals would have us believe. The largest economies continue to conduct most of their business in their home markets – 90 per cent of the US economy, for example, produces goods and services for Americans rather than the export market. The figure is similar in leading European economies. And if judged in terms of where assets, management, ownership, headquarters and R & D funding is principally located, transnational corporations are not as global as first thought. Despite their popular image, they remain largely anchored at home (Gilpin 1996, p. 24).

Fifthly, as one would expect, neo-realists regard the military power of states as being far more important in conditioning international politics than economic globalisation. Strategic or military power is the ultimate projection and expression of the national interest. 'The most important events in international politics are explained by differences in the capabilities of states, not by economic forces operating across states or transcending them.' High levels of economic interdependence early last century failed to prevent the First World War, nor did economic integration forestall the breakup of Yugoslavia at the end of the century. When it comes to inhibiting conflict, neo-realists are in no doubt that nuclear weapons are more effective than shared economic interests. 'The uneven distribution of capabilities continues to be the key to understanding international politics' (Waltz 2000, pp. 1–7).

Finally, whether or not the current wave of Islamic militancy is the latest chapter in a long-standing revolt against the West, it seems premature for liberals to claim that the emergence of Al Qaeda and affiliated groups which perpetrate transnational terrorism constitutes a victory for the deterritorialisation of world politics (Buzan 2003, pp. 297 & 303). Rather as David Harvey notes, 'the war on terror, swiftly followed by the prospect of war with Iraq ... [has] allowed the state to accumulate more power', a claim difficult to refute and one that poses an unexpected new challenge to liberals who believed globalisation was finally eroding the sovereign power of the state and the contemporary relevance of national interests (Harvey 2003, p. 17).

The resuscitation of state power across the industrialised world after the 9/11 attacks has taken numerous forms, including new restrictions on civil liberties, greater powers of surveillance and detention, increased military spending and the expansion of intelligence services. The threats posed by Islamic terror and the dangers of Weapons of Mass

Destruction (WMD) have also been met by an increase in state intervention around the world, in particular by US-led coalitions acting in Afghanistan and Iraq. With each subsequent terrorist assault, states which consider themselves innocent victims have been emboldened to interfere in each others' internal affairs – even pre-emptively. These are developments realists would have little difficulty understanding.

Pre-emption, the disarmament of states alleged to possess WMD, regime change, humanitarianism and the spread of democracy have all been invoked as public justifications for these interventions, although critics have pointed to traditional geostrategic rationales beneath the surface. Regardless of what the true motives for these interventions and restrictions are, the irony of socially conservative, economically neo-liberal governments expanding the reach and size of government should not be lost on anyone. Bigger government deals a heavy blow to those who eagerly anticipated the demise of the state and the end of national interest diplomacy.

The return of the overarching state is an unsurprising response to community calls for protection from non-state terrorism. When citizens of a state require emergency medical relief, as many victims of the Bali bombings did in October 2002, there is little point appealing to market forces for help. Nor can those responsible for attacks such as the Beslan school atrocity in September 2004 be hunted down, disarmed and prosecuted by privately owned transnational companies. Even if the state is no longer prepared to insulate its citizens from the vicissitudes of the world economy, it is still expected to secure them from the threat of terrorism. Only the state can meet these and many other challenges such as 'border protection' and transnational crime. There are no market-based solutions to the dangers posed by what seems to be the latest chapter in the revolt against the West.

To illustrate the enduring relevance of national interests under contemporary forces of economic globalisation, realists also point to the important ongoing role of the state in the negotiation of free trade deals and the regulation of foreign investment. These are always presented to the domestic constituency by leaders as being 'in the national interest', if only because voters in liberal democracies still think politically in national interest terms. The national interest remains an important ingredient of their political and foreign policy discourse.

Modern liberal economic orthodoxy argues that exposing an economy to the efficiency disciplines of market forces is the best way to achieve economic competitiveness and modernity. The pursuit of free trade rather than protectionism is an important means of achieving this outcome. In the Australian context this has been argued forthrightly in the transnationally-owned media, that 'the bottom line is that, regardless of what other countries do, cutting tariffs is in the national interest' (*The Australian*, 11.7.95). According to a former foreign minister, 'it is gradually coming to be appreciated that breaking down such remaining barriers as stand in the way of economic interdependence is a matter of intelligent self-interest; that it is against all experience, as well as all theory, to yearn after autarky in a world increasingly interconnected' (Evans & Grant 1995, p. 12).

However, the fact that this case needs to be made at all is an acknowledgement that the protection of local industries from the rigours of international competition has been, and continues to be seen by some, as justified in national interest terms. Protectionism and other forms of state 'intervention' in the market are an implied acknowledgement that there are national interests which would be threatened by unfettered competition, and therefore need to be supported and insulated by the state. Whether or not this constitutes a concession that free trade produces winners and losers, or that there are sensitive industries and sectors of the economy which must remain under national control, it is clear that national interest considerations require the state to play an important role in the nation's economic development. More generally it must also be acknowledged that trade policy is a site for conflicting views of how the national interest can best be defined and pursued.

Sovereignty and the national interest are also key considerations in the area of foreign investment. The fact that states regulate foreign investment and that governments are especially sensitive about foreign takeovers of local businesses, is an explicit acknowledgement of this.

The Foreign Investment Review Board (FIRB) in the Australian Treasury is the gatekeeper between foreign capital and nationally owned equity and assets. FIRB support for foreign acquisitions of Australian businesses has been routine for over a decade, with estimates in the mid-1990s putting the approval rating as high as 98 per cent, though even a 2 per cent rejection rate was enough to regularly upset other states such as the United States. In 1998–9 100 per cent of foreign takeovers of Australian businesses were approved by the FIRB. And yet the Foreign Investment Review Board is specifically charged with protecting 'the Australian national interest' in cases of foreign takeovers, even though 'the national interest' is not defined in either the board's governing legislation nor in its guidelines for foreign investors. It is ultimately a matter of ministerial discretion.

Critics would argue that governments are either quietly conceding that the nation no longer has any significant interest in who owns its equity, or are admitting that in the era of globalisation it should not or cannot regulate the ownership of Australian assets. However, the mere fact that governments will periodically block foreign takeovers of Australian-owned businesses (e.g. Royal Dutch Shell's bid for Woodside Petroleum in 2001) suggests that they are reluctant to surrender this discretionary power completely. The national interest, in the form of maintaining majority Australian ownership of local enterprises, stands between foreign direct investment and unfettered capital flows and globalisation. Even liberal-minded governments which may wish to dispense with the regulation of foreign investment altogether are unlikely to risk the likely electoral backlash which would follow. They will certainly continue to justify their policy decisions in national interest terms.

Although ultimately aborted in 1998 by nervous governments, the Multilateral Agreement on Investment (MAI) was a vivid illustration of just how keen some states are to surrender their discretionary powers in this area to the markets. OECD members were offering to voluntarily restrict their own ability to discriminate against foreign capital, thus ruling out special treatment or any legislative favours for endogenous capital. The MAI also sought to prevent each member-state from expropriating property owned transnationally (Goodman & Ranald 2000).

When community concerns about the MAI surfaced in Australia in early 1998 – prior to its abandonment a few months later in the OECD – the Australian Government attempted to quell public fear by speaking about the agreement in nationalist terms. Although the Howard Government embraced globalisation as a means of modernising the Australian economy, it recognised that the public were easily spooked by talk of globalisation and economic interconnectedness. Thus the Assistant Treasurer reassured the Australian people that 'we will not sign the [MAI] treaty unless it is demonstrably in Australia's national interest to do so' (Kemp 1998). How this would be done or demonstrated was not explained, but it is significant that a government was still prepared to apply the national interest test as a means of neutralising community concerns about economic globalisation.

Globalisation has undermined the nation-state in several ways. The capacity of each state to control the political loyalties of its citizens has been weakened by an increasing popular awareness of the problems faced by the entire human species. The state cannot prevent its citizens turning to a range of sub-national and transnational agents to secure their political identities and promote their political objectives. Sovereignty is no longer an automatic protection against external interference called 'humanitarian intervention'. And decision-making on a range of environmental, economic and security questions has become internationalised, rendering national administration often much less important than transnational political co-operation (Linklater 1998, pp. 30–1). These are enormously complex issues and contemporary developments which should prompt a re-thinking of what the national interest means in contemporary international politics.

Despite these important changes, realists would nevertheless argue that liberals are premature in announcing the demise of the nation-state or the irrelevance of national interests. They would inform the supporters of globalisation that as a preferred form of political community, the nation-state still has no serious rival. There are currently over 200 nation-states in the world asserting their political independence.

As has been noted, realists cite a number of important powers retained by the state despite globalisation, including monopoly control of the weapons of war and their legitimate use, and the sole right to tax its citizens. They argue that only the nation-state can still demand and command the political allegiances of its citizens or adjudicate in legal disputes between them. They would also remind liberals that it is the nation-state which has the exclusive authority to bind the whole community to international law, including a nascent international court system.

These monopoly powers ensure that governments will continue to speak in terms of national interests in explaining and justifying their diplomatic behaviour. Globalisation has certainly weakened the authority of the nation-state. What liberals regard as its inefficient and corrupting influence in commercial relations is certainly in retreat. National economic planning is no longer as routine as it once was.

However, realists can still persuasively argue that the nation-state remains the pre-eminent actor in international relations and will continue to remain so as long as the international system retains its anarchical character. The character of global politics after the terrorist strikes of September 2001 has been shaped domestically by the growing reach of the state into the civil life of citizens and internationally by conventional great-power behaviour in its most violent form. These developments should be seen as a setback for globalisation.

Even liberals who define the national interest in terms of a desirable decline in national economic sovereignty are forced to concede that self-regulating markets require state intervention; 'for as long as that system is not established, economic liberals must and will unhesi-tatingly call for the intervention of the state in order to establish it, and once established, in order to maintain it' (Chomsky 1993, p. 149). It is therefore premature to consign national interests to history.

Conclusion

In this chapter it has been argued that Morgenthau's early and influential articulation of the principle of the national interest was problematic. It was neither entirely objective nor subjective, variable or invariable. Given his claim that it was a fundamental principle which guided the conduct and understanding of international politics, Morgenthau's suggestion that the interest of a nation can be defined solely in terms of power seemed inadequate, somewhat nebulous, and raised more questions than it answered. Clearly he regarded it as an objective defini-tion of the national interest, even if others did not.

Waltz's belief that a nation's desire for security through the accumu-lation of power could be assumed, overcame much of Morgenthau's apparent confusion and contradiction, and opened up the more inter-esting question of how states pursue their primary interests. Waltz's neo-realism brought greater intellectual rigour and systematic under-standing to the behaviour of states by analysing the issue in systemic rather than reductionist terms. However, the automaticity underlying Waltz's understanding of the term meant that neo-realism's idea of the national interest is largely underdeveloped and insignificant.

Waltz and Morgenthau share a belief that at its most simple, the national interest privileges the survival of the state. But even this is problematic. In recent years states have come into and gone out of existence with the enthusiastic participation and backing of their citizens (e.g. USSR, East and West Germany, Yugoslavia, Czechoslovakia, North and South Yemen, East Timor). Realist and neo-realist assumptions about a national interest in the survival of the state tends to imply an immutability of political boundaries, and fails to sufficiently acknowledge that shifting frontiers are a normal feature of international politics.

Although it is possible to adumbrate a range of nuanced realist versions of the national interest, with variations from Krasner and Gilpin being two important examples, all realists assert the enduring relevance of national interest considerations in the era of globalisation. For as long as the state remains a primary actor in international politics, even the conduct of transnational commerce will not entirely escape the clutches of the state and the interests of nations. This remains true, even if expressions of national interests in the contemporary era of globalisation are, with a few exceptions, somewhat rhetorical. The decline of sovereign economic power has meant that for the state, policies enacted in the national interest may only constitute the increasing transfer of political and economic authority to non-state actors, although the latest wave of Islamist terror may reverse this trend.

Similarly, realists deny the existence of a cosmopolitan ethic which demands that on occasions, the national attachments of individuals within a state should surrender to the higher ethical conviction that their primary loyalties are to the whole of humanity. As will be shown in a subsequent chapter, it is often difficult to explain arms control and disarmament, the resettlement of refugees, overseas aid and development assistance, and human rights diplomacy – each issue with a significant ethical component – in strictly national interest terms. This is a subject that will be explored in a later chapter.

However, it is in the area of global security that the national interest continues to exert its conceptual authority in the discipline of International Relations. For realists, the state must act autonomously from social structural influences because the national community shares a common and indivisible interest in its security and protection from external threats. This was, after all, the promise of the state under the original social contract in exchange for the surrender of important individual freedoms. Given the state remains the preferred form of political organisation under which the world lives, surprisingly little has changed in this specific regard. Any discussion of security issues in international politics cannot entirely avoid realist claims about the enduring importance of the national interest.

3
Critical Perspectives: Marxist and Anarchist Approaches

One of the devices used to obscure plain facts is the concept of the 'national interest', a mystification that serves to conceal the ways in which state policy is formed and executed. Within the nation, there are individuals and groups who have interests, often conflicting ones; furthermore, such groups do not observe national boundaries. Within a particular nation-state, some groups are sufficiently powerful to exert a major, perhaps dominant interest over state policy and the ideological system. Their special interests then become, in effect, 'the national interest'.

(Noam Chomsky, *Language and Politics*)

The pretense is that there really is such a thing as 'the United States', subject to occasional conflicts and quarrels, but fundamentally a community of people with common interests. It is as if there really is a 'national interest', represented in the Constitution, in territorial expansion, in the laws passed by Congress, the decisions of the courts, the development of capitalism, the culture of education and the mass media. ... [But] nations are not communities and never have been. The history of any one country, presented as the history of a family, conceals fierce conflicts of interest (sometimes exploding, most often repressed) between conquerors and conquered, masters and slaves, capitalists and workers, dominators and dominated in race and sex.

(Howard Zinn, *The Twentieth Century: A People's History*)

In modern political discourse, appeals to the national interest are usually made in contrast to claims by sectional interests – the greater national good rather than the domestic group interest. The nation's interest is commonly regarded as the highest political value beyond which there can be no claim: the sum total is considered greater than the individual parts. Appealing to the national interest is also designed to confer legitimacy upon public policy, invoking a sense of patriotism and group loyalty which should not be challenged.

Rarely, however, is the national interest explained or defined. It is mostly presupposed. This is the point at which critical analysis departs from conventional understandings. Critical analysis of foreign policy begins with the question of whether national interests in the context of international relations actually exist.[1]

In this chapter the evolution of critical perspectives of the national interest will be examined, concentrating on the contribution of classical Marxist and anarchist thought in this area, the strengths and weaknesses of critical approaches to the national interest, and concluding with an explication of contemporary critical perspectives.

Introduction

Critical perspectives of the 'national interest' begin by arguing that if we hope to understand anything about the foreign policy of a state, it is important to start by investigating its domestic social structure. Who sets foreign policy? What interests do these people represent? What is the domestic source of their power? In other words, whose interests are defined as the nation's interests? According to critical approaches, it is reasonable to assume that the foreign policy of a state will represent the particular interests of those who design it (Otero 1981, pp. 22–3). Foreign policy is therefore a reflection of the internal political and economic structure of the state – an endogenous interpretation and explanation of external state behaviour.

Critical conceptions claim that the 'national interest' is always articulated by those who control the central economic and political institutions of a nation-state, and that there is therefore no reason to believe that the 'national interest' will reflect the common interests of the whole society. This approach implies that the 'national interest' is

---

[1] The term 'critical' is used here generically to denote more radical approaches to international politics. It includes but does not specifically refer to Critical Theory, a philosophical approach originally associated with the Frankfurt School of Social Research and now a broad philosophical school itself.

largely a propaganda term – part of a process of dissimulation. It is not defined by what is actually in the interests of the entire population. Rather, 'the national interest' comprises what is in the interests of the dominant elites who command the resources which enable them to control the state. According to Magdoff, 'the national interest becomes equated with the interests of those individuals and institutions who, by virtue of their ownership of the decisive wealth of the community, direct and regulate the allocation of economic resources' (Magdoff 1978, p. 186).

From a critical perspective, the conventional understanding and portrayal of the national interest is purposively deceptive. It conceals the fact that governments routinely act to pursue the interests of a small privileged and powerful sector of the community while claiming to act on behalf of the entire population. In the economic domain especially, governments pursue *particular* rather than *common* interests. This is said to be inevitable in class divided societies.

As has been noted, central to conventional understandings of the national interest is the idea that the state can claim to represent the community or public interest – the 'general will' – rather than the private interests of individuals. It is assumed that the state can and does act primarily as a unified actor in international politics. However, according to critical approaches, in capitalist societies the distinction between public interests on one hand, and private interests on the other, is somewhat illusory. 'The state defends the "public" or "community" as if: classes did not exist; the relationship between classes was not exploitative; classes did not have fundamental differences of interest; [and] these differences of interest did not define economic and political life' (Held 1983, p. 25). This is clearly an argument that can be challenged on a number of fronts. As Howard Zinn argues, 'the notion that all our interests are the same (the political leaders and the citizens, the millionaire and the homeless person) deceives us. It is a deception useful to those who run modern societies, where the support of the population is necessary for the smooth operation of the machinery of everyday life and the perpetuation of the present arrangements of wealth and power' (Zinn 1997, p. 339).

The idea of particular classes disguising the pursuit of their own interests while representing their ideas as universally beneficial, is central to critical approaches to foreign policy analysis. In particular, these perspectives argue that the role of the state in defending and promoting the interests of capital should be prominent in any examination of a nation-state's external behaviour.

Adam Smith and the interests of society

In the conclusion of Book I of his *Wealth of Nations*, Adam Smith distinguishes between 'three great, original and constituent orders of every civilised society', those who live by rent, those who live by wages and those who live by profit (Smith 1976, Bk I, Ch. XI, p. 276). Smith defines each group according to whether or not its specific interests are connected with the general interest of the society.

According to Smith, the first two groups – those who live by rent and those who live by wages – are 'strictly and inseparably connected with the general interest of the society' (Smith 1976, Bk I, Ch. XI, pp. 276–7). Rent prices and wages are subject to market pressures from society generally, and cannot be independently set without the risk of being priced out of range altogether. However, the interest of the third order – those who live by profit – 'has not the same connection with the general interest of the society as that of the other two'. According to Smith, the merchants and manufacturers 'are commonly exercised rather about the interest of their own particular branch of business, than about that of the society ... the rate of profit does not, like rent and wages, rise with the prosperity, and fall with the declension, of the society. On the contrary, it is naturally low in rich, and high in poor countries, and it is always highest in the countries which are going fastest to ruin' (Smith 1976, Bk I, Ch. XI, p. 277).

According to Smith, because this third order have a superior knowledge of their own interests than the other two groups, they are more easily able to dominate economic life by manipulating market conditions to their own advantage. By minimising competition, they maximise their own profits at the expense of the public interest. Thus 'the interest of the dealers ... in any particular branch of trade or manufacturers, is always in some respects different from, and even opposite to, that of the public'. Smith warns that any proposal for laws and regulations which come from this group ought to be received with the utmost scepticism. All such proposals 'come from an order of men, whose interest is never exactly the same with that of the public, who have generally an interest to deceive and even to oppress the public, and who accordingly have, upon many occasions, both deceived and oppressed it' (Smith 1976, Bk I, Ch. XI, p. 278).

Smith identifies the mercantile system as an example of where the interests of society are clearly and consciously disaggregated.

> It cannot be very difficult to determine who have been the contrivers
> of this whole mercantile system; not the consumers, we may believe,

whose interest has been entirely neglected; but the producers [merchants and manufacturers], whose interest has been carefully attended to. (Smith 1976, Bk IV, Ch. VIII, p. 180)

The significance of Smith's account is his acknowledgement that there are clear class divisions in early capitalist societies and that these classes do not automatically share common economic interests. In fact, Smith asserts that those who live by profit from their stocks and investments do not have the general interests of society at heart. For him, the opposite case is a more accurate description.

This is perhaps a surprising perspective from someone regularly invoked as the father of classical and liberal economics. Smith is often presented as a champion of free markets which are in turn claimed to be in the best interests of the *whole* society. This is partly true, and his explanation of the 'invisible hand' of the market directing production and labour to its optimal and most efficient use remains a powerful and influential idea. However, his remarks about the disaggregating effects of industrial commerce are less regularly invoked. According to Smith, the creed of those who live by profit is explicitly egoistic rather than civically minded: 'All for ourselves, and nothing for other people, seems, in every age of the world, to have been the vile maxim of the masters of mankind' (Smith 1976, Bk III, Ch. IV, p. 437). It is a theme and an observation which inspired Marx to develop his equally influential thoughts on capitalism.

Marx and international politics

Marx and his analysis of capitalism have been conspicuously absent from the curricula of mainstream International Relations in the West, especially before the 1970s (Linklater 1990). There are three broad reasons for this.

First, in the Western world last century Marxism was closely associated with Communist states such as the USSR, China and Vietnam. It was the self-proclaimed philosophical foundation of the Communist world, which by its very political outlook constituted a threat to Western capitalist states. During the Cold War Marxism was widely portrayed in Western political capitals as expansionist and messianic because it was routinely equated with the foreign policy of Communist states which were thought to represent a strategic challenge to the West (Kubalkova & Cruickshank 1989, part II). Marxist thought and doctrine were rarely separated from the repression and crimes committed in his name by states which were cast in the West as an ideological, economic and security danger (see Halliday 1994, pp. 47–50).

In this atmosphere, which in one form or another lasted from the Bolshevik revolution in 1917 until the collapse of the USSR in the early 1990s, Marxism was tainted by its connection with a number of totalitarian states. This effectively limited the chances that Marx's views would be widely and seriously examined in the West for their insights into the study of international politics, although it must be acknowledged that this was not true for some sectors of the Western Left (Kubalkova & Cruickshank 1985, ch. 10). However, although Communist political movements and states have been discredited, this was not entirely a fate shared with Marxism as a body of ideas. With the collapse of the Soviet threat and the demise of the Communist world generally, Marx's work began to be reconsidered in a fresh light, particularly his views on globalisation or what in the nineteenth century he described as the spread of capitalism.

The second reason for Marx's absence from the International Relations curricula was a belief that Marx had virtually nothing to say about the central concerns of the discipline. The normative basis of the discipline's foundation after the Great War was an examination and understanding of the causes of wars so that lessons could be learned which would prevent a recurrence of violence on such an horrific scale. Despite the failure of this project, the initial central focus of the discipline was the incidence of wars between nation-states. This discussion inevitably involved an examination of the nation-state system, the foreign policy behaviour of states and the role of nationalism, amongst other considerations. On these central subjects, Marx had very little to say. The persistence of the nation-state system has thwarted the pattern of historical development anticipated by Marx, who regarded class divisions as the primary cleavages in human society. Nationalism and nation-states were, for Marx, a passing stage in world history. Unsurprisingly, many scholars in the field regarded, and continue to regard, Marx's work as being an appropriate omission from the discipline's key texts.

Thirdly, according to some Marxists, certain facts and approaches to understanding the causes of the Great War were axiomatically excluded as not belonging to the inquiry at all. Tensions within society, such as class struggles and economic competition between colonial powers – during the 1920s a popular Marxist explanation of the origins of war – were not considered seriously within the discipline in its formative years. One commentator has suggested that the theory of imperialism was deliberately excluded from the early IR curricula because, since it located the causes of war within the nature of the capitalist system, it posed a direct threat to the social order of capitalist states: 'this false doctrine had to be refuted in the interest of stabilising bourgeois society ... the [historians and IR analysts] acted and reflected within the social context of the bourgeois university, which structurally obstructed such revolutionary insights' (Krippendorff 1982, p. 27). In retrospect this view sounds somewhat conspiratorial, although it might explain why the discipline was tightly circumscribed within realist and liberal parameters, to exclude non-conformist and radical theories of international politics from the 'mainstream'.

Within the Enlightenment tradition, Marxism has always been at the radical fringes of political respectability and legitimacy. It has never occupied a secure position in International Relations (Kubalkova & Cruickshank 1985; 1989). Nonetheless, Marx's views form the basis of a critical understanding of what the national interest represents in the analysis of diplomacy and international politics generally. To properly grasp the nature of this critique it is necessary to review both Marx's thoughts on what today is called globalisation, and the interaction of Marxism generally with the discipline of International Relations.

Marx on globalisation

In the middle of the last century, Marx believed that the expansion of capitalism, or what today would be called globalisation, was transforming human society from a collection of separate nation-states to a world capitalist society where the principal form of conflict would be between classes rather than nations. According to Marx, the conflictual properties of capitalism would eventually prove unsustainable: a political revolution led by the working classes would overthrow the capitalist order and usher in a world socialist society free from the alienation, exploitation and estrangement produced by capitalist structures. According to Linklater, 'the structure of world capitalism guaranteed the emergence of the first authentically universal class which would liberate the species from the consequences of estrangement between states and nations' (Linklater 1986, p. 304).

It is worth mentioning again that the trajectory of historical change anticipated by Marx 150 years ago has been undermined by the persistence of the international states system, its propensity for violence, and the grip that nationalism maintains upon the political identities of people across the world. It is tempting, then, to assume that Marx's analysis of capitalism has little of value to say about the contours of world politics at the beginning of the twenty-first century, and specifically the contemporary meaning of 'the national interest'. However, it can be argued that the relevance of Marxism for the current period has significantly increased in the wake of the Cold War and most importantly, with the heightened impact of globalisation upon every advanced industrial society (see Bromley 1999; Renton 2001).

Marx was the first theorist to identify capitalism as the principal driving force behind increasing levels of international interdependence, a process that he believed was both transforming human society and uniting the species. Marx was interested in how the processes of industrialisation shaped the modern world and the way in which capitalism generated specific social formations as it spread across the globe. According to Marx, the interconnections created by the spread of capitalist relations of production would come to both bind the species together and weaken the hold that nationalism had on people's political identities. Capitalism

> produced world history for the first time, insofar as it made all civilised nations and every individual member of them dependent for the satisfaction of their wants on the whole world, thus destroying the former natural exclusiveness of separate nations. (Marx & Engels ElecBook, p. 111)

With remarkable prescience Marx argued that the very essence of capitalism is to 'strive to tear down every barrier to intercourse', to 'conquer the whole earth for its market' and to overcome the tyranny of distance by reducing 'to a minimum the time spent in motion from one place to another' (Marx 1973, p. 539).

Resistance to the spread of capitalism, according to Marx, was futile. National economic planning would become an anachronism as barriers to trade and investment collapsed. In a famous extract from *The Communist Manifesto*, Marx and Engels describe how globalisation prizes open national economies and homogenises economic development across the globe:

> The bourgeoisie has through its exploitation of the world market given a cosmopolitan character to production and consumption in every country ... All old-established national industries have been destroyed or are daily being destroyed. They are dislodged by new industries, whose introduction becomes a life and death question for all civilized nations. ... In place of the old local and national seclusion and self-sufficiency, we have intercourse in every direction, universal inter-dependence of nations. (Marx & Engels 1967, pp. 83–4)

Contrary to the way his views have sometimes been portrayed, Marx saw substantial benefits flowing from economic globalisation. The universalising processes inherent in capitalism promised to bring not only unprecedented levels of human freedom, but also an end to insularity and xenophobia. According to Marx and Engels, under globalisation

national one-sidedness and narrow-mindedness become more and more impossible ... The bourgeoisie, by the rapid improvement of all instruments of production, by the immensely facilitated means of communication, draws all, even the most barbarian nations, into civilization. The cheap prices of its commodities are the heavy artillery with which it batters down all Chinese walls, with which it forces the barbarians' intensely obstinate hatred of foreigners to capitulate. It compels all nations, on pain of extinction, to adopt the bourgeois mode of production; ... In one word, it creates a world after its own image. (Marx & Engels 1967, p. 84)

Unlike economic liberals who regard the collapse of national economic sovereignty as an intrinsically positive development, Marx highlighted the dark side of interdependency, in particular the social and cultural effects of exposure to the rigours of market forces. As early as the 1840s, Marx had noted the social impact of globalisation. People had 'become more and more enslaved under a power alien to them (a pressure which they have conceived of as a dirty trick on the part of the so-called universal spirit, etc.), a power which has become more and more enormous and, in the last instance, turns out to be the world market' (Marx & Engels 1967, pp. 48–9).

According to Marx, the emancipation of human beings from material scarcity and surplus social constraint will take place via the self-liberation of the working class. He is therefore concerned with the estrangement of classes rather than other human groups and identities, such as religions, ethnicities, nations or states. As will be shown, this contrasts with other progressive theoretical traditions. The effect of capitalism in producing specific social formations in the wake of its expansion has important implications for the ways in which individuals come to regard their interests, especially in a global context.

Marx, the state and war in political economy

For Marx, the state functions primarily to maintain and defend class domination and exploitation. It defends the interests of property by sustaining a social order in which the bourgeoisie is the principal beneficiary. The state has become 'a separate entity, beside and outside civil society; but it is nothing more than the form of organisation which the bourgeoisie necessarily adopt both for internal and external purposes, for the mutual guarantee of their property and interests' (Marx & Engels 1967, p. 78).

However, because Marx regarded the state as merely an instrument of class rule – 'the executive of the modern State [is] but a committee for managing the common affairs of the whole bourgeoisie' – he effectively denied that the state could act autonomously of class forces even in the course of pacifying domestic society, resisting external security threats or participating in wars (Marx & Engels 1967, p. 82). This was a major theoretical shortcoming of his analysis.

In the province of political economy, Marx's crude economic reductionism has been acknowledged and, in most cases, modified by those who nevertheless locate themselves in the Marxist tradition. Many self-described neo-Marxists now accept that the nation-state enjoys some degree of autonomy from capital, particularly when it faces national crises such as war and economic depression. The development of the welfare state in most industrialised societies after the Second World War, for example, is widely acknowledged as a significant concession to socialism. The behaviour of the state cannot simply be reduced to an expression of dominant class interests. In broad economic policy the modern state is often forced to make invidious choices between 'fractions' of capital when the interests of the business sector are not homogeneous. For example, debates over free trade versus protectionism can often be characterised as a struggle between nationally-based capital on the one hand, and international capital interests on the other. The state can only pursue a policy of trade liberalisation at the expense of businesses which operate solely in the domestic market and have few if any links to the wider world economy.

According to Poulantzas, for example, the degree of 'relative autonomy' enjoyed by the state at any particular point in time will depend on the state of relations between classes, class fractions and the intensity of inter-class conflict (Poulantzas 1972). Although the state is rarely confronted with a completely unified business community, it will tend to promote and protect the interests of businesses which are seen as being both employment intensive and significant promoters of capital accumulation. Neo-Marxists generally concede that citizens in capitalist states have a common interest in a sustained level of economic activity as the basis of their material standard of living. The modern capitalist state has a vested interest in facilitating capital accumulation – what Claus Offe has called an 'institutional self-interest'. Though it is largely 'excluded' from directly controlling private decisions of production and investment, the state must make policy decisions which are broadly compatible with business-capitalist interests, sustaining a climate of confidence while promoting conditions for accumulation and profitability. Although the state is both excluded from and dependent upon the accumulation process, its intervention is crucial to the maintenance of the process.

The nation-state must therefore represent a broader range of political interests and perspectives than Marx implied: it cannot be dismissed as simply a locus of class power. It must on the one hand sustain the process of capital accumulation and the private appropriation of resources without infringing on managerial prerogatives, because it is dependent on that capital to provide the revenue necessary to satisfy society's increasing demand for government services. On the other hand, it must also preserve society's belief in it as the impartial arbiter of class interests, thereby legitimating its power while fostering broad social acceptance of the whole system. In order to accomplish these tasks, the state must periodically distance itself from dominant class interests. As we shall see, this argument implies that some authentic notion of a 'national interest' might exist in the domain of political economy.

The revisionist debate

An important countervailing, if non-Marxist contribution to this debate was made by historian Gabriel Kolko during the Vietnam War. Kolko argued that it was wrong for pluralist theory to claim that the corporate sector is no more powerful than any other group in US society. Given the 'grossly inequitable distribution of wealth and income', Kolko argued that US business is uniquely placed to shape 'the essential preconditions and functions of the larger American social order' (Kolko 1969, pp. 4–9, 15 & 26):

> It is, of course, the dominant fashion in the study of bureaucracy to ascribe to the structure of decision-making bureaucracy a neutral, independent rationale, and to drain away the class nature of formal institutions – indeed, to deny that men of power are something more than disinterested, perhaps misguided, public servants. The fact, of course, is that men of power do come from specific class and business backgrounds and ultimately have a very tangible material interest in the larger contours of policy. (Kolko 1969, p. xii)

The class-based background of the 'men of power' is for Kolko a significant determinant of state policy and therefore national diplomatic objectives.

> It is in terms of the world economy that the business and economic backgrounds of the men of power become especially germane, for their perception of the world and United States objectives in it reflect their attempt to apply overseas the structural relations which fattened their interests at home. In brief, they see the role of the state as a servant and regulator of economic affairs . . . . (Kolko 1969, p. xiv)

The method by which these interests are expressed is through the exercise of control over the spectrum of legitimate policy options for decision makers. In other words, class preferences manifest themselves as structural power over available policy choices:

> If powerful economic groups are geographically diffuse and often in competition for particular favours from the state, superficially appearing as interest groups rather than as a unified class, what is critical is not who wins or loses but what kind of socioeconomic framework they *all* wish to compete within, and the relationship between themselves and the rest of society in a manner that defines their vital function as a class. It is this class that controls the major policy options and the manner in which the state applies its power. That they disagree on the options is less consequential than that they circumscribe the political universe. (Kolko 1969, pp. 6–7)

It is therefore reasonable to conclude that although the state is not a simple instrument of class rule, an account of its external behaviour and the composition of its 'national interests' would be incomplete without an examination of the interests of those who control the levers of state power. The business class has a predominant role in the determination of foreign policy and is not just one of many competing interest groups. Its power is exerted by setting the parameters in which policy debates take place, hence the incisive description of the foreign policy elite in the US as including businessmen on leave from Wall Street (Kolko & Kolko 1972, p. 23).

And yet as Kolko explains, 'in the history of United States diplomacy specific American economic interests in a country or region have often defined the national interest on the assumption that the nation can identify its welfare with the profits of some of its citizens – whether in oil, cotton, or bananas' (Kolko 1969, pp. 84–5). But does the general population share the interests of businesses in these sectors? Given these profits accrue to the few, it is difficult to see how foreign policy here is being pursued in the common interests of the community.

Clearly some groups have a disproportionate interest in these commercial arrangements which can only be made and maintained with the direct support of the state. Writing in the late 1960s, Kolko argued that 'the contemporary world crisis, in brief, is a by-product of United States response to Third World change and its own definitions of what it must do to preserve and expand its vital national interests,' defined broadly as the economic interests of its business community (Kolko 1969, p. 85).

'The dominant interest of the United States is in world economic stability, and anything that undermines that condition presents a danger to its present hegemony.' Therefore, when the US adopts a policy of 'countering, neutralising and containing ... disturbing political and social trends (e.g. economic nationalism)' which challenge its right to 'define the course of global politics', it does so in direct response to internal social-structural imperatives (Kolko 1969, pp. 55, 85 & 132). These imperatives – the material interests of the ruling business elite – are then enhanced by the ruling group's capacity to define the political consensus which supports them. This consensus is called the 'national interest'.

As will be explored in more detail later, Tucker and other realists have argued that state policy can be explained without introducing 'problematic assumptions about the effects of social structure upon state behaviour' (Linklater 1990, pp. 154–5; Tucker 1971, p. 71). This can be done because Washington's military power extends well beyond its immediate needs of survival and security, allowing it to implement its preferred global vision. Tucker asks 'is it plausible to assume that America's expansion was essentially a response to the structural needs of American capitalism rather than to the dynamics of state competition or the search for a security ... ?' (Tucker 1971, p. 82). It is a rebuttal that is classically realist. The growth of US power around the world after the Second World War is nothing more than would be expected from any Great Power:

By a dialectic as old as the history of statecraft, expansion proved to be the other side of the coin of containment. To contain the expansion of others, or what was perceived as such, it became necessary to expand ourselves. In this manner, the course of containment became the course of empire. In the same manner, the narrower interest containment expressed was submerged in the larger interest of maintaining a stable world order that would ensure the triumph of liberal-capitalist values. (Tucker 1971, p. 109)

In other words, whilst not denying that Washington has an interest in shaping a world that is congenial to US interests, this interest is not driven by economic determinism or the structural needs of US capitalism, but by the normal logic of statecraft. A capitalist world order, controlled and directed by the US, is almost accidental – merely a positive by-product of the fact that the interests of states expand with their power (Tucker 1971, p. 73).

According to Tucker, and realists generally, strategic factors provide the state with a degree of autonomy from social forces. However, this argument begs the question of how a state's global vision is formed in the first place and how this explanation would apply to smaller military powers. It also assumes that in the conduct of foreign economic policy, the business community exerts no more influence than any other section of the community, despite their disproportionate representation in the civilian and military decision-making bureaucracies (Kolko 1969, ch. 2). Kolko's argument that the national interest of the United States is largely determined by the state's business class remains a powerful challenge to realist explanations of US foreign policy during the Cold War.

Marx, the state and war in International Relations

In the province of international relations, Marx's view that the state was merely an instrument of class rule has not been revised by neo-Marxists in the same way as it has been rethought in the field of political economy. The longevity of the international states system and its apparent autonomy, the states-system's propensity for violence, and the grip that nationalism maintains upon political identities, have all defied the pattern of historical development outlined by Marx.

Marx believed that the spread of capitalism guaranteed 'the emergence of a universal class which would liberate the entire species from the consequences of estrangement between states and nations' (Linklater 1986, p. 306). Or as the historian Charles Beard put it, 'class interest cloaking itself in patriotism and national interest must be opposed, the fatherland taken over by the working classes, upper-class interest destroyed, and the way prepared for a reconciliation of nations' (Beard 1934, p. 168).

The high level of order in mid-nineteenth century Europe, however, appears to have deceived Marx into believing that the old world of statecraft and diplomacy was being superseded by the newly globalising forces of capitalism. In the 1840s the problem of war was not a preoccupation for social theorists, it was an 'age of military quiescence' (Gallie 1978, p. 69). Marx's class analysis therefore almost entirely neglected the impact of diplomatic and strategic interaction upon both the process of state formation and the development of capitalism itself (Linklater 1986, p. 302). Marx not only failed to anticipate the increasingly autonomous character of the modern nation-state, he also ignored the crucial relationship between the citizen's concern for territorial security and the state's claim to represent the 'national interest' in its conduct of foreign policy (Linklater 1990, p. 153).

According to Gallie, 'from its first beginnings Marxist overall social theory was defective, through its failure to place and explain the different possible roles of war in human history' (Gallie 1978, p. 99). Insufficient emphasis was given to the impact of war and state-formation upon the internationalisation of capitalism. Similarly, Marx did not foresee that the spread of capitalism would become a major reason for the reproduction of the modern international system of states (Linklater citing Chase-Dunn 1981). Instead, he held to the view that 'as the antagonism between classes within the nation vanishes, the hostility of one nation to another will come to an end' (Marx & Engels 1967, p. 102).

Marxism not only underestimated the importance of the state's monopoly control of the instruments of violence and the autonomous nature of strategic and diplomatic life. It also ignored the crucial role that war played in establishing, shaping and reinforcing bounded political communities. This is because Marx believed that the transformation of the capitalist mode of production alone was the key to eradicating intersocietal estrangement (Linklater 1998, p. 116). Proletarian internationalism would liberate human loyalties and obligations from the confines of parochial nation-states which would 'wither away', to be replaced by a united community of free association. Marxism had little to say about how bounded communities interacted, why and how exclusionary boundaries were developed and maintained, or the obstacles which prevented new forms of political community arising.

Marx's account of international relations can be fairly described as an endogenous approach, where 'the internal structure of states determines not only the form and use of military force but external behaviour generally' (Waltz 1959, p. 125). As Waltz suggests, for Marx war is the external manifestation of the internal class struggle, which makes the problem of war coeval with the existence of capitalist states. If, as Marx suggests, it is capitalist states which cause wars, by abolishing capitalism states will be abolished and therefore international conflict itself will cease (Waltz 1959, pp. 126–7).

However as Michael Howard has suggested, 'the fact remains that most of the serious political movements of our time, however radical, are concerned with remodelling nation-states, if necessary creating new ones, rather than with abolishing them' (Howard 1983, pp. 32–3). The experience of self-proclaimed revolutionary states such as the Soviet Union, and the Sino-Soviet split in the mid-1950s, would suggest that Marx had significantly underestimated both the systemic constraints on new forms of political community and the structural conditioning of the international system upon state behaviour. As Linklater argues, 'Soviet Marxism quickly succumbed to the classical method of power politics, postponing if not altogether abandoning its ideal of a world community in which nationalism and sovereignty would be super-seded, and generating in its own bloc the very forms of nationalism and defence of state sovereignty which it intended to abolish' (Linklater 1986, p. 304). In Waltz's words, 'the socialisation of non-conformist states' by the diplomatic system has proved irresistible – even for self-proclaimed revolutionary regimes (Waltz 1979, p. 128). Neo-realism's claim that the anarchical condition of the international system homogenises foreign policy behaviour – an exogenous approach to international relations – is a major challenge to Marx's belief that the internal conflictual properties of capitalist states will extend the boundaries of political community.

Marx on 'national interests'

Marx and Engels believed that market relations and free trade destroyed the fabric of social harmony by crushing the notion of general society interest. 'When have you done anything out of pure humanity, from consciousness of the futility of the opposition between general and the individual interest?,' Engels berated liberal economists in the 1840s (Renton 2001, pp. 42–3). According to Marx's lifelong collaborator, the market even destroyed the moral economy of family life.

> By dissolving nationalities, the liberal economic system had done its best to universalise enmity, to transform mankind into a horde of ravenous beasts (for what else are competitors?) who devour one another just because each has identical interests with all the others – after this preparatory work there remained but one step to take before

the goal was reached, the dissolution of the family. To accomplish this, economy's own beautiful invention, the factory system, came to its aid. The last vestige of common interests, the community of goods in the possession of the family, has been undermined by the factory system and – at least here in England – is already in the process of dissolution ... What else can result from the separation of interests, such as forms the basis of the free-trade system? (Renton 2001, p. 43)

Marx and Engels were at pains to demonstrate the effects of unfettered capitalism and unrestricted trade on the most vulnerable and exploited class of people. According to Marx, 'if there is anything clearly exposed in political economy, it is the fate attending the working classes under the reign of Free Trade'. Following the rules established by Ricardo, the normal price of labour for a working man is when ' "wages [are] reduced to their minimum – their lowest level"'. Labour is a commodity as well as any other commodity' just like 'pepper and salt' (Renton 2001, pp. 46–7). The laws of political economy are ideally suited to the interests of the property-owning class but for workers, it is a very different story in the short term, if not the long term.

Thus you have to choose: either you must disavow the whole of political economy as it exists at present, or you must allow that under freedom of trade the whole severity of the laws of political economy will be applied to the working classes. Is that to say that we are against Free Trade? No, we are for Free Trade, because by Free Trade all economical laws, with their most astounding con-tradictions, will act upon a larger scale, upon a greater extent of territory, upon the territory of the whole earth; and because from the uniting of all these contradictions into a single group, where they stand face to face, will result the struggle which will itself eventuate in the emancipation of the proletarians. (Renton 2001, pp. 47–8)

According to Marx, the production of consciousness is inextricably linked to an individual's material interests. Ideas, even when freely expressed, cannot have an independent existence: they are always a reflection of material circumstances. It is not just that 'the ideas of the ruling class are in every epoch the ruling ideas: i.e., the class, which is the ruling *material* force of society, is at the same time its ruling *intellectual* force' (Marx & Engels 1967, p. 63). Just as importantly, each new class which puts itself in the place of one ruling before it, is compelled, merely in order to carry through its aim, to represent its interest as the common interest of all members of society, that is, expressed in ideal form: it has to give its ideas the form of universality, and represent them as the only rational, universally valid ones. (Marx & Engels 1967, pp. 61–2)

According to Marx, there is no such thing as the national interest per se. There are, instead, class interests masquerading as the general interest of the community, situations which will only end with the demise of capitalism. As the historian Howard Zinn suggests, 'our Machiavellis, our presidential advisers, our assistants for national security, and our secretaries of state insist they serve "the national interest", "national security", and "national defense". These phrases put everyone in the country under one enormous blanket, camouflaging the differences between the interest of those who run the government and the interest of the average citizen' (Zinn 1997, pp. 339–40).

The overriding importance of the development of class consciousness meant that for Marx, people perceived their individual interests in class terms. It is their location in the production process – workers or capitalists, bourgeoisie or proletariat – which determines their interests. Thus 'interests' for Marx have an objective material reality. The degree of class consciousness an individual has, however, depends upon a subjective awareness of this situation (Bottomore 1991, p. 89). Class membership exists even if it is not always recognised.

As capitalist relations of production spread with globalisation, so too did the breadth and scope of class interests and identity. At the root of class consciousness is the ability to recognise the collective interests of a class and the need to maintain solidarity with those interests. Sometimes alliances will be formed between the same classes in different states (e.g. the solidarity of the World Economic Forum in the face of anti-capitalist protests). At other times there would be competition between the same classes in rival countries (e.g. market competition between the Russian, French and US business classes for Iraqi oil; labour market competition between workers in East Asia for foreign investment). Ultimately, however, conflict between classes on a global scale would be the locomotive of change which would destroy nationalism and the nation-states system in its path (e.g. capital vs. labour, strikes).

Because Marx is almost exclusively concerned with the estrangement of classes, he makes little or no allowance for the residual influences of other modalities of human bonding – sometimes dismissed as 'false consciousness' – which might also determine the manner in which individuals perceive their interests. Membership of other social groups is not denied, but nor is it raised to the level of importance at which class operates to animate human behaviour.

The idea that there can ever be a 'harmony of interests' in capitalist societies was first challenged by Marx. However, the way in which elites couch their particular economic interests in national or 'common' terms was explored in depth by E.H. Carr who, in his seminal discussion of politics in the inter-war period, argued that

> the doctrine of the harmony of interests ... is the natural assumption of a prosperous and privileged class, whose members have a dominant voice in the community and are therefore naturally prone to identify its interest with their own. In virtue of this identification, any assailant of the interests of the dominant group is made to incur the odium of assailing the alleged common interest of the whole community, and is told that in making this assault he is attacking his own higher interests. The doctrine of the harmony of interests thus serves as an ingenious moral device invoked, in perfect sincerity, by privileged groups in order to justify and maintain their dominant position. (Carr 1939; 1981, p. 102)

As Carr reminds us, Marx declared 'that all thought was conditioned by the economic interest and social status of the thinker. This view was unduly restrictive. In particular Marx, who denied the existence of "national interests", underestimated the potency of nationalism as a force conditioning the thought of the individual' (Carr 1939; 1981, p. 66). He could also have said that Marx failed to see nationalism as a powerful determinant of the social bond which simultaneously unites and divides people. Nationalism's capacity to transcend social divisions and blunt class consciousness was not seriously addressed in his writings. Instead, Marx thought that 'national differences and antagonisms between peoples are daily more and more vanishing, owing to the development of the bourgeoisie, to freedom of commerce, to the world market, to uniformity in the mode of production and in the conditions of life corresponding thereto' (Marx & Engels 1967, p. 102).

Marx appeared to believe that the idea of 'national interests' was a hoax because 'while the bourgeoisie of each nation still retained separate national interests, big industry created a class, which in all nations has the same interest and with which nationality is already dead' (Marx & Engels 1967, p. 76).

> The Communists are ... reproached with desiring to abolish countries
> and nationalities. The working men have no country. We cannot
> take from them what they have not got ... National differences and
> antagonisms between peoples are daily more and more vanishing ...
> The supremacy of the proletariat will cause them to vanish still faster.
> (Marx & Engels 1967, pp. 101–3)

Only the bourgeoisie, therefore, thought nationally and sought to pass
off its interests as the interests of the whole community. This was
particularly, though not exclusively the case with respect to economic
interests, especially in matters of finance and trade.

As mentioned earlier, Marx's reluctance to seriously consider the grip
that nationalism holds on an individual's political identity may be
explained by the circumstances of his time. The long peace in Europe from
the middle to the end of the nineteenth century seems to have encouraged
Marx to believe that class-based exclusion was the only motor of history
and to dismiss the ongoing dynamics of strategic interaction, geopolitical
rivalry and inter-state war. He mistakenly regarded the nation-state as a
temporary and transitional form of political community which had
been maintained to further the interests of the dominant bourgeoisie:
nationalism, regarded as a form of false consciousness, was their ruling
ideology. Lenin and Bukharin, writing in the twentieth century, conceded
that there might be a brief digression along the path of nationalism and
war before cosmopolitan aspirations were rediscovered (Linklater 1996,
p. 128). And Gallie has suggested that although Marx's views on war
and nationalism were underdeveloped, there was an 'ever-sharpening
recognition by Marxists of the intrusive and distorting effect which
inter-state rivalries and wars were to play in the predicted transition
from capitalism to socialism' (Gallie 1978, p. 69). Nevertheless, neither
the tenacity of nation-states nor the idea of national interests has been
taken seriously by Marxist students of international relations.

Anarchism and 'national interests'

A parallel critique of the concept of 'national interests' can be found
within the anarchist tradition, perhaps best known for its powerful
anti-statism, of which the following remarks by Michael Bakunin and
Peter Kropotkin are broadly representative:

> The State is the organized authority, domination, and power of the
> possessing classes over the masses ... the most flagrant, the most

cynical, and the most complete negation of humanity. It shatters the universal solidarity of all men on the earth, and brings some of them into association only for the purpose of destroying, conquering, and enslaving all the rest ... This flagrant negation of humanity which constitutes the very essence of the State is, from the standpoint of the State, its supreme duty and its greatest virtue ... Thus, to offend, to oppress, to despoil, to plunder, to assassinate or enslave one's fellowman is ordinarily regarded as a crime. In the public life, on the other hand, from the standpoint of patriotism, when these things are done for the greater glory of the State, for the preservation or extension of its power, it is all transformed into duty and virtue ... This explains why the entire history of ancient and modern states is merely a series of revolting crimes; why kings and ministers, past and present, of all times and all countries – statesmen, diplomats, bureaucrats, and warriors – if judged from the standpoint of simply morality and human justice, have a hundred, a thousand times over earned their sentence to hard labour or to the gallows. There is no horror, no cruelty, sacrilege, or perjury, no imposture, no infamous transaction, no cynical robbery, no bold plunder or shabby betrayal that has not been or is not daily being perpetrated by those representatives of the states, under no other pretext than those elastic words, so convenient and yet so terrible: 'for reasons of state'. (Dolgoff 2002, pp. 133–4)

Man lived in societies for thousands of years before the state had been heard of ... the most glorious periods in man's history are those in which civil liberties and communal life had not yet been destroyed by the state, and in which large numbers of people lived in communes and free federation ... The state is synonymous with war. (Kropotkin 1970, pp. 212 & 246)

Unsurprisingly, this view of the nation-state as a repressive and coercive political community filters through to anarchist critiques of claims that nations can have common interests. In a seminal work *Nationalism and Culture*, Rudolf Rocker dismisses the notion of national interests in terms that Marxists would have clearly recognised and appreciated. Rocker argues that the internal divisions within all societies, but especially capitalist ones, makes the idea of the nation as a community of common interests absurd. According to Rocker, classes which 'cleave the nation with eternal economic and political antagonisms' can never be properly reconciled:

Every nation includes today the most various castes, conditions, classes and parties. These not only pursue their separate interests, but frequently face one another with definite antagonism. The results are countless, never-ending conflicts and inner antagonisms which are infinitely more difficult to overcome than the temporary wars between various states and nations. (Rocker 1937; 1998, p. 260)

Like the Marxists, anarchists regard endogenous conflicts as much more complex and intractable than exogenous wars. For example, Rocker cites the example of the businessman generally, and specifically the behaviour of German industrialists during the inter-war period, to demonstrate the lack of regard which the wealthy have for the fate of their fellow citizens. According to Rocker, the entrepreneur is concerned only for his own welfare; 'personal profit is the deciding factor ... and so-called national interests are only considered when they are not in conflict with personal ones'. Otherwise, 'so called "national interests" have always served as stalking horse for their own ruthless business interests' (Rocker 1937; 1998, pp. 261–2).

The time to test the validity of common national interests is during economic crises when a more even distribution of wealth would spare the desperate and disadvantaged from poverty and hardship. According to Rocker, in Germany during the Great Depression no such concern for the poor emanated from the affluent:

In short, the representatives of heavy industry, of the great estate owners and the stock exchange had never bothered their brains concerning the alleged community of national interests. It never occurred to them that in order to rescue the rest of the nation from helpless despair and misery after the war they might be content with smaller profits. ... The alleged community of national interests does not exist in any country; it is nothing more than a representation of false facts in the interest of small minorities. (Rocker 1937; 1998, p. 264)

Again we find within the anarchist tradition, the notion of the particular interests of the elite being passed off as 'the national interest' – in this instance, a means to avoid their community responsibilities. Anarchists such as Rocker attack the claim for national interests on two fronts. The argument for national interests is flawed, not only by the fact that only particular interests are being represented while others are being exploited, but also by the failure to explain internal struggles, violence and divisions within a community with supposedly common concerns. Thus for Rocker, and for anarchists more generally, it is

> quite meaningless to speak of a community of national interests; for that which the ruling class of every country has up to now defended as national interest has never been anything but the special interest of privileged minorities in society secured by the exploitation and political suppression of the great masses ...
> If the nation were in fact the community of interests which it has been called, then there would not be in modern history revolutions and civil wars, because the people do not resort to the arms of revolt purely for pleasure – just as little do the endless wage fights occur because the working sections of the population are too well off! (Rocker 1937; 1998, p. 269)

Anarchists part company with Marxists on the question of the proletariat being the privileged agents of social and political change, but more importantly on the question of whether state power should ultimately be conquered (Marxists) or dismantled (anarchists). According to Chomsky, 'in one form or another, the problem has arisen repeatedly in the century since, dividing "libertarian" and "authoritarian" socialists' (Chomsky 1973, p. 155). Bakunin's remarks on nineteenth-century attitudes to state power would not have been comfortably embraced by his Marxist contemporaries:

> whatever conduces to the preservation, the grandeur and the power of the State, no matter how sacreligious or morally revolting it may seem, *that is the good*. And conversely, whatever opposes the State's interests, no matter how holy or just otherwise, *that is evil*. Such is the secular morality and practice of every State. (Dolgoff 2002, p. 132)

The anarchist approach to the question of national interests can be compared with a doctor's X-ray of a patient with a broken bone. An initial physical examination of the patient (the nation) reveals little that would sufficiently explain his or her discomfort. An X-ray, however, reveals the patient's skeletal structure (class divisions) and pinpoints the cause of the problem as a fractured bone. Unlike Marxists who believe the state will whither away over time but can be occupied in the intervening period, anarchists regard the state as a fundamental obstacle to human freedom. Nonetheless, despite their fundamental difference of teleology, it is fair to say that Marxists and anarchists share a common critique of the idea of national interests.

National versus class interests

The assertion of 'national interests' is part of the bonding process that nationalism animates: the idea of one people with a common identity and destiny. To critical theorists, those who control this bonding process ultimately become the arbiters of loyalty and patriotism, which are powerful forces in modern life.

Marxists have been relatively slow to acknowledge the power of this process, not just the grip that nationalism has on an individual's political identity but also the extent to which appeals to nationalism and national interests undermine class consciousness and solidarity. According to Vogler, corporatist theory explains how labour in advanced capitalist states comes to believe that it shares common economic interests with capital (Vogler 1985).

The means by which class interests are subordinated to national interests has many strands and theories which cannot be elaborated in detail here. However to briefly summarise critical perspectives, it is helpful to see 'the national interest' as an ideology which socialises labour into an overriding and more powerful nationalist project. Workers are co-opted into collaborating with capital in circumstances where the threat to their welfare is seen to be external (cheap foreign labour, ongoing employment conditional on business profitability which is in turn increasingly dependent on success in internationally competitive markets) rather than internal (struggles for better wages and conditions, boss versus worker) factors. To explicate one example more specifically, workers in one labour market may regard workers in another in competitive rather than solidarist terms. If they cannot compete on an equal footing, meaning the maintenance of investment by their employer, they may look to the state for protection from international competition. This may bind them into a nationalist rather than a class outlook.

Even the 'international competitiveness' of local firms is refracted through a nationalist prism because the only unit or agent which can solve the problem, by restricting imports, introducing quotas or tariffs, is the state. In this way, the state, the employer and the worker are engaged in a common project where class divisions are surrendered to a more immediate and pressing concern. This is the power of socialisation under capitalism, and it has important implications for organised labour. As Vogler explains, 'under the ideological guise of operating in the "national" interests of the whole society, the capitalist state is thought to have incorporated or co-opted national trade union leaders into its own economic policy-making so that they come to act in the interests of capital and against their members' class interests' (Vogler 1985, pp. 56–7).

From a Marxist perspective it has been important to explain how and why subordinate classes in the nation appear to live their daily lives in ways which are consistent with the interests of ruling elites. Or to put it in the present context, why national interests seem to prevail over class solidarity. As has been suggested, corporatism is one possible explanation. The processes of *reification* and *hegemony* also help to explain the dominance of national interests over class interests, even in the economic domain.

Economic systems tend to be naturalised or *reified* in the public discourse. In simple terms, the citizens of a state come to believe that a transitory, historical state of affairs – a particular configuration of political economy, for example – is in fact a permanent and natural condition of their lives. They may not recognise that the current state of political economy under which they live is historically contingent, dynamic and fluid, which may be altered by collective action. According to Block, to naturalise the economy is 'to treat economic arrangements that have a specific history and context as timeless products of the need to economize scarce resources. A method that obscures from view the social, cultural, and political determinants of economic action results in analysis that is ahistorical and, through tautological procedure, continually rediscovers the centrality of purely economic motives' (Block 1990, p. 26). The configuration of political economy is reified just as conceptions of the state and national sovereignty have become regarded as 'natural' or normal aspects of political community for humankind.

People may have no vision of an alternative economic or political order, or at least one that can possibly be obtained. This process of reification, in turn, helps to reinforce and reproduce situations of what the Italian Marxist Gramsci called political *hegemony*, when dominant or ruling classes can rely on the voluntary compliance of subordinate groups, in particular their acceptance of asymmetrical economic and power relations. Hegemony exists when the economic and social structures of a state, which primarily serve the interests of ruling groups, are accepted as broadly legitimate even by those who have least to gain from them. It then becomes a structural force which conditions and constrains debate and discussion about political and economic policy. The political, social and economic order is therefore said to be *legitimate* because there is mass compliance, or at least conditional acceptance of it by the citizens of the state.

False consciousness is an inadequate explanation of why class interests have taken second place to the national interest in explanations of diplomatic behaviour. Loyalties to homeland, common language, culture and ethnicity cannot be easily dismissed or thought to be in terminal decline. The national interest retains powerful resonances long after the state was, according to classical Marxists, supposed to 'wither away'.

Class and foreign policy: the national interest evasion

As has been noted, according to Krippendorff radical and Marxist insights into the causes of wars and international politics generally – with a focus on class analysis, colonial competition, etc. – were systematically excluded from the mainstream of the discipline of International Relations in its formative years because of the challenge they would have posed to the legitimacy of the capitalist order. Capitalism had to be stabilised and protected from internal and external threats, including intellectual challenges to conventional accounts of the causes of the Great War.

According to Marxists, one consequence of this challenge to capitalist states has been for the exercise of power by the ruling classes in their own interests to be either concealed, ignored or denied. Most importantly, the particular interests of one class had to be represented as the common interests of the whole society. In contemporary terms, the influence of the business class in the determination of foreign policy had to be disguised because of the contradiction with democratic processes that this would represent, together with the consequent threat that this would pose to the legitimacy of the liberal-democratic capitalist order (see Brady 1943; Carey 1995).

Looking at the US experience, Chomsky argued that the central question of the influence of corporations in the setting of US foreign policy has been systematically evaded by the discipline which claims jurisdiction over the analysis of foreign policy decision-making. As a result, an accurate understanding of the national interest as an explanatory tool in international politics has been distorted. To support his claim Chomsky cites a rare discussion of the issue of corporations and US foreign policy by political scientist Dennis Ray in 1972. According to Ray,

> [W]e know virtually nothing about the role of corporations in American foreign relations ... [Scholarship has] clarified the influence of Congress, the press, scientists, and non-profit organisations, such as

RAND, on the foreign policy process. The influence of corporations on the foreign policy process, however, remains clouded in mystery. My search through the respectable literature on international relations and U.S. foreign policy shows that less than 5 percent of some two hundred books granted even passing attention to the role of corporations in American foreign relations. From this literature, one might gather that American foreign policy is formulated in a social vacuum, where national interests are protected from external threats by the elaborate machinery of government policymaking. There is virtually no acknowledgement in standard works within the field of international relations and foreign policy of the existence and influence of corporations. (Ray 1972, pp. 80–1; Chomsky 1982, pp. 103–5)

Noting that a concentration on 'respectable literature' excludes from Ray's survey 'advocacy' pieces by corporate executives, business school professors and 'radical and often neo-Marxist analyses', Chomsky claims that the last category is where Ray would have found a discussion of corporations and foreign policy formation if he bothered to look (Chomsky 1982, p. 103). It is significant that Ray doesn't pursue the reasons for this curious gap in the 'respectable literature' or why the lapse doesn't render such analysis less than respectable. Just as interesting is the presumption that accounts from a critical quarter which are likely to focus squarely on the issue at hand are, by definition, excluded because they are not regarded as respectable.

Although Ray reaches the conclusion that 'few if any interest groups, outside of business, have generalised influence on the broad range of foreign policy', the subject of business influence over the national interest remains, according to Chomsky, 'a form of taboo' where there is a 'deep-seated superstitious avoidance of some terrifying question: in this case, the question of how private economic power functions in American society' (Chomsky 1982, p. 104). It seems that even in pluralist accounts of the diplomatic decision-making processes, the role of business is either only mentioned in passing as one of many inputs with relatively equal weighting, or ignored entirely. Chomsky's analysis, though dating from the 1980s, remains relevant today because it reminds us that studies of the national interest specifically (and foreign policy more generally) which focus on class-based explanations may, almost by definition, remain outside the mainstream and on the radical fringes of respectable scholarship.

In many ways the treatment of the business community in foreign-policy making mirrors the way the role of the state is portrayed in domestic economic policy. Though state intervention in the economy is crucial to every state capitalist society, it must be disguised in case it de-legitimates the entire basis of the social order. The state must maintain 'the belief that the collective goals [of the community] can only be properly realised by private individuals acting in competitive isolation and pursuing their sectoral aims with minimal state interference' (Held 1989, p. 71). Providing the state can ensure that the general community interest is equated with the interests of the business community, even if this cannot be openly acknowledged, the class structure of the system is concealed and its legitimacy is maintained.

Under contemporary state capitalism, the state must on the one hand sustain the process of capital accumulation and the private appropriation of resources without infringing on managerial prerogatives, because it is dependent on that capital to provide the revenue necessary to satisfy society's increasing demand for government services. On the other hand, the state must also preserve society's belief in it as the impartial arbiter of class interests, thereby legitimating its power; at the same time fostering social acceptance of the whole system (see Offe 1975; 1984).

According to critical perspectives, the role of the business community in diplomacy is virtually a mirror image of this. The state must defend and promote business interests while actually claiming to represent the interests of all equally, without favour or privilege. The dominant role of business must be partially disguised and presented as just one of many interested stakeholders, none of which is any more influential than any other, be they NGOs, trades unions, churches or corporations. This version of how decision-making occurs in liberal democratic states is what Chomsky calls 'a carefully spun web of pluralist mysticism' (Chomsky 1982, p. 105). It deliberately minimises the overwhelming structural influence of the business class, portraying it as merely one amongst equals rather than first among many.

In conventional IR literature it seems that the integrity of the national interest as an evaluative tool depends on it not being too closely associated with any one domestic player or interest group, regardless of whether this constitutes a misleading and inaccurate portrait of reality.

National interests, Marxism and neo-liberalism

For Marxist and other critical approaches, the idea of common economic interests in a class divided society is oxymoronic. This is particularly so in an era when neo-liberal economic policy has had a significant influence upon public policy-making in the West and when economic globalisation appears to be challenging the sovereign powers of modern nation-states. To make their point, Marxists would cite the push for free trade, widening disparities of wealth and income, and the growing power of the foreign investment community as three contemporary examples of class power which undermine the claim that a state can pursue common national economic interests.

Suggesting that particular interests are commonly shared is not a new practice in politics and government. As Carr explained, 'once industrial capitalism and the class system had become the recognised structure of society, the doctrine of the harmony of interests ... became ... the ideology of a dominant group concerned to maintain its predominance by asserting the identity of its interests with those of the community as a whole' (Carr 1939, p. 58). It was then possible to portray those who opposed the interests of the dominant group as being disloyal or unpatriotic. In the nineteenth century, the British manufacturer, 'having discovered that laissez-faire promoted his own prosperity, was sincerely convinced that it also promoted British prosperity as a whole'. In turn, British statesmen during the same period, 'having discovered that free trade promoted British prosperity, were sincerely convinced that, in doing so, it also promoted the prosperity of the world as a whole' (Carr 1939, p. 103). Unsurprisingly, Carr quotes A.V. Dicey to emphasise his point: 'men come easily to believe that arrangements agreeable to themselves are beneficial to others' (Carr 1939, p. 71).

Invoking the German political economist Friedrich List, Carr points out that while free trade was the logical policy for a nation like Great Britain which was industrially dominant in the nineteenth century, only policies of protection would enable weaker nations to break the stranglehold of British industrial dominance. There was no evidence that the economic nationalism practiced by the United States and Germany had achieved anything less than enabling those states to actually challenge Britain's economic power (Carr 1939, pp. 61 & 72). 'Laissez-faire, in international relations as in those between capital and labour, is the paradise of the economically strong. State control, whether in the form of protective legislation or of protective tariffs, is the weapon of self defence invoked by the economically weak' (Carr 1939, p. 77).

The essential role played by the state in a nation's economic development has been widely acknowledged by economic historians, especially those familiar with the work of Karl Polanyi, Alexander Gerschenkron, Eric Hobsbawm and others. It is a matter of historical record that virtually all industrial societies have entered the phase of 'late development' by radically violating free market principles. The commitment to free market ideology is sometimes only rhetorical, honoured more in the breach than the observance. But as the economist Paul Bairoch has argued, 'it is difficult to find another case where the facts so contradict a dominant theory than the one concerning the negative impact of protectionism'. Bairoch cites the example of the United States, which he refers to as 'the mother country and bastion of modern protectionism', as a case study of what can be achieved when free trade doctrines are explicitly abandoned (Bairoch 1993, pp. 54 & 30).

From its very beginnings, free trade was a middle-class movement. Though in the UK it was only to last until 1931, when free trade was introduced in 1846 it was rightly seen by business activists as a victory for the interests of manufacturers over aristocratic and landed interests. Having discovered that free-trade policies promoted their own prosperity, British manufacturers were convinced – and tried to convince others – that free trade also promoted British prosperity as a whole: their interests were said to be indivisible and 'in harmony' with the general interests of the state. Thus when workers struck for higher pay and better working conditions they damaged the manufacturers and merchants, and by definition, they hurt Britain as a whole. Logically, industrial action could be portrayed as unpatriotic and possibly treacherous behaviour, damaging the whole community.

The class-based nature of free trade advocacy produced bourgeois organisations such as the Anti-Corn Law League which successfully agitated for the repeal of the Corn Laws in 1846 to open up British agriculture to foreign competition. Its victory was rightly described by Cobden as a victory for the middle class over landed interests (Deane 1979, pp. 212–13; Hobsbawm 1969, pp. 106–7 & 137–40). Although it is no longer regarded as advantageous to portray the cause of free trade as being driven by the self-interest of the middle class, in the nineteenth century it would have been absurd to have thought of it in any other terms.

As one leading economic historian explains, free trade is 'believed in only by those who will gain an advantage from it' (Robinson 1966, p. 108). According to Marxists, free trade cannot be in the common interests of the whole society because it produces winners and losers. The losers, however, are rarely compensated. As Lester Thurow points out,

> the theory of free trade admits that there will be sharp income-distribution changes within each participating country. Average incomes will go up with free trade, but there may be millions of

losers in each country ... The theory assumes that the winners will compensate the losers, so that everyone in each country has an incentive to move towards free trade, but in fact such compensation is almost never paid. Without such compensation there are individuals who should rationally oppose free trade as antithetical to their economic self-interest. (Thurow 1992, p. 82)

The losers from free trade include those who would lose their businesses and employment if the enterprises they owned or those for which they worked were suddenly exposed to the chill winds of international competition. They can survive catering to a domestic national market, but would struggle to survive in a global market on a 'level playing field'. They may have no interest in unfettered free trade.

The Australian experience

According to critical perspectives, it is logical for the agents of transnational capital to claim that 'the bottom line is that, regardless of what other countries do, cutting tariffs is in the national interest' for countries such as Australia (*The Australian*, 11.7.95), though this is difficult to reconcile with evidence that the benefits of free trade and globalisation have accrued to a 'very narrow segment of the economy' (*Australian Financial Review*, 2.9.97). It would come as little surprise for Marx to hear a conservative economist such as David Hale claim that current opposition to free trade in the United States is 'heavily influenced by perceptions that voters themselves now view trade issues in terms of a domestic class struggle, not as promoting exports and global integration' (*Australian Financial Review*, 15/16.11.97).

The global measurement of wealth and income distribution, as well as current trends and projections, is a fraught and highly contested activity, especially in the area of statistical methodology. However, given the pro-free trade consensus amongst Western political and economic elites, the 1997 UN Conference on Trade and Development (UNCTAD) report strikes a discordant note for those who equate free trade with common economic interests. The report argues that rising inequality and widening disparities of income between countries in the North and South are becoming a permanent feature of the world economy. They are now so stark they could 'unleash a backlash against global free trade' with 'menacing consequences' (*The Age*, 17.9.97; *Australian Financial Review*, 16.9.97) – a remarkably prescient warning, given the street protests in Seattle, Washington and elsewhere that were soon to follow the report. In contrast to an upbeat World Bank report delivered a week earlier, the UNCTAD paper claims that:

- in 1965, per capita income for the top 20 per cent of the world's population was 30 times that of the poorest 20 per cent – 25 years later the gap had doubled to 60 times;
- the share of income accruing to capital has significantly gained over labour as increased job and income security has spread;
- it was noted that the rules of global free trade have been drawn in favour of the world's richest countries because trade in areas where developing countries have an advantage (e.g. agriculture, labour-intensive manufacturing) remain heavily protected while trade in high-tech goods and services which rich countries produce are low.

The UNCTAD report confirms earlier OECD–World Bank research which identified five countries or regions (mainly African, Caribbean and Pacific countries) which were expected to suffer real income losses from the Uruguay Round and eight which could lose from full free trade, mainly as a result of a deterioration in their terms of trade (Dunkley 1997, pp. 145–6). These figures cast serious doubt on former GATT Director-General Peter Sutherland's claims that the Uruguay Round of multilateral trade negotiations would not produce any losers, only winners (Dunkley 1997, p. 134).

The veracity of the UNCTAD report has been supported by the findings of the United Nations Development Programme's *1999 Human Development Report*, which examined the distribution of benefits from global economic growth since 1975 (http://www.undp.org/hrdo/report. html). While people in the developed world have made strong gains in all areas (longevity, education, wealth) since 1975, these gains have not been evenly shared. The developing world remains a mixture of winners and losers, while the least developed countries (mainly African) have shown little improvement and, in some cases, have declined. Wealthy nations continue to get richer while the poorest become poorer. The richest 20 per cent of the world's population share 86 per cent of the world's GDP, 82 per cent of the world's exports of goods and services and 68 per cent of global foreign direct investment. The equivalent figures for the world's poorest 20 per cent are 1 per cent, 1 per cent and 1 per cent respectively.

If these figures are accurate, and they are contested (see DFAT 2003), they cast doubt on the claim that free trade benefits all sectors of those communities which participate in trade liberalisation. The uneven benefits which flow from free trade remind critics of Marx's injunction about the likely class tensions that flow from its adoption. Les exclus are difficult to hide or ignore.

A significant determinant of every state's economic security is its relationship with the world's money markets. Because most states are incapable of generating sufficient endogenous wealth to finance their economic development (i.e. maintaining the standard of living most of its citizens expect), governments need to provide domestic economic conditions which will attract foreign investment into the country. In a world where capital markets are globally linked and money can be electronically transferred around the world in microseconds, states are judged in terms of their comparative 'hospitality' to foreign capital: that is, they must offer the most attractive investment climates to relatively scarce supplies of money. This gives the foreign investment community significant influence over the course of the nation's economic development, and constitutes a diminution in the country's economic sovereignty. Almost a decade ago, Chomsky wrote that

> the World Bank currently estimates the total resources of international financial institutions at about $US 14 trillion. Not only can European central banks not defend national currencies in the face of this unprecedented private power, but the European Monetary System has 'effectively collapsed' as EC governments 'have experienced the power of today's free-wheeling global capital markets', the *Financial Times* reports in a review of the world economy and finance. The huge and unregulated international capital market controls access to capital, but 'global investors impose a price. If a country's economic policies are not attractive to them' they will use their power to induce changes. Such pressures may not be 'fatal' to the very rich, but for the South, the international capital market is 'no more than an unacceptable arm of economic imperialism', which governments cannot resist in an era when even in the rich countries, governments 'are on the defensive and global investors have gained the upper hand'. (Chomsky 1993a)

The power of transnational finance capital can scarcely be overestimated. The volume of foreign exchange trading in the major financial centres of the world, estimated at $US206 billion per day in 1986 was measured at $US1,971 billion in 1998, and has come to dwarf international trade. In November 1999 the average daily turnover of the Australian dollar against foreign currencies, for example, was $A40.3 billion while the value of daily transactions on the Australian current account of the balance of payments (goods and services, etc.) was $A0.83 billion, meaning that 'for every dollar's worth of "substantive" transactions involving traded goods, services and investments that can be identified, there were forty-five dollars' worth of "virtual" transactions involving trading in the Australian dollar' (Kerr 2001, pp. 16–17).

Capital flows comprising foreign direct investment have multiplied more than forty times over since 1970 when the figure was $US9.2 billion to 1999 when it reached $US827 billion. Over a third of this investment is controlled by one hundred of the world's largest transnational corporations, which in 1997 held $US1,800 billion in foreign assets, sold products worth $US2,100 billion in exports and employed 6 million workers (Kerr 2001, p. 20). Unsurprisingly, they have enormous influence over the economies of host countries, if only because of how significant they are in almost all areas of economic activity. Few, if any countries, can afford to lose the confidence of the international markets.

The brokers on Wall Street and in Tokyo, the 'screen jockeys' in the world's foreign exchange trading houses, and the auditors from credit ratings agencies such as Moody's and Standard & Poors, pass daily judgements on the management of global economies, and signal to the world's financial community the comparative profit opportunities to be found through investment in a particular country. Inappropriate 'interventionary' policies by government can be quickly deterred or penalised with a (threatened) reduction in the nation's credit rating, or a run on the nation's currency. The needs of the international markets need to be anticipated at all times.

This is now a common global phenomenon, with regular examples of the power of the world's financial markets over the nation-state. When the Group of Seven (G7) leading industrial nations met in Naples in July 1994, they effectively conceded that they had lost control of economic policy to the financial markets. The erratic behaviour of the world's bond markets in the weeks leading up to the Naples summit wrought havoc on the monetary policies of most industrialised countries. In Australia, the Government and the Reserve Bank were barely able to hold the line against the enormous pressure exerted on interest rates by bond traders primarily reacting to economic conditions and policies in North America and Western Europe. Discussion of whether the markets were 'right or wrong' soon appeared empty and irrelevant. No matter how loudly the Australian Government protested that domestic 'fundamentals' were 'sound', it was generally conceded that the Government was powerless in the face of such massive cross-border capital flows. Some financial commentators thought this was probably a good thing, believing that markets rather than the governments, know what is in the nation's best interests.

Finance markets are amorphous entities and like their psychology, are difficult to define. The bond markets, for example, have been described as 'a loose confederation of wealthy Americans, bankers, financiers, money managers, rich foreigners, executives of life insurance companies, presidents of universities and non-profit foundations, retirees and people who once kept their money in passbook savings accounts and now buy shares in mutual funds' (*The Australian*, 25.6.94). It is clear that the larger banks and financial institutions, insurance companies, brokers and speculators, are the dominant players. But predicting their behaviour on a daily, if not hourly basis, which is the timeframe of financial speculation, is a perilous activity and only for the stout hearted. The one and only thing that can be said with any confidence about money markets is that they will act in their own interests – as they perceive them. That is to say, they will act to maximise their own wealth. This does not pass unnoticed by the broader community (Pusey 2003).

Marx appears to have anticipated the de-regulation of the world's capital markets and the impact that this would have on states, governments and societies: a process which began in earnest with the Nixon 'shocks' of the 1970s. Far from promoting the common economic interests of all, he was convinced that the rapid flow of money across the world would destabilise many societies and exacerbate class tensions within them. In an address delivered in 1848 he asked,

> what is free trade under the present conditions of society? It is freedom of capital. When you have overthrown the few national barriers which still restrict the progress of capital, you will merely have given it complete freedom of action ... All the destructive phenomena which unlimited competition gives rise to within one country, are reproduced in more gigantic proportions on the world market. It breaks up old nationalities and pushes the antagonism of the proletariat and the bourgeoisie to the extreme point. (Cited in Wheelwright 1993, p. 14)

The argument that contemporary economic de-regulation and neo-liberal economic settings promote the national interests of those states which adopt such approaches, is therefore problematic because the modernising pressure for greater efficiencies has a disaggregating effect on those societies. Change on such a scale cannot occur without the production of winners and losers.

Even more relevant for this study is the absence of national loyalties amongst the foreign investment and trade communities. The changing nature of world trade, the mobility of capital and production, and the global scale of investment opportunities means that the discussion of national interests for these communities is quaint and increasingly anachronistic. Capitalists are no longer bound to their homeland in the way they were when Ricardo's theory of comparative advantage was being developed. Their money can be invested as easily outside the country as it can within. And they are no longer constrained by the need to establish production centres inside their home country. In other words, their national bonds and loyalties to group interests have been weakened to the point where considerations of national interest may inhibit their primary commercial function: profit-making. National attachments no longer constitute the production and investment horizon for the contemporary capitalist.

The Australian experience demonstrates that the idea of governments pursuing national interests is even more difficult to see in an era of economic globalisation when the pressures of competition for shares of global manufacturing and services markets is so intense. Writing in response to the debt crisis faced by Mexico in the mid-1980s, Susan Strange sums up the critical perspective and its enduring relevance for the current era:

> Class structures, in a word, and the nature of wealth explained the differential definition of national interest and the divergent preferences of policy makers faced with a credit crisis. (Strange 1998, p. 108)

Divisible and indivisible interests: a correction to Marx

In an approach which borrows heavily from Marx but which concedes the realist point that Marxism failed to deal adequately with strategic interaction and the state's ability to act autonomously from dominant domestic interests, McGowan and Walker maintain that 'radical' theories of the state are nevertheless useful in explaining foreign policy decisions which produce an unequal distribution of costs and benefits for different groups in the community (Walker & McGowan 1982; Linklater 1990, p. 157).

In the area of tariff policy, for example, there are obvious winners and losers from government decisions: the gains are clearly 'divisible'. Not surprisingly, the state faces pressure from domestic constituents for favourable treatment as the class actors directly concerned mobilise to head off any threats to their interests. This is what happens, for example, when local manufacturers are faced with increased overseas competition as a result of a government's commitment to trade liberalisation. The state must be highly responsive to the most powerful economic interests in the community, as any Marxist account would suggest, and threatens them at its peril. Major difficulties are faced, however, when economic interests pull in opposite directions, as often happens in the case of competition between national-based and transnational capital. Kolko's claim that the power of business to 'circumscribe the political universe' is more important than 'who wins or loses' these debates, may not be a sufficient explanation of the actual policy outcome (Kolko 1969, pp. 6–7).

McGowan and Walker argue that policy in the defence and security domains does not have the same divisible qualities. The costs and benefits of decisions affecting 'power, security and prestige' are equally shared throughout the community – they are 'indivisible'. The citizens of a state stand to gain or lose to the same extent from a government decision to procure new, more highly sophisticated weaponry, for example, because the defence of the homeland from an external threat is a common social concern. This argument is at the heart of the realist conception of 'the national interest'. As McGowan and Walker explain,

> when an issue involves the relatively intangible and indivisible goods of power, security and prestige, then the policy process will correspond to a rational actor model in which the maker of government policy is a relatively monolithic rational decision maker. However, if an issue involves only the distribution, regulation, or redistribution of more tangible goods such as tariffs and export subsidies, then the policy process begins to resemble the domestic interactions of several actors .... (Walker & McGowan 1982, p. 212)

Tangible goods, such as trade preferences, have clearly divisible effects. As a consequence, policy outcomes in these areas are the product of competition between domestic constituents who have different interests at stake despite their common class identity. Globally efficient mineral producers, for example, seek relief from competition with inefficient players who are protected and subsidised by their home governments. Those producers who are 'internationally competitive' have a direct interest in free trade and trade liberalisation, and expect the state to pursue these objectives at both multilateral and regional fora, and to adopt free trade measures unilaterally across all sectors. However, those motor vehicle manufacturers who cater primarily to a domestic market, and who are not efficient by world standards, expect the state to intervene to protect them from unfettered foreign competition. They hold the prospect of disinvestment and higher levels of unemployment as a sword over the heads of democratic governments which fail to protect their profit margins.

Regardless of how this domestic struggle is resolved, perceiving foreign policy – in this case trade policy – as a 'divisible' with costs and benefits varying amongst different domestic groups, allows McGowan and Walker to explain policy outcomes as both a struggle between class 'fractions' and as a process which requires a degree of autonomy from the state. The outcome may be a victory for either nationally-based or transnational capital, depending on which fraction can most successfully mobilise government support. Either way the integrity of a more sophisticated class analysis is preserved. Capital is not monolithic as most neo-Marxists now concede. When the modern state is required to defend the interests of capital it must frequently choose between a variety of fractions – industrial, commercial, finance, local manufacturing, agricultural – which in an increasingly globalised world economy can have divergent economic interests.

McGowan and Walker's model can also explain how the state's specific responsibility for national security policy requires it to act autonomously from dominant class interests. Because they regard national security as an 'indivisible' and 'intangible', the state can more plausibly claim to represent the 'national interest' in its management of this particular aspect of foreign policy. This claim is particularly persuasive when the state faces a direct security threat: avoiding a nuclear holocaust or some ecological catastrophe, for example. In this instance the citizens of a state share a common interest in the territorial integrity of the state, their own physical security and ultimately, their survival. In defending the homeland from foreign invasion or from a threat to the environment's life-support systems, the state represents a broad range of interests and perspectives. In these responses it is clearly not simply an instrument of class rule. In fact it is possible to imagine circumstances where a conflict between the dominant class and the state's national security role will be resolved in favour of the latter.

However, national security policy can also have divisible benefits for certain constituent groups, a point not explored by McGowan and Walker but emphasised by Kolko and others. For example, since the Truman administration, critics of US foreign policy have highlighted the role played by the 'military–industrial complex' in promoting US interventions in the Third World. They have alleged that security policy can be framed by this group in a way which encourages the state to spend enormous public outlays on the research and development of new military technologies as well as to maintain advanced industry sectors – what is sometimes called the Pentagon system or 'military Keynesianism'. Kofsky, for example, has argued that in order for the Truman Administration to inaugurate a huge buildup of military hardware and bailout a near-bankrupt aircraft industry in 1948, an imaginary Soviet war scare was launched upon public opinion and the Congress (Kofsky 1993). Using 'threat inflation' in this way proved to be a consistently successful method of channelling public funds to the private sector during the Cold War. As the radical journalist H.L. Mencken famously explained, 'the whole aim of practical politics is to keep the populace alarmed (and hence clamorous to be led to safety) by menacing it with an endless series of hobgoblins, all of them imaginary' (Nathan & Mencken 1997, p. 14).

Public sector investment and state guaranteed markets for production are, of course, an explicit violation of free market economic principles, although they have been crucial to the development of both the microchip and aviation industries in the United States, to name only two.

Critics would argue that the exaggeration of foreign security threats in the post-war period has distorted public perceptions of international politics by helping to entrench political dichotomies and a sense of 'bonding by exclusion': making 'otherness' – in the West during the Cold War the ever-present but grossly exaggerated 'Soviet threat' – appear normal and permanent. As Dalby and others have explained, the construction of foreign threats during the Cold War by constituent groups such as the Committee on the Present Danger, served specific domestic political and economic interests, suggesting national security policy is more divisible than either realists or McGowan and Walker are prepared to concede (Dalby 1990).

Constructivists have similarly argued that national interests are not inscribed in some objective reality but constructed by agents within military/security discursive frameworks. So called 'common security threats' may in fact be more imagined than real, or rendered more objective and immutable than need be. According to Dalby, aspects of the anti-Communist discourse in the West during the Cold War, for example, were as much about the construction of the United States as a free democratic society as they were about the USSR. Campbell similarly argues that political identity and the discourse of security in the United

States can only be properly understood if it is seen as constituted by perceptions of 'foreign-ness' and the 'writing of a threat' (Campbell 1992). Common security interests cannot, therefore, automatically be presumed to be common: they may be sourced from beyond the frontier and may be complicit in the limiting of domestic political identities. Or they may simply be confected by elites and 'sold' to a dependent public.

As a correction to the crude economic reductionism of Marx's original account, McGowan and Walker's model demonstrates an awareness of the realist critique. It provides a challenging explanation of when and why the state responds to powerful domestic interests in the conduct of foreign policy, and conversely it also explains when and why the state can act in the common interests of the nation, even if this advantages some sectors of the community. It explains why the state often appears as an impartial arbiter or referee in the formulation of policy, and why at other times it seems to be hostage to dominant class interests.

Conclusion

Conventional approaches to the national interest, such as realism, clearly overestimate the extent to which a state's external policies are autonomous from its internal social complexion, particularly in the economic domain. Even a great power's preponderant influence in the international system does not give it sufficient room to ignore the needs of its dominant domestic constituency. The power of Marxist and anarchist insights rests on their ability to expose the deep, irreconcilable and internal tensions within capitalist societies which cannot be easily concealed with appeals to the common interests of all. The good of the part should not be mistaken for the benefit of the whole.

On the other hand, critical approaches such as Marxism have often failed to acknowledge the nature of state autonomy in the formulation and implementation of national security policy. A tendency to reduce all state behaviour to dominant class preferences has left these analyses blind to the fact that a state's national security role may actually bring it into conflict with members of the dominant class. McGowan and Walker's approach to the 'national interest' is both a recognition of the vulnerability of critical approaches to realism and a more promising avenue of research which is both informed by critical Marxism but consonant of the residual power of the realist tradition.

For Marxists and anarchists, the conventional presentation of national interests is always a subjective formulation unless they are referring to specific class interests which they presume to be an objective fact. The foreign policy preferences of the ruling class may change over time. To that extent, following Frankel and Rosenau's distinction between objective and subjective national interests, the means to achieve diplomatic goals will vary in a subjective sense. However, the disproportionate influence of ruling groups and their ability to extract benefits from state policy is an subjective, class-based assessment. A capitalist nation cannot have common objective interests.

The previous chapter concluded that any discussion of security issues in international politics cannot avoid realist claims about the enduring importance of the national interest. This chapter emphasises the limitations of realist conceptions of the national interest particularly in the explanation of economic policy, exposed by Marxists and anarchist thinkers as often merely an elegant disguise for particular rather than common interests. This chapter also demonstrates than even in the area of security policy where the state enjoys relative autonomy from societal interests, some groups in the community have a greater stake than others in exaggerating the threat posed by outside forces.

4
Progressive Perspectives: Liberal Approaches

> I have never known much good done by those who affected to trade for the public good. It is an affectation, indeed. Not very common among merchants, and very few words need be employed in dissuading them from it.
>
> (Adam Smith, *An Inquiry into the Nature and Causes of the Wealth of Nations*)

> Jesus Christ is Free Trade and Free Trade is Jesus Christ.
>
> (John Bowring, English diplomat, cited in B. Anderson, *The Alfred Deakin Lectures*)

Liberalism is one of two great progressive philosophical traditions to have come out of the European Enlightenment, the other being Marxism. Its ideas have had a profound impact on the political shape of all modern industrial societies. Liberalism has championed limited government and scientific rationality, believing individuals should be free from arbitrary state power, persecution and superstition. It has advocated political freedom, democracy, human and constitutionally guaranteed rights, and privileged the liberty of the individual and equality before the law. Liberalism has also argued for individual competition in civil society and claimed that market capitalism best promotes the general welfare of all by most efficiently allocating scarce resources. To the extent that its ideas have been realised in recent democratic transitions in both hemispheres and manifested in the globalisation of the world economy, liberalism remains a powerful and influential doctrine.

Because it is such a broad philosophical church, liberalism contains within its boundaries a number of sometimes conflicting and contradictory sub-groups and traditions. These include economic liberals who focus on the promotion of market relations as the optimal form of economic organisation, political liberals who regard the spread of liberal-democracy as an antidote to conflict in the international system, and moral liberals who believe that the universal adoption of human rights benchmarks will gradually improve the condition of the species. These are not necessarily discrete factions within liberalism, though Macpherson has characterised conflict within liberal philosophy as a division between the market view of human beings as consumers maximising their utilities and the ethical view of humans striving to realise their potential (Macpherson 1973, p. 24; see also Richardson 1997).

The tension between these various schools and their intersection with conservative political ideology accounts for a variety of attitudes towards the nation-state as an actor in international politics, and to national interests as the primary objective of diplomacy. Although this analysis will concentrate on the anti-statist, pro-market philosophical stream within liberal thought (sometimes called the neo-liberal school), and how it conceives of the idea of national interests, it will also note a range of alternative conceptions which are inherent within other branches of the tradition.

The chapter will begin with an explanation of Adam Smith's classical theory of the national interest, which underwrites market liberalism generally. The revival of liberal international thought after the Cold War will then be assessed. The role of the nation-state within traditional liberal attitudes to war and the importance of democracy and human rights in liberal internationalism will be examined for the extent to which modern liberalism has redefined the idea of the national interest. The chapter will conclude with an assessment of how liberalism understands the idea of national interests within debates over contemporary economic globalisation.

Adam Smith's invisible hand

At the basis of Adam Smith's conception of the national interest is his claim that the pursuit of material self-gain is the normal condition of humankind. This 'natural disposition', which is unique to humans, determines the very structure of economy and society:

> The division of labour ... is the necessary, though very slow and gradual, consequence of a certain propensity in human nature which has in view no such extensive utility; the propensity to truck, barter and exchange one thing for another. (Smith 1976, Bk I, Ch. II, p. 17)

Understanding the overriding importance of individual self-interest by liberating the acquisitive instincts of the species, not only enables Smith to explain the importance of the division of labour in maximising economic efficiency. It is also the basis of his concerns about the state, which at root is the view that a person has a clearer sense of their own interests than the state could ever have: 'every individual, it is evident, can, in his local situation, judge much better than any statesman or lawgiver can do for him' (Smith 1976, Bk IV, Ch. II, p. 478). The danger posed by the state, according to Smith, is its capacity to break the nexus between self-interest and individual commercial actions. However, Smith's understanding of human nature also provides a guide to rational social behaviour:

> But man has almost constant occasion for the help of his brethren, and it is in vain for him to expect it from their benevolence only. He will be more likely to prevail if he can interest their self-love in his favour, and show them that it is for their own advantage to do for him what he requires of them .... It is not from the benevolence of the butcher, the brewer, or the baker, that we expect our dinner, but from their regard to their own interest. (Smith 1976, Bk I, Ch. II, p. 18)

The challenge Smith set for himself was to extrapolate from this model of individual action with its explanation of basic economic motivation to an account of how the larger human community should be organised economically. Or to put it more specifically, what are the implications of Smith's theory of economic self-interest for the state as the largest form of political and economic organisation? It is a measure of his achievement that, far from arguing for them separately, Smith's most famous dictum is that individual and public interest are effectively one and the same thing. To best serve the latter, individuals need only pursue what comes naturally to them – their own self-interest. They need not even be aware of how their own behaviour connects with the general good of their society or intend their actions in that direction. In fact it would be better if they did not directly aim to promote the public interest:

> As every individual, therefore, endeavours as much as he can both to employ his capital in the support of domestic industry, and so to direct that industry that its produce may be of the greatest value; every individual necessarily labours to render the annual revenue of the society as great as he can. He generally, indeed, neither intends to promote the public interest, nor knows how much he is promoting

it. By preferring the support of domestic to that of foreign industry, he intends only his own security; and by directing that industry in such a manner as its produce may be of greatest value, he intends only his own gain, and he is in this, as in many other cases, led by an invisible hand to promote an end which was no part of his intention. Nor is it always the worse for the society that it was no part of it. By pursuing his own interest he frequently promotes that of the society more effectually than when he really intends to promote it. (Smith 1976, Bk IV, Ch. II, pp. 477–8)

Individuals, motivated by self-interest – the *primum mobile* of life – and with a clear objective sense of this interest and how to realise it, enhance the wealth of the entire nation unintentionally by pursuing what comes naturally to them. They are led to serve the greater good by the 'invisible hand' of competition which turns self-regarding behaviour into the common good of the society.

The national interest, as defined by Smith, is simply the accumulation of each individual's self-interest – a natural state produced without conscious thought or planning. According to Carr, Smith's conception of the national interest revolves around a symbiosis of particular and community interest. It 'achieves this synthesis by maintaining that the highest interest of the individual and the highest interest of the community naturally coincide. In pursuing his own interest, the individual pursues that of the community, and in promoting the interest of the community he promotes his own. This is the famous doctrine of the harmony of interests' (Carr 1939; 1981, p. 43).

As will be shown, Smith's ideas were extrapolated further to optimise relations between states on the basis of free trade and the non-intervention of the state in commercial relations between individuals across the world. According to the tradition Smith is often said to have founded, free markets not only enhanced the prosperity of people everywhere by allowing them to pursue their own interests without interference. They also promoted peace between states because free trade was a powerful antidote to wars fought over commercial rivalry, suspicion and competition for colonial possessions. A powerful theme which runs through liberal philosophy argues that economic links between people are a uniting and pacifying force in international politics. Conversely, protectionism and barriers to trade are a cause of conflict. As Smith argues, 'Commerce, which ought naturally to be, among nations, as among individuals, a bond of union and friendship, has become the most fertile source of discord and animosity' (Smith 1976, Bk IV, Ch. III, Pt II, p. 519).

It is a mistake, however, to regard Smith as an unqualified free trader who always opposed any meaningful role for the state in the economic life of the nation. Although rarely cited, Smith lists two important exceptions to the rule that the individual's pursuit of self-interest must be unfettered by the state.

> There seem, however, to be two cases in which it will generally be advantageous to lay some burden upon foreign, for the encouragement of domestic industry. The first is, when some particular sort of industry is necessary for the defence of the country .... The act of navigation [Navigation Act of 1660], therefore, very properly endeavours to give the sailors and shipping of Great Britain the monopoly of the trade of their own country, in some cases, by absolute prohibitions, and in others by heavy burdens upon the shipping of foreign countries. (Smith 1976, Bk IV, Ch. II, pp. 484–5)

Goods required for national security should, according to Smith, be exempted from the normal rules of commercial exchange which privilege their market value. Free trade cannot exist where 'national animosity' threatens the very survival of the state, a common occurrence because states 'being neighbours ... are necessarily enemies' (Smith 1976, Bk IV, Ch. III, Pt II, p. 522). Security must come before prosperity:

> The act of navigation is not favourable to foreign commerce, or to the growth of that opulence which can arise from it ... defence, however, is of much more importance than opulence. (Smith 1976, Bk IV, Ch. II, pp. 86–7)

This first exception is a major qualification to Smith's underlying thesis, given the important role that the visible hand of the state is expected to play in defending the population from foreign invasion. It almost redefines Smith's conception of the national interest. For one scholar this exception is enough to suggest that the Scottish moral philosopher had a 'fundamentally realist view of international relations [because] ... for Smith, power politics ruled in international affairs (Walter 1996, pp. 149 & 162). This may exaggerate the priority which Smith awards to the state but it is an important reminder that for liberals, free trade, national security and a strong state are not necessarily incompatible. According to Beard,

> The exception of national defence and security from economic free play, for practical purposes, destroys the validity of the whole thesis

of individual interest in the age of technological warfare. Moreover, the very navy which Adam Smith regarded as necessary to the security of Great Britain had sprung largely from commercial advantage; it controlled trade routes and bases in the British interest, and was, with its various ship-building and supply adjuncts and its bureaucratic appendages, an economic and political engine of immense potency, a special collective interest as distinguished from an aggregation of individual interests. (Beard 1935, p. 163)

Nor, according to Smith, is the state merely reduced to the role of keeping order and providing domestic protection to individuals – a necessary evil. Although Smith is widely regarded as a champion of the minimal state, he was quite explicit about its necessary role:

> According to the system of natural liberty, the sovereign has only three duties to attend to; three duties of great importance, indeed, but plain and intelligible to common understandings; first, the duty of protecting the society from the violence and invasion of other independent societies; secondly, the duty of protecting, as far as possible, every member of the society from the injustice or oppression of every other member of it, or the duty of establishing an exact administration of justice; and, thirdly, the duty of erecting and maintaining certain public works and certain public institutions, which it can never be for the interest of any individual, or small number of individuals, to erect and maintain; because the profit could never repay the expense to any individual or small number of individuals, though it may frequently do much more than repay it to a great society. (Smith 1976, Bk IV, Ch. IX, pp. 208–9)

As a consequence, Beard is encouraged to extend the logic of Smith's argument to the international domain:

> Thus after all, in classical theory, nations are not mere aggregations of individuals trading freely with one another, regardless of national boundaries. Nations as such exist and they seek to preserve their nationality, to defend it against aggression, and 'wisely' make such exceptions to the law of freedom for individual interests as may be necessary to a supreme national interest – security and defence. Hence it would seem that nations must also place restraints on such commercial operations of their nationals as may lead to distant adventures likely to put all the powers of defence in jeopardy. (Beard 1935, p. 163)

The second exception to laissez-faire is when a case can be made for protective reciprocity because other states act to protect their local industries from cheaper imports. According to Smith:

> The second case, in which it will generally be advantageous to lay some burden upon foreign for the encouragement of domestic industry, is, when some tax is imposed at home upon the produce of the latter. In this case, it seems reasonable that an equal tax should be imposed upon the like produce of the former. (Smith 1976, Bk IV, Ch. II, p. 487)

A reciprocal tax 'would leave competition between foreign and domestic industry, after the tax, as nearly as possible upon the same footing as before it', providing a war of escalating protectionism is not triggered (Smith 1976, Bk IV, Ch. II, p. 487). The revenue raised by these taxes should, according to Smith, be put to the benefit of the general public. Thus society may collectively benefit from levies, tariffs and taxes applied to imported goods. This constitutes another important exception to the rule that foreign trade and international exchange must always be free of state interference.

Smith defends the decision of one state to retaliate against another nation restricting imports if it leads to the abolition of restrictions, as well as the need to gradually and progressively restore free trade, rather than unilaterally and immediately removing all regulations which would impose severe adjustment costs. Here it is almost as if Smith is acknowledging the gap between what he believes works best in the national interest and what in reality will actually prevail in commercial relations between states. In a remarkable passage which would be appreciated by those with a critical perspective of the national interest, he expresses a profound pessimism that free trade in anything like its idealised form will ever come to describe commercial exchanges between nations:

> To expect, indeed, that freedom of trade should ever be entirely restored in Great Britain, is as absurd as to expect that an Oceana or Utopia should ever be established in it. Not only the prejudices of the public, but what is much more unconquerable, the private interests of many individuals, irresistibly oppose it. (Smith 1976, Bk IV, Ch. II, p. 493)

To read Smith's treatise as a celebration of unfettered free trade and the liberation of individual commercial interests from the intrusive and corrupting influence of the state, is to paint an inaccurate portrait of his conception of the national interest. It is not even necessary to agree with Beard that 'the classical conception of national interest as an aggregation of individual interests guided by "an invisible hand" is vitiated, if not entirely destroyed, by reservations and exceptions', to acknowledge that Smith's account is not as simple or pure as some have portrayed it (Beard 1935, pp. 163–4). Nor is it necessary to consider Smith more a realist than a liberal. Smith always acknowledged that the state played a positive role in economic life beyond that of nightwatchman. It is important, therefore, not to simply equate his view of the national interest with a preference for laissez-faire. It was a much more flexible construction, as Beard notes:

> When national 'security' or 'defence' is introduced as a value or reality superior to and supreme over private interests and the opulence which those interests create and accumulate, it is made a primordal consideration of policy. The maxim of freedom for the international circulation of commodities under the impetus of individual interests is abrogated, or at least subordinated, to the exigencies of security and defence. Moreover, when taxes are imposed on domestic production for public purposes – in realisation of social policy – the maxim of freedom is also restricted in application, and another primordial beyond the scope of private interest is brought into operation, namely social policy for which taxes are levied. Full reliance upon the *primum mobile* of individual interest which, under the 'invisible hand,' brings about the general interest is thus repudiated. Even the grand object of interest, opulence, is subordinated to another value, security, which is not measurable in the pecuniary terms of private interest. The State is thus restored to economy, the unity or integrity of the nation is posited as datum, and a national interest superior to the pursuit of individual interests is made the supreme concern of domestic and foreign policy. (Beard 1935, p. 164)

It is important to accept that Smith's influential account of the national interest – that self-regarding behaviour maximises the common interests of society – is qualified by the need to place the security of the nation before the affluence of society, and by the need to respond in kind to protectionist measures introduced by states which are commercial competitors. As will be seen, those within the liberal tradition who sought to develop Smith's ideas into general rules for international exchange and the conduct of international relations generally, tended to narrow his understanding of the national interest by emphasising his theory of the 'invisible hand' without acknowledging the important qualifications he made to his own general rule.

Liberal antidotes to war: democracy and free trade

The foundations of contemporary liberal prescriptions for a peaceful world order were laid in the eighteenth and nineteenth centuries. In summary they concluded that the prospects for the elimination of war lay with a preference for democracy over aristocracy, free trade over autarky, and collective security over the balance of power system. In this section each of these arguments will be examined in turn for the extent to which they have informed contemporary liberal thinking about the national interest.

Prospects for peace

For liberals, peace is the normal state of affairs: in Kant's words, peace can be perpetual. The laws of nature dictated harmony and co-operation between peoples. War is therefore both unnatural and irrational, an artificial contrivance and not a product of some peculiarity of human nature. Liberals have a belief in progress and the perfectibility of the human condition. Through their faith in the power of human reason and the capacity of human beings to realise their inner potential, they remain confident that the stain of war can be removed from human experience (see Zacher & Matthew 1995; Gardner 1990; Hoffmann 1995).

A common thread running through liberal thought, from Rousseau, Kant and Cobden, to Schumpeter and Doyle, is that wars were created by militaristic and undemocratic governments for their own vested interests. Wars were engineered by a warrior class bent on extending their power and wealth through territorial conquest. According to Paine in *The Rights of Man*, the '"war system" was contrived to preserve the power and the employment of princes, statesmen, soldiers, diplomats and armaments manufacturers, and to bind their tyranny ever more firmly upon the necks of the people' (Howard 1978, p. 31). Wars provided governments with excuses to raise taxes, expand their bureaucratic apparatus and thus increase their control over their citizens. The people, on the other hand, were peace-loving by nature, and only plunged into conflict by the whims of unrepresentative rulers who did not have their interests at heart.

War was a cancer on the body politic. But it was an ailment that human beings, themselves, had the capacity to cure. The treatment which liberals began prescribing in the eighteenth century has remained consistent: the disease of war could be successfully treated with the twin medicines of *democracy* and *free trade*. Democratic processes and institutions would break the power of the ruling elites, and curb their propensity for violence. Free trade and commerce would overcome the artificial barriers erected between individuals and unite them everywhere into one human community.

For liberals like Schumpeter, war was the product of the aggressive instincts of unrepresentative elites. The warlike disposition of these rulers drove the reluctant masses into violent conflicts which, while profitable for the arms industries and the military aristocrats, were disastrous for those who did the fighting. For Kant, the establishment of republican forms of government in which rulers were accountable and individual rights were respected would lead to peaceful international relations because the ultimate consent for war would rest with the citizens of the state (Kant 1970, p. 100). For both Kant and Schumpeter, war was the outcome of minority rule, though Kant was no champion of democratic government. Liberal states, founded on individual rights such as equality before the law, free speech and civil liberty, respect for private property and representative government, would not have the same appetite for conflict and war. Peace was fundamentally a question of establishing legitimate domestic orders throughout the world. 'When the citizens who bear the burdens of war elect their governments, wars become impossible' (Doyle 1986, p. 1151).

The dual themes of domestic legitimacy and the extent to which liberal-democratic states exercise restraint and peaceful intentions in their foreign policy have been taken up more recently by Doyle and Russett. In a restatement of Kant's argument that a 'pacific federation' (*foedus pacificum*) can be built by expanding the number of states with democratic constitutions, Doyle claims that liberal-democracies are unique in their ability and willingness to establish peaceful relations between themselves. This pacification of foreign relations among liberal states is said to be a direct product of their shared legitimate political orders based on democratic principles and institutions. The reciprocal recognition of these common principles – a commitment to the rule of law, individual rights and equality before the law, representative government based on popular consent – means that liberal democracies evince little interest in conflict with each other and have no grounds on which to contest each other's legitimacy: they have constructed a 'separate peace' (Doyle 1986, p. 1161). This does not mean that they are less inclined to make war with non-democratic states, and Doyle points out that democracies maintain a healthy appetite for conflicts with authoritarian states. But it does suggest that the best prospect for bringing an end to war between states lies with the spread of liberal-democratic governments across the globe. The expansion of the zone of peace from the core to the periphery is the basis of Francis Fukuyama's optimism about the post-Communist era (Doyle 1986; Fukuyama 1992; Russett 1993; Doyle 1997). This is an argument extended by Rawls, who claims that liberal societies are also 'less likely to engage in war with nonliberal outlaw states, except on grounds of legitimate self-defence (or in the defence of their legitimate allies), or intervention in severe cases to protect human rights' (Rawls 1999, p. 49). The inference is clear. For liberals the national interest can only be properly represented by a state with a liberal-democratic political order and the spread of these arrangements is most likely to pacify the international system.

A related argument by Mueller claims that we are already witnessing the obsolescence of war between the major powers. Reviving the liberal faith in the capacity of people to improve the moral and material conditions of their lives, Mueller attempts to demonstrate that, just as duelling and slavery were eventually seen as morally unacceptable, war is increasingly viewed in the developed world as repulsive, immoral and uncivilised. That violence is more widely seen as an anachronistic form of social intercourse is not due to any change in human nature or the structure of the international system. According to Mueller, the obsolescence of major war in the late twentieth century is the product of moral learning, a shift in ethical consciousness away from coercive forms of social behaviour. Because war brings more costs than gains and is no longer seen as a romantic or noble pursuit, it has become 'rationally unthinkable' (Mueller 1989).

The long peace between states of the industrialised world is a cause of profound optimism for liberals such as Mueller and Fukuyama, who are confident that the world has already entered a period in which war as an instrument of international diplomacy is becoming obsolete. But if war has been an important factor in nation-building, as Giddens, Mann and Tilly have argued, the fact that states are learning to curb their propensity for violence will also have important consequences for forms of political community which are likely to emerge in the industrial centres of the world. The end of war between the great powers may have the ironic effect of weakening the rigidity of their political boundaries and inspiring a wave of sub-national revolts. If war has been a binding as well as destructive force in international relations, the problem of maintaining cohesive communities will be a major challenge for metropolitan centres.

Far from sharing the optimism of the liberals, neo-realists such as Waltz and Mearsheimer are profoundly disturbed by the collapse of

Soviet strategic power and directly challenge the post-Cold War optimism of Fukuyama and Doyle. If mutual nuclear deterrence between the United States and the Soviet Union accounted for the high level of international stability in the post-war period, the end of bipolarity casts an ominous shadow over the future world order. Because there is no obvious replacement for the Soviet Union which can restore the balance of strategic power, the world has entered an uncertain and dangerous phase. As Waltz concedes, 'in international politics, unbalanced power constitutes a danger even when it is American power that is out of balance ... both friends and foes will react as countries always have to threatened or real preponderance of one among them: they will work to right the balance. The present condition of international politics is unnatural' (Waltz 1991, p. 670; Waltz 2000, pp. 55–6).

Waltz and Mearsheimer continue to stress the importance of strategic interaction in shaping the contours of international relations. For them, the distribution and character of military power remain the root causes of war and peace: the national interest has little to do with the internal political complexion of the state (Mearsheimer 1990, p. 6). Instead of highlighting the spread of liberal-democracy and a concomitant zone of peace, they regard the sudden demise of bipolarity in the early 1990s as the single most dramatic change in contemporary world politics. The pacification of the core, while desirable and perhaps even encouraging, is merely a transient stage which needs to be superseded by a restoration of the strategic balance amongst the great powers. Echoing Carr's critique of liberal utopianism on the eve of the Second World War, Waltz believes that the peace and justice which liberals claim is spreading beyond the central core 'will be defined to the liking of the powerful' (Waltz 1991, p. 669).

According to Waltz and Mearsheimer, the recurrent features of international relations, most notably the struggle for power and security, will eventually reassert themselves: 'in international politics, overwhelming power repels and leads others to try to balance against it' (Waltz 1991, p. 669). However, the absence of a countervailing power to the United States means there are few clues about how the current period will develop. According to Mearsheimer, the long peace of the Cold War was a result of three factors: the bipolar distribution of military power in continental Europe, the rough equality of military power between the United States and the Soviet Union, and the pacifying effect of the presence of nuclear weapons (Mearsheimer 1990, pp. 6–7). The collapse of the Soviet Union removed the central pillar upon which the bipolar stability was built. Multipolar systems, on the other hand, are notoriously less stable than bipolar systems because the number of potential bilateral conflicts is greater, deterrence is more difficult to achieve, and the potential for misunderstandings and miscalculations of power and motive is increased (Mearsheimer 1990, pp. 14–19). Based on the experience of previous multipolar systems, in particular both pre world war periods, the post-Cold War era is more a cause for concern than celebration.

Recent conflicts in the Persian Gulf, the Balkans and the former Soviet Union, as well as US responses to terrorism in Central Asia and the Middle East – all involving major industrial powers – are a reminder that the post-Cold War period remains volatile and suggest that war may not yet have lost its efficacy in international diplomacy. None of these constitute conflicts between democratic states but they are no less important to the maintenance of world order. These and other conflicts in so called 'failed states' such as Somalia, possibly Indonesia, Papua New Guinea and a range of South-West Pacific states, highlight the fact that the fragmentation of nation-states and civil wars arising from secessionist movements have not been given the same attention by liberals as more conventional inter-state wars. In fact liberals who stress the importance of the spread of democracy to the pacification of international politics have very little to say about these issues.

Neo-realists have regarded nuclear weapons, and the rough parity between East and West, as a source of stability and pacification during the Cold War. They provided security to both blocs, generated caution amongst decision makers, imposed a rough equality, and created a clarity of relative power between both camps (Mearsheimer 1990, p. 32). The absence of a first-strike capability and the destructive potential of a direct conflict forced the United States and the Soviet Union to learn to manage their differences without recourse to violence. In addition, the binding force of having a common enemy imposed a discipline upon and within each bloc. According to Mearsheimer, if this level of stability is to be reached in the multipolar environment, the 'carefully managed proliferation' of nuclear weapons in Europe may be required to preserve the peace, or at least keep a check on the strategic primacy of the United States (Mearsheimer 1990, pp. 7–8).

Maintaining strategic stability in Europe in a multipolar environment is just one of many major challenges for liberals. On the question of how liberal states should conduct themselves with non-liberal states, Fukuyama and Doyle are equally and surprisingly silent. Rawls, on the other hand, is concerned with the extent to which liberal and non-liberal peoples can be equal participants in a 'Society of Peoples'. He argues that principles and norms of international law and practice – the 'Law of Peoples' – can be developed and shared by both liberal and non-liberal or decent hierarchical societies, without an expectation that liberal democracy is the terminus for all. The guidelines and principal basis for establishing harmonious relations between liberal and non-liberal peoples under a common Law of Peoples, takes liberal international theory in a more sophisticated direction because it explicitly acknowledges the need for utopian thought to be realistic (Rawls 1999, pp. 11–23).

As the number of East Asian and Islamic societies which reject the normative superiority of liberal-democracy becomes more apparent, considerable doubt is cast on the belief that the non-European world is seeking to imitate the Western route to political modernisation. Perhaps the answer here, as Linklater suggests, is not so much the spread of liberal-democracy per se, 'but the idea of limited power which is present within, but not entirely synonymous with, liberal democracy' (Linklater 1993, pp. 33–6; Rawls 1999). The notion of limited power and respect for the rule of law contained within the idea of 'constitutionalism' may be one means of solving the exclusionary character of the liberal zone of peace. It is a less ambitious project and potentially more sensitive to the cultural and political differences among states in the current international system. It may avoid the danger of the system bifurcating into a privileged inner circle and a disadvantaged and disaffected outer circle (Linklater 1993, p. 33). The greatest barrier to the expansion of the zone of peace from the core is the perception within the periphery that this constitutes little more than the domination of one culture by another. These suspicions are well founded given that peripheral states have consistently been the victims of Western intervention.

The confidence liberals have that the democratisation of the state will purify the national interest and pacify international relations must also be assessed against the relative failure of recent democratic transitions in Southeast Asia to improve the life circumstances of the citizens of a number of states. According to Anderson, the modern histories of Thailand, the Philippines and Indonesia demonstrate that, in of itself, a democratic political system with free and fair elections is no panacea to poverty, inequality and underdevelopment (Anderson 2001).

Democratic institutions may well place a break on the propensity of unaccountable elites to drive their unwilling populations into international conflicts, and Doyle's observation that liberal-democracies eschew war in their relations is a correlation that generally appears to hold true. However, as the recent behaviour of the United States in Central America, Central Asia, the Middle East and Southern Europe suggests, liberal-democratic Great Powers have shown little reluctance to avoid conflict with non-democratic adversaries. Democratising the state may be an important precondition for the construction of a legitimate national interest, but it remains an insufficient prescription for a more peaceful world order and a rather poor guide to the future diplomatic behaviour of states.

The spirit of commerce

Adam Smith's conception of the national interest had a profound influence upon liberals who believed that not only was an individual's motivation for private gain rooted in human nature, it was also the basis upon which global peace could be constructed. If the acquisitive instincts of the species were unfettered by the interference of government, a policy of international free trade would bring an end to conflict and war between states.

Eighteenth- and nineteenth-century liberals felt that the spirits of war and commerce were mutually incompatible. Many wars were fought by states to achieve their selfish mercantilist goals. According to Carr, 'the aim of mercantilism ... was not to promote the welfare of the community and its members, but to augment the power of the state, of which the sovereign was the embodiment ... wealth was the source of power, or more specifically of fitness for war'. Until the Napoleonic wars,

> wealth, conceived in its simplest form as bullion, was brought in by exports; and since, in the static conception of society prevailing at this period, export markets were a fixed quantity not susceptible of increase as a whole, the only way for a nation to expand its markets and therefore its wealth was to capture them from some other nation, if necessary by waging a trade war. (Carr 1945, pp. 5–6)

Free trade, however, was said to be a more peaceful means of achieving national wealth because, according to the theory of comparative advantage, each economy would be materially better off than if it had been pursuing nationalism and self-sufficiency (autarky). Importantly, free trade would also break down suspicion and the divisions between states to unite individuals everywhere in one community. Artificial barriers to commerce distort perceptions and relations between individuals, thereby causing international tension. Free trade would expand the range of contacts and levels of understanding between the peoples of the world and encourage international friendship, cosmopolitan thinking and understanding. According to Kant, unhindered commerce between the peoples of the world would unite them in a common, peaceful enterprise.

'Trade ... would increase the wealth and power of the peace-loving, productive sections of the population at the expense of the war-orientated aristocracy, and ... would bring men of different nations into constant contact with one another; contact which would make clear to all of them their fundamental community of interests' (Howard 1978, p. 20; see also Walter 1996). Similarly Ricardo believed that free trade 'binds together, by one common tie of interest and intercourse, the universal society of nations throughout the civilised world' (Ricardo 1911, p. 114).

The national interest should not, therefore, be defined in provincial or even national terms. Ultimately, the national interest should result in the abolition of national economic barriers which are a product of the division of the species into a multiplicity of separate and exclusive political communities.

Conflicts were often caused by states erecting barriers which distorted and concealed a natural harmony of interests commonly shared by individuals across the world. The solution to the problem, argued Adam Smith and Tom Paine, was the free movement of commodities, capital and labour. 'If commerce were permitted to act to the universal extent it is capable, it would extirpate the system of war and produce a revolution in the uncivilised state of governments' (Howard 1978, p. 29). Writing in 1848, John Stuart Mill also claimed free trade was the means to bring about the end of war: 'it is commerce which is rapidly rendering war obsolete, by strengthening and multiplying the personal interests which act in natural opposition to it' (Howard 1978, p. 37). The spread of markets would place societies on an entirely new foundation. Instead of conflicts over limited resources such as land, the industrial revolution raised the prospect of unlimited and unprecedented prosperity for all: material production, so long as it was freely exchanged, would bring human progress. Trade would create relations of mutual dependence which would foster understanding between peoples and reduce conflict. Economic self-interest would then be a powerful disincentive for war.

Free trade, according to Cobden, was 'eternal in its truth and universal in its application'. It was the key to global harmony and peace: 'the triumph of free trade was a triumph of pacific principles between all nations of the earth' (Arblaster 1984, p. 261). 'The colonial policy of Europe', claimed Cobden, 'has been the chief source of wars for the last hundred and fifty years. Again, free trade, by perfecting the intercourse, must inevitably snatch the power from governments to plunge their people into wars' (Beard 1935, p. 161). As it was understood by Bright, free trade was the means for 'undermining the nationalist ambitions of nation-states by encouraging cosmopolitanism (meaning free from national limitations), and making nations so interdependent that wars and military budgets became unthinkable. Imperialism and autarky were regarded by liberals as the work of illiberal and reactionary forces and as a direct cause of wars' (Gamble 1981, pp. 81–2). Free trade, said Cobden, meant

> breaking down the barriers that separate nations; those barriers behind which nestle feelings of pride, revenge, hatred and jealousy which every now and then break their bonds and deluge whole countries with blood; those feelings which nourish the poison of war and conquest, which assert that without conquest we can have no trade, which foster that lust for conquest and dominion which sends forth your warrior chiefs to sanction devastation through other lands. (Howard 1978, p. 43)

It was felt that unfettered free commercial exchange would encourage links across frontiers and shift loyalties away from the nation-state. In effect, national interests as they are conventionally understood, would gradually give way to global interests. Leaders would eventually come to recognise that the benefits of free trade outweighed the costs of territorial conquest and colonial expansion. The attraction of going to war to promote mercantilist interests would be weakened as societies learn that war can only disrupt trade and therefore the prospects for economic prosperity.

It was thought that free trade would also reduce misunderstandings between states, because the often contentious issues of industrial production and distribution would be taken from the jurisdiction of the state and handed over to the market. States would then be removed from direct responsibility for commercial behaviour which might upset, or threaten a rival state. State officials and commercial interests would be free to establish 'crosscutting transnational ties that serve as lobbies for mutual accommodation' (Doyle 1986, p. 1161). Interdependence would replace national competition and defuse unilateral acts of aggression and reciprocal retaliation.

Interdependence and liberal institutionalism

Free trade and the removal of barriers to commerce is at the heart of modern interdependency theory. The rise of regional economic integration in Europe, for example, was inspired by the belief that the likelihood of conflict between states would be reduced by creating a common interest in trade and economic collaboration amongst members of the same geographical region. This would encourage states which traditionally resolved their differences militarily, such as France and Germany, to co-operate within a commonly agreed economic and political framework for their mutual benefit. States would then have a joint stake in each other's peace and prosperity. They would be forced to think less in a narrow national interest framework and more in terms of mutual and regional benefits. The European Union is the best example of economic integration engendering closer economic and political co-operation in a region historically bedevilled by national conflicts.

As Mitrany argued in his important functionalist approach, initially co-operation between states would be achieved in technical areas where it was mutually convenient, but once successful it could 'spill over' into other functional areas where states found that mutual advantages could be gained (Mitrany 1948, pp. 350–63). In a development of this argument, Keohane and Nye have explained how, via membership of international institutions, states can significantly broaden their conceptions of self-interest in order to widen the scope for co-operation. Compliance with the rules of these organisations not only discourages the narrow pursuit of national interests, it also weakens the meaning and appeal of state sovereignty (Keohane & Nye 1977). This suggests that the international system is more normatively regulated than realists would have us believe, a position further developed by the English School such as Wight and Bull.

A development of this argument can be found in liberal-institutionalism which shares with neo-realism an acceptance of the importance of the state and the anarchical condition of the international system, though liberal-institutionalists argue that the prospects for co-operation, even in an anarchical world, are greater than neo-realists would have us believe (Nye 1988; Powell 1994). Accepting the broad strictures of neo-realism, but employing rational choice and game theory to anticipate the behaviour of states, liberal-institutionalists seek to demonstrate that co-operation between states can be enhanced even without the presence of a hegemonic player which can enforce compliance with agreements. For them, anarchy is mitigated by regimes and institutional co-operation which brings higher levels of regularity and predictability to international relations. Regimes constrain state behaviour by formalising the expectations of each party to an agreement where there is a shared interest. Institutions then assume the role of encouraging co-operative habits, monitoring compliance and sanctioning defectors.

Neo-realists and neo-liberals disagree about how states conceive of their own interests. Whereas neo-realists, such as Waltz, argue that states are concerned with 'relative gains' – meaning gains are assessed in comparative terms (who will gain more?), neo-liberals such as Keohane claim that states are concerned with maximising their 'absolute gains' – an assessment of their own welfare rather than their rivals (what will gain me the most?). Accordingly, neo-realists argue that states will baulk at co-operation if they expect to gain less than their rivals. Liberal-institutionalists, on the other hand, believe international relations does not need to be a zero-sum game, as many states feel secure enough to maximise their own gains regardless of what accrues to others. Mutual benefits arising out of co-operation are possible because states are not always preoccupied with relative gains. The debate between relative gains and absolute gains points to a significant divergence between the way realists and liberals understand and define the national interest (see Reus-Smit 2001, p. 212).

Liberal-institutionalists acknowledge that co-operation between states is likely to be fragile, particularly where enforcement procedures are weak. However, in an environment of growing regional and global integration, states can often discover – with or without the encouragement of a hegemon – a coincidence of strategic and economic interests which can be turned into a formalised agreement determining the rules of conduct.

According to Rosecrance, the growth of economic interdependency has been matched by a corresponding decline in the value and importance of territorial conquest for states. In the contemporary world the benefits of trade and co-operation among states greatly exceed that of military competition and territorial control. Nation-states have traditionally regarded the acquisition of territory as the principal means of increasing national wealth. In recent years, however, it has become apparent that additional territory does not necessarily help states to compete in an international system where the 'trading state' rather than the 'military state' is becoming dominant (Rosecrance 1986). In the 1970s state elites began to realise that wealth is determined by their share of the world market in value-added goods and services. This understanding has had two significant effects. First, the age of the independent, self-sufficient state seems to be over. Complex layers of economic interdependency ensure that states cannot act aggressively without risking economic penalties imposed by other members of the international community. It also makes little sense for a state to threaten its commercial partners, whose markets and capital investment are essential for its own economic growth. Secondly, territorial conquest in the nuclear age is both dangerous and costly for non-compliant states. The alternative, economic development through trade and foreign investment, is a much more attractive and potentially beneficial strategy. In an environment of free and open trade, the conquest of territory would not only be burdensome, it would also undermine the system upon which economic success in the global economy rests (Rosecrance 1986; Strange 1991, pp. 30–1).

Neo-realists have two responses to the liberal claim that economic interdependency is pacifying international relations. First, they argue that in any struggle between competing disciplines, the anarchic environment and the insecurity it engenders will always take priority over the quest for economic prosperity. Economic interdependency will never take precedence over strategic security because states must be primarily concerned with their survival. The national interest, defined in strategic terms, is primary. The capacity of states to explore avenues of economic co-operation will therefore be limited by how secure they feel, and the extent to which they are required to engage in military competition with others. Secondly, the idea of economic interdependence implies a misleading degree of equality and shared vulnerability to economic forces in the global economy. Interdependence does not eliminate hegemony and dependency in interstate relations because power is very unevenly distributed throughout the world's trade and financial markets. Dominant players such as the United States have usually framed the rules under which interdependency has flourished. Conflict and co-operation is therefore unlikely to disappear, though it may be channelled into more peaceful forms.

Secret diplomacy, the balance of power and collective security

As much as any other factor, liberals argue for democracy because they are profoundly suspicious of concentrated forms of power, especially state power. After all, liberalism from the time of Adam Smith has expressed a preference for the minimalist state. When they looked at the international system, liberals of the nineteenth and early twentieth centuries saw power being exercised in the interests of governing elites and against the wishes of the masses. 'Secret diplomacy' was the name they gave to the way unrepresentative elites practiced international relations in the pre-democratic era. Liberals disputed the view that foreign policy was a specialised art which was best made by professional diplomats behind closed doors and away from the influences of national politics. If the democratisation of domestic politics could produce important economic and social reforms there would be a commensurate improvement in the conduct of foreign policy as a result of popular participation

(Clark 1989, pp. 147–8). And if popular consent was to be fully realised in the liberal state, there would need to be an adequate machinery for ensuring the democratic control of foreign policy. Elite secret diplomacy was the antithesis of government in the national interest.

From the time of Bright and Cobden, liberals have regarded the balance of power as the most pernicious aspect of 'secret diplomacy'. It was, in Bright's words, 'a foul thing' which gave no credence to the common interests of humankind and the just claims of small nations seeking self-determination. The balance of power was the product of elite collusion which resulted in international relations being 'arranged' to suit the interests of those who ruled Great Powers. For Cobden the 'balance of power' was both the veil behind which the armaments industries enriched themselves through state expenditure on weapons of war and a smokescreen which concealed British imperial interests (Kauppi & Viotti 1992, pp. 208–9).

Consistent with their preference for the minimalist state was liberal belief that governments get in the way of peaceful relations between individuals, hence Cobden's call for 'as little intercourse as possible between Governments, as much connection as possible between nations of the world'. To realise their world view, liberals wanted to replace autocratic regimes with ones based on democratic accountability and values. However, a major obstacle to the transformation of international relations was the balance of power system, which helped to sustain tyrannical regimes by denying nationalities the opportunity to over-throw the structures of state power. Empires and authoritarian governments were propped up by those with vested interests in main-taining the integrity of the European states-system, regardless of the political aspirations of the peoples of Europe.

The balance of power is normally defined as the absence of a prepon-derant military power in the international system. As it operated in Europe, the balance of power system described the process whereby smaller powers would form temporary alliances of convenience which would act as a countervailing power to the dominant military state in the region. Membership of these alliances would change over time as new hegemons emerged, and from time to time war would be necessary to cut down the dominant state and distribute strategic power in the region more evenly. To defenders of the balance of power, conflict was a regrettable but necessary and sometimes even a desirable feature of the international system.

Liberal critics of the balance of power claim the concept is vague and unintelligible and the method by which great powers pursue their commercial and strategic interests at the expense of small powers is often in violation of international law. Realist defenders of the concept, on the other hand, argue that liberals have missed the point of the system. The principal function of the balance of power is not to preserve peace, but to preserve the system of states. On certain occasions war may in fact be necessary to recalibrate the differentials of power in the international system. Smaller powers may be absorbed or partitioned in the process, and international law may be sporadically breached, but this is the necessary cost of keeping order in the system (Bull 1977, pp. 106–12).

Until 1914 most scholars and statesmen assumed that the 'balance of power' was a self-regulating system, the political equivalent of the law of economics. The First World War discredited the laws of both economics and politics. The self-operating laws had failed to prevent the most destructive conflict in human history. The balance of power had failed to prevent the war because, instead of allowing for the flexibility of realigning each other against the aggressor, the great powers had locked themselves into two antagonistic blocs. The liberal alternative idea of collective security was designed to prevent this situation recurring by ensuring that in the future, the aggressor would be confronted by all other states. In other words, a balance of power would be institutionalised. According to its proponents, collective security would have two beneficial results. First, it would make the balance of power more effective because there would be less chance of a preponderant power emerging. Secondly, it would ensure that violence, if necessary, would always be used in a legitimate manner. Since power is vested in the international community, it would not be abused in the way it was by individual nation states. Henceforth, all members of the international community would take collective responsibility for keeping the peace. This responsibility would be formally enshrined in the institutional form of the League of Nations.

In summary, liberals believed that national interests should focus on the pursuit of peace – a harmony between nations. This could only be realised by replacing balance of power diplomacy with collective security arrangements. Realists, on the other hand, believed national interests should have a more narrow concern for power – national power – and that peace would be an incidental by-product of a balance of power between states, not a primary pursuit in itself.

Consistent with the view that peace depended on the spread of democracy, collective security was an attempt to reproduce the concepts and processes of domestic law at the international level. Liberals believed that the destructive forces of international anarchy could only be brought to an end if the international system was regulated in the same way as domestic society. Then there would no longer be any need for covert alliances between governments because secret diplomacy would be replaced by open discussion within the Assembly of the League. The commitment of member states to the principle of collective security would override any other alliance or strategic obligations. States would formally renounce the use of force as a means of settling international disputes.

The idea of collective security failed in the 1930s because it depended on the general acceptance by states of a particular configuration of international power: a distribution of influence, territory and military potential that clearly favoured the victors of the First World War at the expense of the defeated powers. Why should Germany, for example, accept forever the injustice of a discriminatory peace settlement imposed on them in 1918? To those states which lost the First World War, and who wished to revise the frontiers and conditions imposed by the Versailles settlement, the League of Nations seemed dedicated to the preservation of the status quo rather than the preservation of peace. As Carr was soon to point out, the insecurity states feel in the international system does not afford them the luxury of forswearing the use of violence to uphold a principle. States are extremely reluctant to reduce their freedom of manoeuvre in an anarchical international environment. They continued to see international life from the perspective of their interests rather than the interests of the broader human community or an ethical interest in global peace.

And what could be done about states which did not accept these new diplomatic norms, such as the rule of law, controls on the use of force in international disputes, and the authority of the collective security organisation? When Japan occupied Manchuria in 1931 and Italy invaded Abyssinia in 1935–6, the League of Nations lacked both the collective will and the enforcement power to reverse these acts of aggression. Collective security was seen as inherently contradictory, if not hypocritical. If its principal motivation was outlawing the recourse to war, should the enforcement of its provisions in the final instance be dependent on the threat of the use of force?

Ironically, although the League of Nations was properly seen as one of the principal instruments of collective security, its creation had the effect of consolidating conceptions of national sovereignty and the national interest as the 'natural' political condition of humankind. Far from representing a stage beyond the nation-state as a representation of political community, the League operated on the principle that 'statehood' was universally applicable: it should be extended to most ethnic and national groups. As a critique of the balance of power as the principal guarantor of sovereignty, the League of Nations was an alternative means of legitimating national sovereignty, not an alternative *to* national sovereignty. The restructured territorial divisions which arose as a result of the new entitlement to statehood merely ensured that, after 1918, hostilities between ethnic or national minorities would become conflicts between states (Giddens 1985, pp. 258–61).

Liberal internationalists had been wrong to assume that there was a self-evident value system, committed to international harmony and co-operation, which had universal validity. As Carr commented, 'these supposedly absolute and universal principles were not principles at all, but the unconscious reflections of national policy based on a particular interpretation of national interest at a particular time' (Carr 1939, p. 87). Collective security, as it was practiced in the early phase of the inter-war years, was little more than the preservation of the status quo congenial to the interests of the victorious powers.

At the very least, a collective security system requires 'a degree of mutual confidence, a homogeneity of values and a coincidence of perceived interests' (Howard 1978, p. 132). This level of cultural homogeneity is never easy to find in the international system. Later in the century collective defence would prove to be more successful when attempted at the regional level, especially in limited strategic alliances against a common enemy.

Challenging liberalism

Challenges to Adam Smith's arguments for laissez-faire and his conception of the national interest, as well as critiques of free trade advocacy by Ricardo, Cobden and others, fall into two broad categories.

The first group focuses upon liberal attempts to construct a 'market society' in nineteenth-century Britain, and the implications for both the social fabric and Smith's original book. The second category challenges the allegedly benign and mutually beneficial effects of free trade. Both groups challenge the claim that the national interest is best achieved by the individual's self-regard for his or her personal interest.

Society and the 'free market'

In his seminal account of the abandonment of laissez-faire capitalism, Karl Polanyi argued that contrary to economic orthodoxy, the arrival of laissez-faire in the early nineteenth century was neither inevitable nor the result of an evolutionary process. According to Polanyi, it was the product of deliberate state policy and 'nothing less than a self-regulating market on a world scale' could ensure its proper functioning. The crucial step towards the laissez-faire economy was the commodification of land and labour in the eighteenth century, while the expansion of the market system in the nineteenth century was dependent on the spread of international free trade, the creation of a competitive (national) labour market, and the linking of the currency to the gold standard (Polanyi 1944, pp. 137–9).

Polanyi sought to explode a number of myths which underwrite economic liberalism and the claims it makes for market capitalism on the basis of human nature.

The first of these is the suggestion that the pursuit of material self-gain is the natural condition of humankind. This has been an article of faith for economic liberals who, since the time of Adam Smith, have argued that society comprises individuals with an innate propensity to 'truck, barter and exchange'. Polanyi argues that the pursuit of material self-gain is not innate but became an institutionally enforced incentive. 'Only in the nineteenth-century self-regulating market did economic self-interest become the dominant principle of social life, and both liberalism and Marxism made the ahistorical error of assuming that what was dominant in that society had been dominant throughout human history' (Block & Somers 1984, p. 63). According to Polanyi, 'the pursuit of material gain compelled by laissez-faire market rules is still not seen as behaviour forced on people as the only way to earn a living in a market system, but as an expression of their inner being; individualism is regarded as the norm, and society remains invisible as a cluster of individual persons who happen to live together without responsibility for anyone other than kin' (Polanyi 1968, p. xxvii). There is nothing natural about material acquisitiveness and no reason to believe that self-interest is a more dominant force in human nature than altruism.

Secondly, according to Polanyi laissez-faire capitalism was a unique and transitory event, given birth in England between 1750 and 1850, but dying in Europe and America during the 1930s and 1940s (Dalton 1968, pp. i & xxx). Polanyi claims that the great achievement of economic liberals has been to present a transitory, historical state of economic and social relations as if they were permanent, neutral and eternal. 'The market mechanism ... created the delusion of economic determinism as a general law for all human society', he says (Polanyi 1968, p. 70).

Thirdly, according to Polanyi the discipline of Economics was invented on the assumption of an artificial and misleading separation of the polity and the economy. As Block points out, 'the neo-classical insistence that the economy is analytically distinct from the rest of society makes it logical to see government regulation of business or government provision of welfare as an external interference with a market economy. While economists may disagree as to whether particular types of interference are benign or malignant, they share the view that they are external' (Block 1990, p. 39). This view of the state's unnatural role in the economy has been very influential despite Smith's own exceptions to the rule of laissez-faire.

Paradoxically, the expansion of the market system after the Industrial Revolution could only be maintained by state intervention. According to Polanyi, 'the road to the free market was opened and kept open by an enormous increase in continuous, centrally organised and controlled intervention'. Despite the claims of liberals that laissez-faire was a natural, organic development, 'there was nothing natural about laissez-faire; free markets could never have come into being merely by allowing things to take their course' (Polanyi 1944, pp. 139–40). The liberal preference for the non-intervention of the state in economic life disguised the extent to which governments were expected to maintain conditions for markets to function.

Markets appear to often be the products of states, not their alternatives or rivals. 'Economic history reveals that the emergence of national markets was in no way the result of the gradual and spontaneous emancipation of the economic sphere from governmental control. On the contrary, the market has been the outcome of a conscious and often violent intervention on the part of government which imposed the market organisation on a society for non-economic needs' (Chomsky 1993, p. 250). Gramsci endorsed this view, claiming that 'it must be made clear that laissez-faire too is a form of State "regulation", introduced and maintained by legislative and coercive means. It is a deliberate policy, conscious of its own ends, and not the spontaneous, automatic expression of economic facts' (Gramsci 1971, p. 160). Another observer agrees, adding that 'in the last analysis, markets come out of the barrel of a gun, and to establish an integrated world economy on capitalist lines requires the international mobilisation of political power' (Hodgson 1984, p. 79).

Importantly, as Chomsky has noted, economic historians such as Alexander Gerschenkron have long been arguing that a sharp departure from neo-liberal doctrines was a prerequisite for economic development in the twentieth century. In fact in the post-war period, the experience of Japan and the other once dynamic economies of East Asia has demonstrated that 'late development' would appear to be critically dependent on state intervention in the economy (Gershenkron 1962). There appear to be few, if any examples of laissez-faire transitions to economic development. This view of economic development runs directly counter to much neo-liberal orthodoxy.

According to Polanyi, the abandonment of market principles and the protective intervention of the state in late nineteenth-century Britain arose out of the need to safeguard the public from the more odious conditions of modern industrial life: 'the market economy was a threat to the human and natural components of the social fabric', and 'to allow the market mechanism to be the sole director of the fate of human beings and their natural environment, indeed, even of the amount and use of purchasing power, would result in the demolition of society ... ' (Polanyi 1944, p. 73).

Far from being 'strangled by shortsighted trade unionists, Marxist intellectuals, greedy manufacturers and reactionary landlords', the abandonment of laissez-faire principles was demanded by a public which required protection from the perils inherent within the market system (Polanyi 1944, p. 150; Calleo & Rowland 1973, pp. 23–4). The public had a national interest in the regulation of the market. Social legislation covering working hours, public health, factory conditions and trades unions were acts of community self-defence. They were a response of both the organised working class and the middle class protecting their own respective interests. 'Paradoxically enough, not human beings and natural resources only but also the organisation of capitalistic production itself had to be sheltered from the devastating effects of a self-regulating market' (Polanyi 1944, p. 132).

Adam Smith anticipated this challenge. The invisible hand, he wrote, will destroy the possibility of a decent human existence 'unless government takes pains to prevent' this outcome, as must be assured in 'every improved and civilised society' (Smith 1976 Bk V, Ch. 1, Pt III, Art II, p. 303). Smith's warnings have been widely ignored by those free market advocates inspired by a more narrow interpretation of his ideas. Laissez-faire capitalism in the nineteenth century collapsed because of the free operation of the self-regulating market, which in turn prompted calls for state protection – an authentic expression of community fear that without state intervention, society would be annihilated by the market (Polanyi 1944, p. 73).

Whilst it is possible for liberals to support the market on grounds of economic efficiency, it is more difficult to defend market society on moral grounds. The devastating effects of unrestricted economic competition in nineteenth-century Britain were only overcome by protecting society from market forces. In the post-Cold War period, however, protectionism is widely demonised: in the discourse of many industrialised societies it is a pejorative term, associated with intrusive and inefficient government. Attempts to create a 'market society' on a global scale may not be as socially desirable as some liberals believe, though as Macpherson suggests they are a measure of 'how deeply the market assumptions about the nature of man and society have penetrated liberal-democratic theory' (Macpherson 1977, p. 21). The basis of Adam Smith's conception of the national interest – his idea of basic individual motivation – may be socially generated rather than part of the human condition.

Free trade imperialism

Two of the difficulties produced by the term 'free trade' are its benign symbolism and the gap which often exists between the rhetoric of its progenitors and the reality of their behaviour. As will be shown later, in contemporary world politics free trade agreements, for example, are rarely 'free' nor are they specifically about 'trade'. Moreover, the most prominent advocates of free trade often behave as if the idea was non-reciprocal: it is a policy often honoured more in the breach than in the observance. As Gabriel Kolko wrote about US policy in 1969,

> Although the United States for over two decades has advocated that all nations sharply lower their tariffs and rely on a world economy of essentially free trade, it has never been willing to implement this policy when it was not to the interest of powerful American industries. This American refusal to open fully its own economy to the world, which would undoubtedly gain thereby, is the vital difference between a desire to dominate the world economy – a new imperialism – and a theory of free trade or 'Open Door'. (Kolko 1969, p. 62)

To those societies which have had the 'beneficence' of free trade thrust upon them by metropolitan powers, the policy can appear anything but benign. After all, free trade and market forces tend to overwhelm and even dissolve traditional social relations and institutions: they are a powerful source of social and political change. The introduction of free trade and market relations produces a competition for efficiency which drives out the inefficient and forces all members of society to adapt to new ways. Free trade also affects the distribution of wealth and power within and between societies, establishing new hierarchies, dependencies and power relationships. Within states, community life is partly transformed into market life, in accordance with the requirements of efficient production, export earnings and the international division of labour. Outside, in the international system, not all states are able to take advantage of the opportunities presented by free trade or capable of influencing market forces to their own advantage. Only wealthy societies seem capable of harnessing the power of the market, and sometimes even they struggle to do so.

Recipients may view free trade as a rationale for the exploitation of subordinate sectors by rich and powerful states determined to secure domestic economic advantages for themselves. 'Free trade undermines national autonomy and state control by exposing the economy to the vicissitudes and instabilities of the world market and exploitation by other, more powerful economies' (Gilpin 1987, p. 183). This argument was first articulated during the middle of the nineteenth century, the so called 'golden age' of liberalism when British colonialism and industrial expansion was at its peak (Gallagher & Robinson 1953, pp. 1–15).

The case of those who felt the malign effects of 'free trade' has been argued by political economists such as Friedrich List who regarded free trade in the mid-nineteenth century as merely the 'veil behind which the British state ruthlessly pursued its own national interests and exploited its particular advantages – the great productivity of its industries and their consequent dominance of world trade' (Gamble 1981, p. 145). In other words, free trade was less a philosophical conviction which cast national interests into history and more an economic strategy designed to enhance the national interests of the dominant state of the time.

It was not until 1846 that British manufacturers were sufficiently powerful to allow the Corn Laws to be repealed, confident in the knowledge that free trade policies would now serve their particular interests. According to List, the British used the power of the state to protect their infant industries against foreign competition while weakening their opponents by military force, and only became champions of free trade after having achieved technological and industrial supremacy over their rivals. They had pursued protectionist policies until British industry was strong enough to out-compete all of its rivals. Having reached this point, they then sought to advance their own 'national' economic interests by gaining unimpeded access to foreign markets through free trade (Gilpin 1987, p. 181). 'In contemporary terms, once they had established the "level playing field" to their incontestable advantage, nothing seemed more high-minded than an "open world" with no irrational and arbitrary interference with the honest entrepreneur, seeking the welfare of all' (Chomsky 1993, p. 10). Free trade, as List argued, may well have been the correct policy for an industrially dominant nation like Great Britain in the nineteenth century, but only policies of protection could enable weaker powers to challenge the hegemon's supremacy.

From the very beginning free trade was a middle class movement. Though it was only to last until 1931, when free trade was introduced in Britain in 1846 it was rightly seen by Cobden as a victory for the interests of manufacturers over aristocratic and landed interests. Having discovered that free trade policies promoted their own prosperity, British manufacturers were convinced that free trade also promoted British prosperity as a whole: their interests were said to be indivisible and 'in harmony' with the interests of the whole society. According to Marx, 'the assertion that free competition is the final form of development of productive forces, and thus of human freedom, means only that the domination of the middle class is the end of world history' (Marx 1970, p. 153). Thus when workers struck for higher pay and better working conditions they damaged the manufacturers and merchants, and therefore by definition, they hurt Britain. Logically, industrial action became treacherous behaviour.

Few economic historians would contest the view that the rise of Britain to industrial and commercial superiority in the nineteenth century had little to do with methods guided by free trade principles: hence the suffix 'imperialism' was attached by critics of 'free trade' to the original description of international market relations. As one American commentator declared in 1866, 'free trade was a system devised by England to enable her [middle class] to plunder the world' (Arblaster 1984, p. 262). Little needs to be added to the truism that all the modern advanced societies also industrialised behind protective walls (the US in 1816 and most advanced states by the 1880s): so 'it seems altogether rash to suppose that economic nationalism is necessarily detrimental to states which practice it' (Carr 1939, p. 72). On this subject, economic history remains surprisingly uniform.

However, what is not generally acknowledged in the scholarly literature is the dual standards of economic development which hegemonic states apply on the one hand to themselves, and on the other to economically subordinate societies: evidence of a residual preoccupation with national interests at the expense of others. Nowhere is this more graphically illustrated than in the post-war period where the means by which the burgeoning US had climbed to economic maturity were to be denied to later entrants in the race.

The creation of a liberal free trading regime by the United States in the post-war period was a conscious act of state policy. The United States emerged from the Second World War with 'preponderant power' and in an unprecedented position to reconstruct the world economy 'so American business could trade, operate and profit without restrictions everywhere' (Leffler 1992, pp. 12 & 19; Kolko & Kolko 1972, p. 2). This meant creating an open world economy conducive to the free movement of goods, capital and technology. US planners wanted to break down England's sterling bloc, create convertible currencies, and establish conditions for free trade. Crucially, raw materials had to be made available to all nations, though particularly to the advanced industrialised states, without discrimination. It was clear from official statements that the US was ready to assume Britain's former role as the world's financial hegemon, and realised this could only be achieved by exercising considerable state power (Leffler 1992, p. 16).

The regions of the world would have to be 'opened' – to investment, the repatriation of profits, access to resources, and so on – and dominated by the United States (Leffler 1992, p. 16). It flows from this analysis that the Soviet Union was considered by US planners to be the major threat to the liberal international order because of its very existence as a great power controlling an imperial system that could not be incorporated within the US sphere (Chomsky 1989, p. 25). A country or bloc which succeeded in exempting itself from the US-dominated system might expect hostility from the United States because this would constitute a reduction in the potential resource base and market opportunities available to the hegemonic economy. 'We believe passionately', Acheson stated, 'that the dissemination of free enterprise abroad was essential to its preservation at home' (Leffler 1992, p. 63). If necessary the doors barring access to US capital may need to be opened by force.

The historical record suggests two fundamental exceptions to the free trade model of the national interest and economic development. The doors which barred free and non-discriminatory access to raw materials, and which blocked the path to currency convertibility, could only be pushed open by the state, in the post-war period the United States. Left alone they would have remained shut. As Calleo and Rowland have argued, 'it is, in fact, difficult to sustain any free trade system without a concomitant political hegemony' (Calleo & Rowland 1973, p. 12). Beyond that, the markets so necessary to absorb America's vast industrial production at the end of the Second World War had to be helped into existence by the state. Foreign trade had to be subsidised. The reconstruction of the economies of Western Europe was therefore only partially altruistic. At one level it was designed to deal decisively with the Franco-German problem. But it was also the only way US capitalism could expand at the necessary rate in its conversion to a civilian economy.

Secondly, the distinction between the state and the private economy is more blurred than the liberals have argued. Not only does the state periodically intervene on behalf of private companies; transnational corporations frequently return the compliment. As Leffler argues, 'in a world free of barriers to the movement of goods and capital ... the private sector could serve as an instrument, albeit not a docile one, of state power'. Thus US-based multinational oil companies could help ensure American control over the world's most important raw material (Leffler 1992, p. 16).

The critique of 'free trade imperialism' exposes both the double standards of states which espouse free trade and the extent to which the economic world order advocated by liberals paradoxically requires state intervention for its realisation. Free trade has never been embraced as enthusiastically in developing societies as it has by the elites in wealthy industrial states. They tend to see free trade as a weapon used by dominant players to open up their societies to resource exploitation, foreign investment, access to raw materials and the repatriation of profits. Invariably this means that free trade can lead to a diminution in their economic sovereignty, at the same time blocking paths to alternative forms of economic development.

More importantly for this study, the history of free trade advocacy exposes its inseparability from national interests. Free trade, whether it be at a regional or global level, seems to be only possible if it is promoted by a strong state, often using coercive methods for its own ends rather than for the welfare of all. It doesn't emerge spontaneously to reflect human nature or as a desire to produce a harmony of interests between nations. In some cases where it has been imposed on unwilling states, the opposite appears to be true. Free trade appears to be conceived and argued for in national interest terms – a policy which advances the interest of a particular political community or a group within a community – rather than a universal principle which benefits all nations.

The liberal revival

The demise of Soviet Communism at the beginning of the 1990s enhanced the influence of liberal theories of international relations within the academy, a theoretical tradition long thought to have been discredited by realist perspectives which emphasise the recurrent features of international relations. In a confident reassertion of the teleology of liberalism, Fukuyama claimed that the collapse of the Soviet Union proved that liberal democracy had no serious ideological competitor: it was 'the end point of mankind's ideological evolution' and the 'final form of human government'. It is an argument that has been strengthened by recent transitions to democracy in Africa, East Asia and Latin America.

For Fukuyama the end of the Cold War represented the triumph of the 'ideal state' and a particular form of political economy, 'liberal capitalism', which 'cannot be improved upon': there can be 'no further progress in the development of underlying principles and institutions'. According to Fukuyama, the end of the East–West conflict confirmed that liberal capitalism was unchallenged as a model of, and endpoint for, humankind's political and economic development. Like many liberals he sees history as progressive, linear and 'directional', and is convinced that 'there is a fundamental process at work that dictates a common evolutionary pattern for *all* human societies – in short, something like a Universal History of mankind in the direction of liberal democracy' (Fukuyama 1992, pp. xi–xii & 48).

Fukuyama's belief that Western forms of government and political economy are the ultimate destination which the entire human race will eventually reach poses a number of challenges for orthodoxy within International Relations. First, his claim that political and economic development always terminates at liberal-capitalist democracy assumes that the non-Western world is striving to imitate the Western route to modernisation: to put in another way, that the Western path to modernity no longer faces a universal challenge of the kind posed by communism, and will eventually command global consent.

Secondly, Fukuyama's argument assumes that the West is the progenitor of moral and political truths which progress will oblige all societies to observe, regardless of national and cultural distinction.

Thirdly, Fukuyama's observation that the spread of capitalism now faces little or no resistance raises vital questions about governance and political community. What are the implications of globalisation for nation-states and their sovereign powers? Does the national interest have to be redefined or abolished entirely?

Fourthly, Fukuyama believes that progress in human history can be measured by the elimination of global conflict and the adoption of principles of legitimacy which have evolved over time in domestic political orders. This constitutes an 'inside-out' approach to international relations, where the exogenous behaviour of states can be explained by examining their endogenous political and economic arrangements. It also leads to Doyle's claim that 'liberal democracies are uniquely willing to eschew the use of force in their relations with one another', a view which refutes the realist contention that the anarchical nature of the international system means states are trapped in a struggle for power and security (Linklater 1993, p. 29).

Fukuyama revives a long-held view amongst liberal-internationalists that the spread of legitimate domestic political orders will eventually bring an end to international conflict. This neo-Kantian position assumes that particular states, with liberal democratic credentials, constitute an ideal which the rest of the world will emulate. Fukuyama is struck by the extent to which liberal democracies have transcended their violent instincts and institutionalised norms which pacify relations between each other. He is particularly impressed with the emergence of shared principles of legitimacy amongst the great powers, a trend which can be expected to continue now that the ideological contest of the Cold War has passed into history. The projection of liberal-democratic principles to the international realm is said to provide the best prospect for a peaceful world order because 'a world made up of liberal democracies ... should have much less incentive for war, since all nations would reciprocally recognise one another's legitimacy' (Fukuyama 1992, p. xx).

As has been shown, this approach is rejected by neo-realists who claim that the moral aspirations of states are thwarted by the absence of an overarching authority which regulates their behaviour towards each other. The anarchical nature of the international system homogenises foreign policy behaviour by socialising states into the system of power politics. The requirements of strategic power and security are paramount in an insecure world, and they soon override the ethical pursuits of states, regardless of their domestic political complexions. Waltz, for example, highlights the similarity of foreign policy behaviour amongst states with diverse political orders, and argues that if any state was to become a model for the rest of the world, one would have to conclude that 'most of the impetus behind foreign policy is internally generated'. The similarity of United States and Soviet foreign policy during the Cold War would suggest that this is unlikely, and that their common location in the international system is a superior explanation (Waltz 1991, p. 667; Linklater 1993, pp. 29–31).

By stressing the importance of legitimate domestic orders in explaining foreign policy behaviour, Waltz believes that liberals such as Fukuyama and Doyle are guilty of 'reductionism' when they should be highlighting the 'systemic' features of international relations. This conflict between 'inside-out' and 'outside-in' approaches to international relations has become an important line of demarcation in modern international theory.

Fukuyama's argument is not simply a celebration of the fact that liberal capitalism has survived the threat posed by Marxism. It also implies that neo-realism has overlooked the 'the foremost macropolitical trend in contemporary world politics: the expansion of the liberal zone of peace' (Linklater 1993, p. 29). Challenging the view that the nature of anarchy conditions international behaviour is Doyle's argument that there is a growing core of pacific states which have learnt to resolve their differences without resorting to violence. The likely expansion of this pacific realm is said to be the most significant feature of the post-Communist landscape. If this claim can be upheld it will constitute a significant comeback for an international theory widely thought to have been seriously challenged by Carr in his critique of liberal utopianism in the 1930s. It will also pose a serious challenge to a discipline which until recently has been dominated by assumptions that war is a recurrent and endemic feature of international life. States would indeed have a national interest in promoting liberal democratic political order across the world.

Regrettably, in Fukuyama's celebration of liberal democracy and market capitalism little is said about national interests beyond a criticism of realism's ability to explain current trends. This is presumably because unlike some more devout neo-liberals, Fukuyama does not regard the demise of the nation-state as the inevitable consequence of the triumph of economic globalisation. In fact he is largely concerned with its internal political complexion. On the question of national interests, a clear division exists within liberal philosophy between those like Fukuyama who acknowledge a key role for the state in the global spread of capitalism, and those such as Ohmae who believe globalisation presages the end of the nation-state and the idea of national interests. Paradoxically, both schools claim to be the natural inheritors of Adam Smith's wisdom.

Globalisation and national interests

To a significant extent, the globalisation of the world economy coincided with a renaissance of neo-liberal thinking in the western world. The political triumph of the 'New Right' in Britain and the United States in particular during the late 1970s and 1980s, was achieved at the expense of Keynesianism, the first coherent philosophy of state intervention in economic life. According to the Keynesian formula, the state intervened in the economy to smooth out the business cycle, provide a degree of social equity and security, and maintain full employment. Neo-liberals, who had always favoured the free play of 'market forces' and a minimal role for the state in economic life, wanted to 'roll back' the welfare state, in the process challenging the social-democratic consensus established in most Western states during the post-war period.

Just as the ideological predilection of Western governments became more concerned with efficiency and productivity and less concerned with welfare and social justice, the power of the state to regulate the market was eroded by the forces of economic globalisation, in particular the de-regulation of finance and currency markets. The means by which domestic societies could be managed to reduce inequalities produced by inherited social structures and accentuated by the natural workings of the market, declined.

In addition, the disappearance of many traditional industries in Western economies, the effects of technological change, increased competition for investment and production, and the mobility of capital, undermined the bargaining power of labour. The sovereignty of capital began to reign over both the interventionary behaviour of the state and the collective power of organised working people. This has had a profound effect upon the way national interests were now understood. As Scholte explains,

> states have also changed in current times of globalisation with regard to the constituencies that they serve. The sovereign state of old generally represented so-called 'domestic' or 'national' interests. It sought to advance the pursuits of its citizens in the wider world and to defend them against harmful so-called 'external' or 'foreign' intrusions. To be sure, sovereign states often favoured the interests of certain sectors of their resident populace more than others, for example particular classes, religious denominations or ethnic groups. However, such privileged constituencies almost always reside within the given state's territory and among its citizens.
>
> Under the influence of contemporary globalisation, a state has become less consistent in holding a territorial line of defence of its 'inside' against its 'outside'. States no longer always clearly promote 'domestic' interests against those of 'foreigners'. Instead, post-sovereign states have tended to become arenas of collaboration and competition between a complex array of territorial and supraterritorial interests. (Scholte 2000, p. 138)

Globalisation has effectively widened the range of constituent interest groups which governments must be cognisant of, while blurring the lines between what are actually domestic interests on the one hand and international interests on the other. Out of this tension, the so-called 'democratic deficit' has grown. In liberal democracies, governments are being held responsible for economic outcomes over which they may have little influence, while unaccountable market players who are not elected and who owe no allegiance to any particular state, are holding considerable sway over government policies. To say that a particular policy is 'in the national interest' therefore increasingly begs the question of how the concept can now be defined. As Horsman and Marshall argue,

> The concept of a 'national interest' becomes all the more impossible to sustain when it is evident that the concept of 'national' community is increasingly empty. The growing salience of local, regional and ethnic interest groups is one factor. Another is the presence of immigrant communities with little in common with their host country who are still entitled to citizenship. However, the widest discrepancies in the concept of national interest are revealed by differences of opinion over involvement in the global economy, which brings such great benefits to some and such huge costs to others that a single expression of 'interest' is meaningless. For many, its expression might be available jobs, goods in stores, reliable communications, adequate health care, good roads, efficient public transportation, a social safety net. For others, it might mean affordable credit, laissez-faire regulations, lower taxes, flexible work rules. But just how much can a national government deliver on these or any other demands? Every policy directed at the definition and distribution of public goods within a national economy – and it is the state's primary function so to define and distribute – will be judged by and through the market. Governments, alone, cannot buck the system, at least not for long. That does not mean they cannot do some of those things citizens clamour for. But more than just citizens will sit in judgement. (Horsman & Marshall 1994, p. 221)

Credit ratings, floating exchange rates, interest rates and foreign invest-ment, to name only the most accessible indices, are all vulnerable to expressions of external displeasure about government policies even though they will ultimately be seen by voters as indicators of a govern-ment's own performance. For governments, 'the "national interest" becomes almost impossible to define as a web of connections tie different elements of the nation to parts of the globe that are geographically and culturally distant' (Horsman & Marshall 1994, p. 200).

There is much debate over globalisation, both between liberals who believe it constitutes a fundamentally new phase of capitalism and statists who are sceptical of such claims, and within liberalism itself between market and statist liberals (Held, McGrew et al. 1999, intro; Held & McGrew 2000, intro). A number of market liberals point to the increasing irrelevance of national borders to the conduct and organisation of economic activity. They focus on the growth of free trade, the capacity of transnational corporations to escape political regulation and national legal jurisdictions, and the liberation of capital from national and territorial constraints (Ohmae 1995; Friedman 2000; Mickelwait & Wooldridge 2000).

Sceptics, on the other hand, claim that the world was less open and globalised at the end of the twentieth century than it was in the nineteenth. They suggest that the volume of world trade relative to the size of the world economy is much the same as it was in 1914, though they concede that the enormous explosion of short-term speculative capital transfers since the collapse of the Bretton Woods system in the early 1970s has restricted the planning options for national governments. Significantly, sceptics want to distinguish between the idea of an international economy with growing links between separate national economies – which they concede, and a single global political economy without meaningful national borders or divisions – which they deny (Weiss 1998; Chomsky 1999; Hirst & Thompson 1999; Hobsbawm 2000).

This final section will examine the claims made by liberals and sceptics about the relevance of national interests in a globalised economy. As in previous chapters, it will focus on the contemporary nature of world trade and the question of sovereignty and foreign investment.

'Free trade' and the national interest

For neo- or market liberals, the principles of free trade first enunciated by Smith and Ricardo continue to have contemporary relevance. Commercial traders should be allowed to exchange money and goods without concern for national barriers. There should be few legal constraints on international commerce, and no artificial protection or subsidies constraining the freedom to exchange. An open global market, where goods and services can pass freely across national boundaries, should be the objective of policy makers in all nation-states. Only free trade will maximise economic growth and generate the competition that will promote the most efficient use of resources, people and capital.

Conversely, 'protectionism' is seen as a pernicious influence on the body politic: some regard 'protectionism as sin' (Luttwak 1999, pp. 184–6). Policies which protect uncompetitive industries from market principles corrupt international trade, distort market demand, artificially lower prices and encourage inefficiency, while penalising fair traders. Protection is the cry of special or vested interests in society and should be resisted by governments in the broader national interest. It penalises developing nations by excluding them from entry into the global marketplace where they can exploit their domestic advantage in cheap labour. Regrettably, those seeking subsidies, tariffs and other protections from market competition often enjoy 'disproportionate political clout' within the state's decision-making councils (Ohmae 1995, p. 63).

The cornerstone of the free-trade argument is the theory of 'comparative advantage', which discourages national self-sufficiency and autarky by advising states to specialise in goods and services they can produce most cheaply – their 'factor endowments'. They can then exchange their goods for what is produced more cheaply elsewhere. As everything is then produced most efficiently according to the price mechanism, the production of wealth is maximised and everyone is better off. For Smith, the 'invisible hand' of market forces directs every member of society in every state to the most advantageous position in the global economy. The self-interest of one becomes the general interest of all.

According to market liberals such as Ohmae, 'in a borderless world, traditional national interest – which has become little more than a cloak for subsidy and protection – has no meaningful place'. This is because 'more and more ... "national interest" gets used as a knee-jerk defence of special interests, not of a people's interests' (Ohmae 1995, pp. 64 & 62). According to Ohmae, 'wrapping outdated industry in the mantle of national interest is the last refuge of the economically dispossessed ... in economic terms, pleading national interest is the declining cottage industry of those who have been bypassed by the global economy' (Ohmae 1995, p. 62). Thus for market liberals, national interests are inconsistent with the drive towards economic modernity. Trade must be free from interference and regulation by increasingly irrelevant political structures if economic development is to be maximised. States which continue to manage their resources in terms of the national interest 'wall themselves off from the most powerful engines of growth' in the world economy (Ohmae 1995, p. 60).

However, the relevance of the theory of comparative advantage in the era of globalisation has recently come under question (Strange 1985; Daly & Cobb 1994; Bairoch 1993). The first charge is that it was devised at time when there were national controls on capital movements. Ricardo and Smith assumed capital was immobile and only available for national investment. They also considered capitalists first and foremost members of a national political community, which was the context in which they established their commercial identities: Smith's 'invisible hand' presupposed the internal relations and bondings of community, so that capitalists feel a 'natural disinclination' to invest abroad. Smith and Ricardo could not have foreseen 'a world of cosmopolitan money managers and transnational corporations which, in addition to having limited liability and immorality conferred on them by national governments, have now transcended those very governments and no longer see the national community as their context'. The emergence of capitalists who had freed themselves from community obligations and loyalties, and who had no 'natural disinclination' to invest abroad, would have appeared absurd (Daly & Cobb 1989; 1994, pp. 215 and 209–35). Highly mobile and volatile capital markets are a major challenge for the theory of comparative advantage.

The second problem arises from the fact that the forms of international trade have dramatically changed over recent decades. The idea of national, sovereign states trading with each other as discrete economic units is becoming an anachronism. Intra-industry or intra-firm trade dominates the manufacturing sector of the world economy. Over 40 per cent of all trade now comprises intra-firm transactions, which are centrally managed interchanges within transnational corporations (that cross international borders) guided by a highly 'visible hand', to quote Alfred Chandler: these are what Robert Reich has called a 'global web' of linkages and exchanges (Chandler 1977; Lazonick 1991). Intra-firm trade runs counter to the theory of comparative advantage which advises nations to specialise in products where factor endowments provide a comparative cost advantage. The mobility of capital and technology, and the extent to which firms trade with each other, means that 'governments in virtually all industrial societies now take an active interest in trying to facilitate links between their own domestic firms – including offshoots of multinationals – and the global networks' in the strategic industries. They can no longer remain at arms length from business as neo-liberal economic theory demands (Emy 1993, p. 173).

Similarly, the globalisation of the world economy has seen the spread of manufacturing industries to many developing countries and the relocation of transnational manufacturing centres to what are often low wage, high repression areas – regions with low health and safety standards where organised labour is frequently suppressed or illegal. Transnational corporations are becoming increasingly adept at finding ways of circumventing national borders in their search for cheap labour and access to raw materials, and few states can refuse to play host to them. The creation of new centres of production occurs wherever profit opportunities can be maximised because investment decisions are governed by absolute profitability and no longer by comparative advantage, and manufacturing is so mobile. For liberals, this is the best way of encouraging much needed foreign investment in the developing world and establishing a trade profile for countries which might otherwise be excluded from world trade altogether.

Modern trading conditions have also diverged from the assumptions which underpin the neo-liberal analysis of how markets and trade actually work. The internationalisation of production, the mobility of capital and the dominance of transnational corporations (20 per cent of world production, 70 per cent of world trade) are just three developments which render theories of comparative advantage somewhat questionable. The idea of national sovereign states trading with each other as discrete economic units is steadily becoming the exception rather than the rule. Neo-mercantilist theory, which stresses the maximisation of national wealth, also fails to explain contemporary trade realities. A more accurate description might be 'corporate mercantilism', with 'managed commercial interactions within and among huge corporate groupings, and regular state intervention in the three major Northern blocs to subsidise and protect domestically-based international corporations and financial institutions' (Chomsky 1993, p. 95). If there is still such a thing as a nation's comparative economic advantage it is clearly a human achievement and certainly not a gift of nature, though this view remains unorthodox within powerful economic circles.

The third challenge to the relevance of the theory of comparative advantage is the steady erosion of the rules which have underpinned multilateral trade in the post-war era. Whilst there has been a reduction in barriers to trade *within* blocs such as the EU and NAFTA, they have been raised *between* blocs. Tariffs have come down but they have been replaced by a wide assortment of non-tariff barriers, including import quotas and voluntary restraint agreements. This is a concern to small, 'fair' traders which are incapable of matching the subsidies provided by Europeans and North Americans. States which unilaterally adopt free market doctrines while leading industrial societies head in the opposite direction, place themselves in a vulnerable position within the world economy. But regardless of whether tariff and non-tariff barriers were dismantled, the world market would not be 'free' in any meaningful sense, because of the power of the transnational corporations to control and distort markets through transfer pricing and other devices.

State liberals would argue for the continuing relevance of the state in the promotion of free trade and market economics generally. Global and regional trade groupings such as the WTO or APEC comprise representatives of states. IMF bailouts and World Bank loans are directed through the agency of the state. Even developing societies which are expected to adopt a free market blueprint by their Western financial backers (sometimes called the 'Washington consensus') – opening their economies up to foreign investment, financial de-regulation, reductions in government expenditure and budgetary deficits, the privatisation of government-owned enterprises, the abolition of protection and subsidies, developing export-orientated economies – are represented by state authorities in their negotiations (Stiglitz 2002, pp. 73–4).

Even governments which embrace a free-trade agenda presumably have some conception of what their nation's national economic interests are, especially when they are involved in international negotiations. No government says, 'we have no national interests, let the market rip'. Thus it is possible to support liberal, free-trade policies while recognising an important, ongoing role for the state in implementing those policies. According to Hall and Soskice, the shape of a nation's national interests in the twenty-first century depends primarily upon the ability of that country to sustain the comparative institutional advantages provided by its specific variety of capitalism. In this sense 'institutions' include industrial innovation, vocational training, legal systems, firm structure and behaviour, banking systems, education, labour-market de-regulation and corporate governance (Hall & Soskice 2001, pp. 9 & 52). State representatives must ask themselves which policies will keep unemployment and inflation low, maximise economic growth, satisfy dominant domestic interests and allow local forms to be competitive while optimising the national economy's overall comparative advantages. The state may be the agency which clears the way for the market to operate freely, but its role – promoting the national interest – remains, even if this may ultimately be to the advantage of a national business class.

It is possible to exaggerate the division between market and state liberals. Their differences are primarily of degrees of state involvement in the economy, not fundamental principles. Some hold on to the idea of a minimal state, others see it losing most of its economic functions, to be replaced by a global market where questions of governance are handled at a local level. Neither, however, will mourn the passing of nationalism and xenophobia cast as national interests. As Fukuyama says,

> it is curious why people believe that a phenomenon of such recent historical provenance as nationalism will henceforth be so permanent a feature of the human social landscape. Economic forces encouraged nationalism by replacing class with national boundaries and created centralised, linguistically homogenous entities in the process. Those same economic forces are now encouraging the breakdown of national boundaries through the creation of a single, integrated world market.

The fact that the final political neutralisation of nationalism may not occur in this generation or the next does not affect the prospect of its ultimately taking place. (Fukuyama 1992, p. 275)

Sovereignty, foreign investment and the national interest

The enormous volumes of unregulated capital liberated by the collapse of the Bretton-Woods system in the early 1970s, have transformed the relationships between states and markets. Credit (bonds and loans), investment (FDI) and money (foreign exchange) now flow more freely across the world than commodities. The resulting increase in the power of transnational capital and the diminution of national economic sovereignty is perhaps the most dramatic realisation of liberal economic ideas (Strange 1996; 1998).

For market liberals, political borders in this field have become either irrelevant or an obstacle to economic efficiency. Transnational capital flows have significantly challenged national economic sovereignty because states can no longer control the movement of capital across their borders without incurring a financial penalty in the form of disinvestment – a capital 'strike'. Moreover, the national interest has become something of a psychological barrier which blocks countries from enjoying the fruits of economic integration which, in the modern world, is the principal engine of economic growth (Ohmae 1995, p. 60).

The relationship between a nation's economic prosperity and the world's money markets is decisive. Because most states are incapable of generating sufficient endogenous wealth to finance their economic development, governments need to provide domestic economic conditions which will attract foreign investment into their countries. Again, government plays an important role in paving the way for foreign capital. In a world where capital markets are globally linked and money can be electronically transferred around the world in microseconds, states are judges in terms of their comparative 'hospitality' to foreign capital: that is, they must offer the most attractive investment climates to relatively scarce supplies of money. This gives the foreign investment community significant leverage over policy settings and the course of a nation's economic development generally, and constitutes a diminution in the country's economic sovereignty and a defining control over the national interest.

The power of transnational finance capital in the modern period can scarcely be overestimated. The volume of foreign exchange trading in the major financial centres of the world, estimated at over $US 1.5 trillion per day, has come to dwarf international trade by at least 60 times. Recent UN statistics suggest that the world's 100 largest transnational corporations, with assets of over \$US4.6 trillion, account for a third of the total foreign direct investment of their home states, giving them increasing influence over the economies of host countries.

The brokers on Wall Street and in Tokyo, the clients of the 'screen jockeys' in the foreign exchange rooms, and the auditors from credit ratings agencies such as Moody's and Standard & Poors, can now pass daily judgements on the management of individual economies, and signal to the world's financial community the comparative profit opportunities to be found in a particular country. Inappropriate interventionary policies by government can be quickly deterred or penalised with a (threatened) reduction in the nation's credit rating, a 'run' (sell off) on its currency or an investment 'strike'. The requirements of the international markets can only be ignored at a nation's economic peril. Not only have nation-states lost much direct control over the value of their currencies and the movements of capital around the world, they can no longer determine by themselves the institutional settings in which capital markets operate. Many neo-liberal financial commentators regard this development as a positive change, believing that markets rather than the governments know what is in peoples' best economic interests. Smith's residual anti-statism and 'hidden hand' remain a potent influence in much liberal thinking. As Stiglitz argues,

> They genuinely believe the agenda they are pursuing is in the *general interest*. In spite of the evidence to the contrary, many trade and finance ministers, and even some political leaders, believe that everyone will eventually benefit from trade and capital market liberalisation. Many believe this so strongly that they support forcing countries to accept these 'reforms,' through whatever means they can, even if there is little popular support for such measures. (Stiglitz 2002, p. 216)

Finance markets, dominated by large banks and financial institutions, insurance companies, brokers and speculators, exist to maximise their own wealth and the wealth of their clients. There is no reason for them to act in the interests of a state. Governments which cede economic sovereignty to these global players in the name of free trade and commerce do so in the knowledge that it will be very difficult to regain that authority in the future.

When the foreign investment community is largely unencumbered by state barriers and controls, and able to choose the most profitable location for its capital, it has the effect of homogenising the economic development of nation-states across the globe. In what is effectively a bidding war for much needed infusions of capital, states are driven by the lowest common denominator effect to reduce their regulations, standards, wages and conditions, in order to appear attractive to the investor community: in contemporary parlance, this is what is meant by 'international competitiveness'. Priority is given to the drive for efficiency and profits. The threat of disinvestment becomes the stick for markets to wield over the heads of government. For liberals this is a realisation of their view of modern history which most see as a struggle for liberation from the clutches of arbitrary state power. Ironically, in many instances the key to attracting overseas investment is for the host government to provide the transnational investor with subsidies and protection from market forces. In some cases this is the only way states can win and maintain the confidence of global markets.

There are many other examples which highlight the shift of economic power in the contemporary period. To take two, interest rate settings, which are nominally set by central banks, are now ultimately determined by the pressures of highly integrated global financial markets, over which even the most powerful economies have limited control or influence. The demand for the liberalisation of finance and services by the investment community allows transnational banks to displace domestic rivals so that it is difficult for developing economies to carry out the kind of national economic planning that enabled most Western countries to develop. This is another example of changing state and market differentials.

As was mentioned in an earlier chapter, the ill-fated Multilateral Agreement on Investments (MAI) was a vivid illustration of just how far governments in the developed world (the OECD) were prepared to surrender their discretionary economic power to the markets by voluntarily restricting their ability to discriminate against foreign capital. The MAI is a reminder that economic globalisation is not the result of the spontaneous emancipation of the economic sphere from government control, but in fact the product of decisive intervention by advanced capitalist states. Paradoxically, markets can only be freed by states.

The defeat of the MAI by reluctant governments and popular opposition suggests there is still some gap between elite support for liberal economic prescriptions in the area of global finance and public thinking which links the regulation of foreign investment with state intervention. The failure of the MAI is a reminder of the power of national interest thinking, even if economic reality is starting to pass it by, although attempts to resuscitate it as a General Agreement on Investments (GAI) through the World Trade Organisation suggests the issue is not finalised.

During the current phase of globalisation national economic sovereignty been either enthusiastically given away by governments committed to neo-liberalism or begrudgingly surrendered. Although sometimes exaggerated by neo-liberals, the state's capacity to direct the national economy has been significantly undercut by the globalisation of relations of production and exchange. Sovereign power has been ceded to bond holders, funds managers, currency traders, speculators, transnational banks and insurance companies – groups that by definition are democratically unaccountable in any national jurisdiction, and therefore unconstrained by considerations of national interest.

In effect, the world economy has come to resemble the global strategic environment. It has become anarchic in character and, as a consequence, the competition for economic security is as intense as the search for strategic security. The traditional requirements of liberal internationalism have been partly achieved. The distorting power of the state to interfere in commercial relations between individuals has been curtailed. The sovereignty of the state has, in part, been replaced by the sovereignty of capital.

In the areas of free trade and foreign investment, the national interest enjoys an ambivalent status amongst liberals. Market liberals see it as an excuse to insulate a state's national economy from integration with the world economy. This diminishes competitive pressures and leads to the corruption and distortion of market forces that if released from the interference of the state, would deliver optimal outcomes to the whole community. Like Marxists, this group looks forward to the day when the state and national interests wither away. Although they see regional and global groupings as a substitute for national economic entities, they are almost silent about alternative forms of political community. It is not clear how they imagine politics beyond the state. On the question of governance after the nation-state, they are conspicuously silent.

State liberals, however, whilst retaining a preference for a minimalist role, acknowledge that the agency of the state is vital in two respects. First, despite all of its imperfections the state remains the only form of organisation which is likely to maintain a liberal-democratic political culture. Although they are always vigilant about the state's capacity to encroach upon the individual's civil liberties, this group remains sceptical that superior forms of political community, such as regional bodies, can be found in the short run. Secondly, state liberals believe trade liberalisation and economic globalisation in general is largely dependent upon the state. In other words, their vision of the national interest comprises the state's role in securing policies such as free trade and foreign direct investment which could not be achieved without its agency. The guarantee of property rights, efficient and regulated capital markets, infrastructure services, an educated workforce, and the protection of intellectual property rights are just some of the important functions which the state must perform. The state and national interest are not so much the antithesis of the free market but more the agency for its realisation and maintenance.

Conclusion

Adopting Frankel and Rosenau's division into objective and subjective national interests, it could be argued that liberals generally agree about the 'objective' goals of foreign policy (minimal state, free trade, unfettered commerce) but are highly suspicious of 'subjective' claims which invariably reflect sectional interests. For liberals, subjective interests – government interpretation of the policy means to the policy end – are invariably captured by dominant groups, and therefore frustrate the community's objective interest in market-based solutions to economic challenges. Only self-regarding individuals have true interests that can be objectively known. Subjective interests are almost always rationalisations for why objective interests cannot be realised.

The globalisation of the world economy means there are decreasingly few obstacles to international trade. Liberals have long sought to remove the influence of the state in commercial relations between businesses and individuals, and the decline of national economic sovereignty is an indication that the corrupting influence of the state is diminishing. Transnational corporations and capital markets wield unprecedented influence over the shape of the world economy, in the process homogenising the political economies of every member-state of the international community. The objective of creating a market society on a global scale is closer than ever.

The same is also true of global capital flows, which are now largely (though not totally) unencumbered by state regulations thanks to market demands for investment, profit opportunities for currency speculators and developments in information technology. The globalisation of the world economy has also increased the power of transnational corporations and financial markets, which have become unchallenged and largely unaccountable to players outside the global markets.

As liberals have intended since the time of Adam Smith, globalisation has weakened the authority of nation-states. Its inefficient and distorting influence in commercial relations is being removed. National economic planning is no longer an obvious option. The replacement of national interests with self-regarding individualism no longer seems utopian.

There is some division amongst liberals, however, between those who want the state to disappear and those who regard it as an important agent of governance and liberalisation. This division reflects the exceptions in Smith's own thesis to his general advocacy of the 'invisible hand'. As has been shown, for some these exceptions undermine his entire argument for self-regarding individualisation. For others, they are minor qualifications to a broader argument for free markets and unfettered global exchange. Regardless of its philosophical divisions, liberalism has mounted a significant challenge to the claim that national interests have an ongoing significance in international politics.

5
Progressive Perspectives: the English School

> [George] Kennan is really a Rationalist because he maintains that national interest should be guided by justice; he advocates a non-interventionist policy against the Soviet Union; and he argues that war is the breakdown of policy.
>
> (Martin Wight, *International Theory: the Three Traditions – Martin Wight*)

The realist tradition in international politics paints the world as inherently conflictual and resistant to change, a place in which moral principles do not significantly influence state behaviour and where there is clear distinction between domestic and international politics. Cosmopolitan and more radical approaches imagine a world where progress and change are possible and necessary, in which the gap between the domestic and international is closed and where shared moral principles play an important role in governing international behaviour.

The English-School approach, which is associated with classical thinkers such as Grotius and Vattel, and modern thinkers such as Wight, Bull and Vincent, occupies the space between realism and cosmopolitan approaches, while sharing some of the features of both: what Wight called the 'via media' or 'golden mean' between realism and revolutionism (Wight 1966).

The aspect of the English School which most clearly distinguishes it from the polar opposites of realist and revolutionary approaches to international politics, is its emphasis on the presence of an international society which the English School believes has evolved out of an acknowledgement by states that order needs to be preserved in the international system. As will be shown in this chapter, an important

feature of international society is the requirement that states significantly broaden the way they have traditionally conceived their national
interests.

According to the English School, a narrow egoism which prevents
states from looking beyond their immediate self-interest and concerns,
is no longer a viable way of defining national interests. A wider, more
enlightened self-interest is vital to the maintenance of international
society and the preservation of a world order which maximises the
prospects of state survival and security. This chapter will examine the
concept of order, the notion of international society and, according to
the English School, the role that national interests play in contemporary
international politics. It will then focus on examples of the way states
have redefined their national interests to acknowledge both their
obligations to international society and their broader duties to humanity.

The English School and order

Although the English School, or rationalism, has been portrayed by some
critics such as George as a minor variant or subset of realism, the extent
to which it substantially qualifies realism's portrait of international
relations as a stark world of anarchy establishes its credentials for separate
theoretical treatment (George 1997).

Like realism 'rationalism begins with the condition of anarchy but it
is more inclined than realism to emphasise the ways in which the sense of
belonging to the community of humankind has had its civilising effect
on international relations' (Linklater 2001, p. 104). While recognising
that the prospects of radical structural changes to the international system
are limited, the English School nevertheless believes that progress in
the forms of higher levels of global social justice and greater respect for
universal human rights are both possible and necessary. While they are
not optimistic about the likelihood that the world can be remade in a
new image as some cosmopolitans may desire, the English School argues
that there is a lot more to international relations than the stark and
sterile anarchy portrayed by realists.

Given that states acknowledge no higher political authority than
themselves and are forced to exist in an inherently dangerous environment without guarantees for their survival, adherents to the English
School are struck by the high degree of order which exists in this world of
ungoverned anarchy. By international order, English-School theorists such
as Bull mean the 'pattern of activity that sustains the elementary or primary goals of the society of states, or international society' including 'the

goal of the preservation of the system and society of states itself ... the goal of maintaining the independence or external sovereignty of individual states ... the goal of peace ... as the normal condition of their [states] relationship ... [and] the common goals of all social life: limitation of violence resulting in death or bodily harm, the keeping of promises and the stabilisation of possession by rules of property' (Bull 1977, pp. 8 & 16–19). The English School concentrates on how these conditions of international order have evolved, the challenges which exist to them, and the prospects for their further development.

Even though states must provide for their own security, demand a monopoly on the use of violence and are not required to submit to an overarching power, the English School is keen to understand why the international system is not in a constant state of war. They argue that states have a common interest in placing restraints on the use of force and have developed an ability to compromise and accommodate themselves in the wider interest of maintaining international order.

Alderson and Hurrell (2000) argue that the English School's support for international order and the need for co-existence rests on three general considerations. The first is a recognition of the importance of power in the international system with a particular priority given to the maintenance of the balance of power. On the question of power and its importance in international politics, there are few differences between the English School and realists.

The second factor is the English School's belief in the existence of common interests among states. This is defined as the capacity of all states in the international system to gain from the establishment of rules and conventions which place limits on their behaviour. The English School believes that states recognise they have shared interests which favour all, including a reduction in uncertainty and the provision of higher levels of predictability in the international system. This common recognition of shared interests has produced functional and utilitarian outcomes such as the international diplomatic system, which facilitates and protects the ability of states to communicate with each other. For host governments the immunity from prosecution of diplomatic personnel, for example, is at times a frustrating legal right, but states have long recognised its reciprocal benefits for international order and are very reluctant to breach or deny it.

Thirdly, states have also recognised that international order relies upon some shared values which are mostly procedural rather than substantive or cultural. The English School believes states can co-operate with each other without the need for any substantive consensus on societal or cultural values. What is necessary, however, is a shared commitment to dialogue and common rules and institutions for the mediation of conflict. It is therefore possible to have a universal diplomatic culture in a world of cultural heterogeneity (Alderson & Hurrell 2000, pp. 1–19).

Given that it must be present in an environment without a global sovereign authority, order is a precarious achievement which should not be taken for granted. The self-interest of states cannot always be kept at bay and thus order is never a permanent state of affairs (Linklater 2001, p. 105). The task for the English School is 'identifying and strengthening the foundations of international order' within a world where nation-states remain primary authorities (Bull 1969 in Alderson & Hurrell 2000, p. 137).

International society

There is an English-School view within international theory which argues that it is wrong for nation-states to pursue their strategic and economic interests without regard for international morality and international law. An Australian foreign minister once claimed that these broader considerations constituted a third category of national interests (apart from state security and economic prosperity) called 'good international citizenship' or what he said was a state's interest in pursuing what Hedley Bull called 'purposes beyond ourselves' (Evans 1989, pp. 9–10). In arguing for 'good international citizenship', Gareth Evans suggested that a state's pursuit of national interests in the narrow, realist sense of the concept could no longer be sustained and needed to be supplemented by more elevated concerns such as promoting world order, encouraging global reform and honouring duties to humanity (Linklater 1991). This is the central focus of much of Hedley Bull's work, and the basis of the English School's critique of the realist tradition.

The English School offers a substantial qualification to realism's contention that conflict and competition are endemic in the international system. The English School believes that nation-states form a self-regulating international society with common interests and values, rules, laws and institutions. In this international society conflict between states is mollified by their common need for co-existence. International law, inter-governmental dialogue, international organisations and a common respect for national sovereignty form part of a growing framework of norms, rules and institutions comprising an international diplomatic culture. One of the intriguing aspects of this international society is that although it is voluntary and not always codified in formal terms, states act as if they are subject to its authority. Clearly they see the maintenance of international society as the key to the preservation of international order.

Beyond the struggle for power and security, but well short of a universal human community, lies the international society of states. According to Wight, international society

> is the habitual intercourse of independent communities, beginning in the Christendom of Western Europe and gradually extending throughout the world. It is manifest in the diplomatic system; in the conscious maintenance of the balance of power to preserve the independence of the member-communities; in the regular operations of international law, whose binding force is accepted over a wide though politically unimportant range of subjects; in economic, social and technical interdependence and the functional international institutions established latterly to regulate it. All these presuppose an international social consciousness, a world-wide community-sentiment. (Wight 1966, pp. 96–7)

Bull defines international society in a similarly historical way. First in the late 1950s:

> the sovereign states of today have inherited from renaissance Europe an ordered system for the conduct of their relations which may be called an international society. For though sovereign states are without a common government, they are not in a condition of anarchy; like Locke in his account of the state of nature they are a society without government. This society is an imperfect one; its justice is crude and uncertain, as each state is judge of its own cause; and it gives rise to recurrent tragedy in the form of war; but it produces order, regularity, predictability and long periods of peace, without involving the tyranny of a universal state. (Bull 1959 in Alderson & Hurrell 2000, pp. 3–4)

And in his most famous work, *The Anarchical Society*:

> A society of states (or international society) exists when a group of states, conscious of certain common interests and common values, form a society in the sense that they conceive themselves to be bound by a common set of rules in their relations with one another, and share in the working of common institutions. (Bull 1977, p. 13)

According to Bull, there is a recognition by states of their common interests, some common values and a duty to work within a common framework of rules and institutions for the benefit of all states. Because they want order to be sustained, states acknowledge that they are bound by rules which govern their relationships with one another, including 'respect [for] one another's claims to independence, that they should honour agreements into which they enter, and that they should be subject to certain limitations in exercising force against one another' (Bull 1977, p. 13). This is quite different from neo-realist conceptions of anarchy, where the structure of the international system and its most significant condition – anarchy – forces states to maximise their relative power before any other considerations. Beyond the preservation of a balance of power, neo-realism denies the capacity of states to informally regulate the international system in ways which will ameliorate its harshest and most dangerous features. Whereas neo-realists argue that states must define national interests in relation to the stark, self-help world of anarchy which they can do little to modify, the English School thinks states must conceive of their interests in a much broader way to take of account of their numerous obligations to international society.

One of the defining characteristics of international society is that while realists deny its existence, revolutionists want to destroy it. According to Bull, both the pluralist and solidarist wings of the English-School approach

> assert the existence of an international society and of laws which are binding on its member states in their relations with one another. Both are opposed to the tradition of Realpolitik, according to which there is no international society but rather an international state of nature in which states are without binding obligations in their relations with one another. And both are hostile also to that doctrine according to which the standards to which appeal may be made in international politics enjoin not the preservation of international society, but its subversion and replacement by a universal empire or cosmopolitan society. (Bull 1966 in Alderson & Hurrell 2000, p. 98)

The English School seeks to occupy the middle ground between what might be said are the realist and revolutionist 'bookends' of international relations theory.

The English School places great emphasis upon legitimacy and international order, and does not necessarily consider these to be antithetical to considerations of justice and human rights in the international system.

Whereas realists would argue that one cannot 'weave good international citizenship into the foreign policy culture of states' because 'conditions of profound insecurity for states do not permit ethical and humane considerations to over-ride their primary national considerations', the English School would claim that human rights, justice and international law are essential to the maintenance of international order (Linklater 1992). The English School rejects the contention that morality and self-interest are incompatible and just as importantly, that self-interest and altruism are always antonyms, as realism often implies.

Perhaps the most interesting aspect of the English-School approach is its claim that co-operation and even a degree of unity between states can be achieved without the requirement for world government. States can enjoy the benefits of society without submitting to a higher authority. The English School conceives of humankind as a global community where the moral and social bonds which are created across political and geographical frontiers lead to a society rather than a government. According to the English School, moral obligations to people everywhere are the key to a more peaceful world order. Because inter-subjective understandings can bring a measure of civility to international relations, international society can exist in the absence of cultural homogeneity.

The English School argues that a high degree of order and co-operation can exist between states which do not feel they belong to a common culture or civilisation. States with very different cultures and belief systems can meet together in a society of states because they share the primary goals of sovereign independence and a belief that international society is the only legitimate form of world political organisation. A pragmatic need to co-exist is sufficient to produce what Bull called a 'diplomatic culture' – that is, a system of conventions and institutions which preserve order between states with radically different aspirations and domestic social and political complexions. According to John Vincent, this international society is 'functional' or utilitarian rather than 'cultural' or moral in character: this is one of the keys to its success (Linklater 2001, p. 107). The English School is not in favour of imposing one set of values, Western or otherwise, upon all peoples because they recognise this would be fiercely resisted. The evolution of international society and its spread in the post-colonial era depends upon it not being identified closely with one state or one group of states.

According to the English School, international order is the most propitious context in which states can pursue and achieve common purposes. As previously explained, the foundations of international order, according to Bull, requires every society to protect the three 'primary goals' of (a) placing constraints on the use of force, (b) upholding property rights, and (c) ensuring agreements are kept (Linklater 2001, p. 108). From this base, transcultural values and ethical standards can be progressively developed between states within the society.

Importantly, an open dialogue which places emphasis on order rather than stability, can bridge many of the differences between different states such as Australia and Indonesia, for example. Diplomacy can be the means through which the different, the suspicious and even the hostile reach some common ground. Cultural convergence is neither necessary nor desirable, particularly in the current phase of globalisation. Appeasement or estrangement is always a false dichotomy for the English School, especially within particular bilateral relationships. Accommodation and compromise within agreed parameters are more likely to produce advances, bringing greater levels of civility, understanding and tolerance to the relationship. In this way order and international society can be enriched.

The English School: morality and interests

E.H. Carr believed that the doctrine of a 'harmony of interests' was a liberal attempt to reconcile national interests with a broader sense of obligation to humanity as a whole. According to Carr, the doctrine of the harmony of interests 'identifies the good of the whole with the security of those in possession' (Carr 1939; 1981, p. 150). Satisfied states simply clothe their 'own interest in the guise of a universal interest for the purpose of imposing it on the rest of the world' (Carr 1939; 1981, p. 71).

According to Carr, liberals impute common interests to states; interests which are not as widely shared as dominant powers like to think. In the inter-war period a number of liberals claimed that every nation had an identical interest in peace and that any state which behaved aggressively or failed to respect the peace was acting irrationally and immorally. According to Carr, this was in fact little more than an expression of the 'satisfied powers' with a vested interest in the preservation of the 'status quo' (Carr 1939; 1981, p. 51). The post-World War One system had been created by the victors of the war, and it was an arrangement from which they stood to gain the most at the expense of those later described as 'revisionist' powers. 'The post-war utopia became the tool of vested interests and was perverted into a bulwark of the status quo ... a cloak for the vested interests of the privileged.' The rhetoric of liberal internationalism, if it were to be taken seriously, was based on 'the illusion of a world society possessing interests and sympathies in common'

(Carr 1939; 1981, p. 76). In reality the post-war order reflected the specific interests of 'satisfied powers', and was therefore unlikely to receive the support of those states, such as Germany, which clearly felt aggrieved by the 1918 Versailles settlement.

Carr refutes the liberals' belief that international concord could be achieved by the widest possible application of their views. This is because 'these supposedly absolute and universal principles (peace, harmony of interests, collective security, free trade) were not principles at all, but the unconscious reflexions of national policy based on a particular interpretation of national interest at a particular time' (Carr 1939; 1981, p. 80).

Liberal internationalists had been wrong to assume that there was a self-evident value system, committed to international harmony and co-operation, which had universal validity. Collective security, as it was expressed in the League of Nations and practiced in the early phase of the inter-war years, was little more than the preservation of a status quo congenial to the interests of the victorious powers.

According to Bull the problem with Carr's argument is that his 'relativism denied all independent validity to moral argument, and [his argument contained] an instrumentalism which asserted that international law and morality were merely the tool of the ruling group and excluded the elaboration of the notion of the good of international society as a whole' (Bull 1969 in Alderson & Hurrell 2000, pp. 129–30). This prevented Carr from an 'elaboration of the notion of the good of international society as a whole' (ibid., p. 137). Carr's own Marxism seemed to lead him to the view that all norms and values in international politics were simply epiphenomenal expressions of ruling class interests. He seemed to be staking a claim for moral relativism by arguing that there were no independent or disinterested standards from which political behaviour can be judged. This raises a number of issues, not the least important of which is the moral basis of Carr's argument.

Wight, and later Bull, was clearly dissatisfied with Carr's realism–idealism (utopianism) dualism. Wight's trichotomy of traditions – realism, rationalism (English School) and revolutionism – was an early rejection of Carr's binary model and the foundation of claims for a middle way which put moral claims at the forefront of philosophical thought about international relations (Wight 1991). Bull was particularly keen to reject Carr's claim that moral claims in international politics can be little more than expressions of ruling class rule. In doing so, Bull opened up the possibility of national interests which were not merely a guise for the pursuit of elite interests.

The fact that all moral beliefs are socially or historically conditioned does not mean that they have no independent causal force, nor should it be taken to imply that moral disagreements cannot be settled by rational discussion. The fact that moral principles may serve as the instrument of a dominant group within a society does not mean that they cannot also function so as to fulfill purposes recognised by the society as a whole .... . A principle like *pacta sunt servanda* (one which Carr singles out for special criticism) will be upheld by particular powers (and rejected by others) at particular times for their own special reasons, but it derives not from the interests simply of the ruling group, but from the perceived interests of all states in securing the elementary conditions of social coexistence. (Bull 1969 in Alderson & Hurrell 2000, p. 130)

Bull thinks it is churlish of Carr to dismiss the notion of moral values in international politics as nothing more than a charade for imposing the will of dominant states. He seems to be implying here that regardless of what common interests they may share in a range of other domains, be they economic, cultural or strategic, the citizens of a state can share a common national interest as part of international society: they have a joint stake in its preservation and expansion. Even preponderant states are forced to widen their conception of national interest to take account of their responsibility for global leadership and the impact their behaviour has on the wider world community. According to Bull,

in the 1940s and 1950s the United States became heir to the tendency to identify its interests with those of the world at large ... the association of American policy with such ideologies [anti-communism] and organizations ... helps to broaden the American conception of the national interest and so to facilitate the willing acquiescence of many countries in a system of world order which, while it reflects an American hegemony, also provides a large part of the world with a large part of what it wants. (Bull 1969 in Alderson & Hurrell 2000, p. 131)

Order has an unambiguous moral value for states in an anarchical international environment where Carr believes, conflicts of interest are 'real and inevitable' (Carr 1939; 1981 p. 77). States have therefore created an international society on their own volition rather than out of coercion, because they recognise its common benefits, particularly in the avoidance of unnecessary conflict. International law, the English School concedes, may not have the status of domestic law with its compulsory jurisdiction and strong compliance provisions, but what is significant is that states so frequently feel obliged to voluntarily conform to it. According to the English School, it is striking that states will adhere to the rules and norms of international society even when these conflict with their non-vital interests. International law therefore confirms the existence of international morality.

The English School and national interests

Is there a distinctly English-School concept of the national interest? Whilst it is reasonable to expect some variation within a broad school of philosophical thought, it is possible to distill an English-School position which differs significantly from both realist-conventional and Marxist-critical conceptions.

According to Linklater, what Gareth Evans described as 'good international citizenship' promises to overcome the 'conflict between citizenship and humanity which has been such a recurrent feature of the theory and practice of international relations' (Linklater 1992, p. 22). Expressed another way, 'the conviction that the state marks the outer limits of our moral and political obligations has never been able to prevail' (ibid., p. 25). Nor is there much evidence that a global harmony of interests, a world moral community or a civitas maxima has ever enjoyed international recognition. Consequently, the English School seeks a mid-point between the extremes of realism and what Wight called 'revolutionist' positions.

For the English School, human obligations transcend the division of the species into separate sovereign states. The exclusionary character of the modern state mitigates against both cosmopolitan loyalties and the extension of political community both below to the sub-national level and above to global humanitarian obligations.

The challenge is to strike a balance between the inclusive and the exclusive, the universal and the particular, the national interest and cosmopolitan aspirations. Examining the ways in which states define their moral rights and duties in relation to the rest of the world is the starting point. According to Linklater,

> For Vattel, the good international citizen is the state which is prepared to put the welfare of the international society ahead of the relentless pursuit of its own national interests. It does not sacrifice its own national independence in the process, nor is it legally obliged to act in ways which will jeopardise its survival or endanger its vital national

interests, but it is beholden to other states to place the survival of order before the satisfaction of minimal national advantages. (Linklater 1992, pp. 28–9)

Vattel speaks of states in a pluralist way – the purpose of diplomacy, he believes, is to balance the interests of different states. Each state needs to look after its citizens but recognise that all other states have obligations to do the same for their populations. The challenge is to find ways in which each state can do the best for its people without placing great costs or burdens on others. The state has to moderate its claims and sacrifice some of its interests for the sake of order and co-existence.

Vattel was discussing states and was an arch-defender of their sovereignty. For him, international order is order between states but there is a cosmopolitan element to his thinking because if every state does the best it can for its citizens while respecting the duty of all others to do the same, then the entire human race will be better off: in a way, an extension of Adam Smith's invisible hand to the global political sphere. It is possible to sense the same theme in Bull's last work when he says that international order is not just order between states but an order that should protect the needs of individuals. International order contributes to world order.

According to Linklater, the *Oxford English Dictionary* identifies two forms of cosmopolitanism.

The first holds that provincial attachments should yield to the allegedly higher ethical conviction that our primary loyalties are to the whole of humanity. The second does not reject national ties, but opposes them when they ignore the legitimate interests of outsiders. The *cosmophil*, which the OED defines as someone who is 'friendly to the world in general' exemplifies this second approach. On this view, one should not defend or celebrate national affiliations and cultural differences when they burden outsiders with intolerable costs. On this view, cosmopolitans need to combine loyalties to co-nationals with moral obligations to the members of other societies which include the duty to do no harm. (Linklater 2001a, p. 263)

A cosmophil, therefore, is not against national affiliations but is against them when they become indifferent to the interests of alien outsiders. This is what Vattel can be taken to be saying and it is important to note this strain of cosmopolitanism in English-School thought. Clearly there is an overlap between both approaches.

The approaches of the English School and cosmopolitanism diverge if cosmophilia means taking the side of alien outsiders when they are oppressed by their own government. As a strong supporter of sovereign rights, Vattel did not want states interfering in the domestic affairs of others. There are national interests (although he did not use this term) and international interests in preserving order but cosmopolitan interests in protecting individuals from human rights violations do not feature in his thought. A cosmophil feels obligations to distant strangers who suffer harm – and that might mean intervention or certain interference in some cases. Vattel seems to be saying that rather than abandon sovereignty and the protections it affords, the cosmophil's noble aspirations are best realised by ensuring respect for sovereignty and not by encouraging its erosion. On this account, the principle difference between the English School and cosmopolitans is about means rather than ends.

For the English School, then, states should define their national interests, not in isolation from other states but in ways which are cognisant of the interests of other states and aware of the impact of their actions upon the broader international society. Vattel appears to be arguing that states can divide their interests into vital and non-vital categories, the former being non-negotiable because they go to the very heart of national survival, the latter being much more flexible and accommodating to other states.

Wight argues that this boils down to states defining their national interests as enlightened self-interest rather than in more selfish, narrow, isolationist and realist terms where conflicts of interest are inevitable. Wight defines this perspective in the following terms:

> Enlightened self-interest is that which calculates all obstacles and contingencies in the path to fulfillment ... a selfishness which, negatively, seeks not to violate or affront the self-interest of others. It is a self-interest so intelligent and penetrating that it recognises that one of the chief obstacles on the path to fulfillment is the reactions of other persons or states, and therefore seeks to avoid stirring up trouble ... a selfishness which gives positive consideration to the interests of other persons or states, and consents to modify and limit itself out of respect for these other interests, because it recognises their right to exist. (Wight 1991, p. 120)

This is a more sophisticated definition of national interests because it recognises that states are more likely to achieve their objectives if they take account of the interests and goals of others. If they are prepared to moderate and modify their behaviour out of a joint interest in co-existence, they are more likely to avoid conflicts which threaten their own interests.

According to Wight, realists believe that 'no power can, or may, define another power's interests or duty; it has neither the capacity nor the right to do so' (Wight 1991, p. 113). The English School, on the other hand, argues that up to a point it is possible for states to know the interests of others, though Wight adheres to Bentham's notion that each person is ultimately the best judge of their own interests. The English School 'presupposes that you can estimate the interests of those towards whom you are being generous, moderate and considerate' (Wight 1991, p. 120). This allows and encourages states to co-operate on a range of levels that realists believe are barred due to a natural antagonism.

For the English School, moral behaviour in the international domain depends on the domestic analogy: that is, the ethics of behaviour within a state should apply to international (state) behaviour. This means endowing the state with personal attributes: declaring or imagining the state to be a moral agent. Just as individuals can learn to behave ethically, states, too, can demonstrate moral behaviour by being prepared to live by values that are not strictly self-interested. If individuals can form an ethical viewpoint because of their capacity to imagine themselves in the positions of others, surely states can do the same?

According to Wight, states are like individual humans in society in that 'we have a distinct conception of the general interest within which their interests can be accommodated to our own' (Wight 1991, p. 121). States should cultivate 'a self-interest intelligent enough to recognise that reactions of other states are among the complexities of the situation in which national self-interest must be pursued' (Wight 1991, p. 125). The need is for awareness of the predictable consequences of each state's behaviour upon other states and on international society more generally.

The English School believes that states must broaden the definition of their own interests to include their impact on other states, regional stability more widely and global order generally, to name only a few considerations. In the language of German critical theory, states must develop 'a constitutive interest in the preservation and expansion of the intersubjectivity of action-orienting mutual understanding' (Habermas 1971, p. 310). This has been done in the past on moral issues such as the abolition of the slave trade, and in some cases the surrender of territory under de-colonisation, neither of which fit into a conventional-realist definition of the national interest behaviour.

For the English School, diplomacy is the means states use to avoid conflicts while pursuing their core interests. According to Wight,

> the rationalist doctrine of national interest, then, assumes a tension of interest between states which sometimes but not normally rises into a conflict of interests, but it asserts a wide possibility of mutually adjusting these interests. The great aim of statecraft, of foreign policy, is to pursue and safeguard the national interest within the setting of a respect for the interests of others, or of international society as a whole ... [the key challenge for diplomats is to show] how and with what discrimination they struck the balance between national interest and wider interests. (Wight 1991, p. 126)

The English School does not ignore or pretend that conflicts of national interests between states do not occur, only that they need not rise to the level of military hostilities. The most successful way of preventing wars is for states to remain aware of the interests of others – to imagine themselves in the shoes of their rivals and competitors – who have an equal interest in survival. This can be accomplished by expanding the levels of economic, political and social intercourse between states.

Whereas realists have a tendency to turn all interests into vital interests, adherents of the English School 'minimise the number of particular interests that are designated as vital' so that states maintain the maximum degree of flexibility in discharging their international responsibilities and pursuing their national interests (Wight 1991, p. 126).

Nor is the English School utopian or idealist in believing that a global concord is imminent or even likely, however desirable it might be. 'Rationalists are led to assume the accommodatability of interests wishfully, and assertions about a harmony of interests are always statements of aspiration, not of fact' (Wight 1991, p. 127). They locate themselves firmly in the middle of the debate with a conception of relations between states that 'is not a conflict of interests, nor an immanent solidarity of interests, but a partially resoluble tension of interests, open to reconciliation' (Wight 1991, p. 127).

One of the strengths of the realist approach has been to define a nation's interests in narrow terms relating to security and survival, with power being the means to achieve these basic objectives. This is said to be a constant national concern common to all citizens. The English School, on the other hand, broadens the scope of its political horizons to incorporate additional features beyond strategic considerations. 'Whereas the Realist identifies security with power and makes security a function of power', says Wight, 'the rationalist separates power from security ... Security consists in other factors besides national power: the strength and reliability of allies, and the absence of conflicting interests ...' (Wight 1991, p. 129). The benefit of this is that in increasing levels of security in this way, individual state behaviour is less threatening to neighbours and rivals.

The English School has a 'presumption in favour of small powers ... [which] have been truer spokesmen of civilised values than great ones' (Wight 1991, p. 130). Because they do not possess the deterrent effect of overwhelming military strength, small and medium powers are forced to seek the protections afforded by international society. Thus they have a greater stake in the development of rules, conventions and institutions which increase order, predictability and harmony while reducing their vulnerability to naked aggression. 'The constitutional co-operation between states, in Concerts, Leagues, UNs, is the corresponding mode whereby the Rationalist works, not towards civitas maximus, but towards mitigating international anarchy' (Wight 1991, p. 131). Whereas neo-realists argue that anarchy is a structural condition of the international system which states can do little if anything to modify, the English School claims that international society substantially qualifies the stark and sterile world which realists describe. For the English School there is a lot more to international relations than anarchy and endemic conflict.

A hope and belief that diplomacy is the vehicle through which wars and violence are headed off is a constant theme in English-School thought. States retain their national interests but are encouraged to distinguish between core or vital interests which cannot be negotiated away, and non-core interests which can be modified or sacrificed in the interests of international society. As Wight explains (in a way which reverses Frankel's objective/subjective categorisation),

> In rationalist theory, therefore, there is a resoluble tension of interests between powers, a balance between the interests of inter-national society as a whole and individual powers. The criteria of statecraft are skill, judgement, and moral insight in estimating other powers' interests and those of international society as a whole. There is a middle path between the Realist doctrine of the absolute autonomy and subjectivity of national interest, and the Revolutionist doctrine of the dogmatic objectivity of national interest, defined by doc-trinal authority. In the Rationalist conception, while it may be impertinent to define another power's interests and duties, it is possible to make broad statements of a common international interest, which

includes particular interests, especially through the constitutional machinery and organisations of international society. 'The task of the diplomatic agent is to reconcile the interests of his own nation with those of others'. (Wight 1991, p. 128)

Initially, Bull defines the English-School position on the national interest in similar terms to Wight, though subsequently there is a shift in ground. Writing in 1969, Bull argued that the

> Wilsonian notion of an ultimate identity of interests among the peoples of the world, of which the United States was the best interpreter, has always been more truly represented in the communist world, where the doctrine that the interests of all people, when truly interpreted by communist parties, do not admit of any conflict has provided an obstacle, of a sort that does not arise within the Western world, to the adjustment of conflicts between the Soviet Union and its allies. (Bull 1969 in Alderson & Hurrell 2000, p. 132)

Clearly divisions within the communist world during the Cold War and the evident stratification of each communist society puts paid to the claim that the interests of all citizens of the Soviet Union, for example, were equally represented by the Communist Party of the USSR. Whilst communist states may not have shared the same class divisions as their capitalist counterparts, this did not mean, of course, that they were societies with undivided interests. Again, Bull places the Western experience firmly between the poles of realism and revolutionist positions.

> The principal diplomatic tradition of the West is one which rejects both the idea of an identity of national interests and the idea that these interests are necessarily exclusive of each other, and affirms the notion of national interests which are different but which overlap in some areas, the business of diplomacy being to determine what these areas are. (Bull 1969 in Alderson & Hurrell 2000, p. 132)

As we have seen, in a later assessment (1977), Bull makes a deliberate distinction between means and ends in a discussion of the national interest. In any political community, says Bull, individuals have common interests in the primary goals of social life which both define and are sustained by order. These include 'restricting violence' (to maximise personal security), 'respect for agreements' (because of their interdependence for material needs), and 'the stabilisation of possession' (as a consequence of scarce resources and limits to human altruism). These common interests might be driven by fear or enlightened self-interest, but they emphasise the difference between process and outcome or means and ends (Bull 1977, pp. 53–4). According to Bull,

> the criterion of 'national interest', or 'interest of state', in itself provides us with no specific guidance either in interpreting the behaviour of states or in prescribing how they should behave – unless we are told what concrete ends or objectives states do or should pursue: security, prosperity, ideological objectives or whatever. Still less does it provide us with a criterion that is objective, in the sense of being independent of the way state ends or purposes are perceived by particular decision-makers. It does not even provide a basis for distinguishing moral or ideological considerations in a country's foreign policy from non-moral or non-ideological ones. (Bull 1977, p. 66)

Merely to claim that something is in someone's interest is only to say that it 'serves as a means to some end that he is pursuing', a matter of objective fact, according to Bull. But whether or not something actually is in someone's interest will depend on the ends that he is pursuing. Thus the idea of interest 'is an empty or vacuous guide, both as to what a person does do and as to what he should do. To provide such a guide we need to know what ends he does or should pursue, and the conception of interest in itself tells us nothing about either' (Bull 1977, p. 66).

Once the ends of state policy are defined and have the consent of the broader community, the conception of national interests becomes meaningful. It then represents the political means most likely to realise the policy ends. The national interest comprises a 'rational plan of action' to achieve agreed ends, which can be contrasted with policies based on sectional interests, the interests of alliances and international organisations, or the ad hoc and uncritical pursuit of established policy (Bull 1977, pp. 66–7). For Bull, determining the national interest is a policy debate, whereas the primary goals of social life are the same for every state. Secondary goals, on the other hand, are more flexible and presumably can be adjusted to accommodate the wider interests of international society.

According to Bull, 'the idea of international society – of common interests and common values perceived in common by modern states, and of rules and institutions deriving from them – is scarcely recognised' by Carr (Bull 1969 in Alderson & Hurrell 2000, p. 137). One of the principal reasons for this is Carr's economic Marxism. It is obvious from his attack on the idea of a harmony of interests that Carr regarded the idea of common economic interests within a class-divided capitalist society to be largely a myth propagated by those who benefit most from the existing arrangements. They have vested interests in masking their privilege in language which implies social cohesion, harmony and acceptance. The idea of a harmony of interests denies that states have both conflicting internal and external interests.

However, as Bull reminds us,

> another of Carr's themes that is relevant to the present time is that the world is divided between Have and Have Not states, between whom there existed little or no real community of interest, and that the Have states were guided by an ideology which obscured this fact, just as within modern states in the late nineteenth and early twentieth centuries, Capital had been guided by an ideology which asserted a spurious community of interest with Labour. (Bull 1969 in Alderson & Hurrell 2000, p. 134)

Bull did not accept that class interests were so irreconcilable they invalidated any notion of national interests. Nor did he think that disparities of wealth and income between states prevented any prospect of a community of humankind. However, he did recognise in his later works that closing the gap between 'haves' and 'have-nots' was an important moral issue which impinged directly on the maintenance of world order. As will be shown, Bull came to believe that in the long term, order and justice were symbiotic notions. Denying or failing to address the claims of those who were revolting against the economic and cultural dominance of the West could threaten the very order upon which international society depended.

The English School: pluralist and solidarist conceptions

It is important to note that the English-School tradition is not an homogeneous one. In the mid-1960s, Hedley Bull identified two different conceptions of international society, what he called the *pluralist* and *solidarist* approaches (Bull 1966 in Alderson & Hurrell 2000, pp. 96–117).

The pluralist approach, most closely associated with Vattel and Oppenheim, is the more minimal and less ambitious position. Pluralists argue that states 'are capable of agreeing only for certain minimum purposes which fall short of that of enforcement of ... [international] law' (Bull 1966 in Alderson & Hurrell 2000, p. 97). Beyond what is necessary for co-existence, the prospects for solidarity between states is limited. States rather than individuals are the basic members of international society and they can only co-operate for the purpose of maintaining their independence and international order more generally.

The solidarist approach, originally associated with Grotius, is the more ambitious and radical conception. It has at its base an assumption of 'solidarity, or potential solidarity, of the states comprising international society, with respect to the enforcement of ... [international] law' (Bull 1966 in Alderson & Hurrell 2000, p. 97). For solidarists, the interests of individuals and humanity as a whole should, on occasion, come before the independence of states. States are capable of co-operating well beyond the basic requirements of co-existence, exhibiting a solidarity which privileges international law and co-operation above state sovereignty.

The distinctions between pluralist and solidarist conceptions of international society are explained by Mayall:

> By pluralism, I mean the view that states, like individuals, can and do have differing interests and values, and consequently that international society is limited to the creation of a framework that will allow them to coexist in relative harmony. It is the recognition by pluralists that it is possible for many, if not all, conflicting values to be accommodated within such a framework that distinguishes their position from indiscriminant relativism. By solidarism, I mean the view that humanity is one, and that the task of diplomacy is to translate this latent or immature solidarity of interests and values into reality. For pluralists, one of the features that distinguishes international society from any other form of social organisation is its procedural and hence non-developmental character. Solidarists, on the other hand, believe in the possibility of international constitutional reform and convergence. (Mayall 2000, p. 14)

The distinction between the two conceptions should not be seen as clearly demarcated or discrete. Even within the work of one scholar, both approaches can be evident. Writing in the early 1960s, Bull took an 'unfavourable view of Grotius .... I am objecting to the specifically Grotian ... assumption of the solidarity or potential solidarity of the members of international society – the notion that all states are able to recognise common sets of rules' (Bull 1962 in Alderson & Hurrell 2000, pp. 119 & 120). By the mid-1980s, however, Bull had shifted from this pluralist outlook to a much more solidarist position, believing that the more minimalist position was insufficient to deal with contemporary international issues and the increasing demands made by citizens of their governments: 'whatever rights are due to states or other actors in international relations, they are subject to and limited by the rights of the international community. The rights of sovereign states, and of sovereign peoples or nations, derive from the rules of the international community or society and are limited by them' (Bull 1984, p. 11; see also Wheeler & Dunne 1996).

The pluralist/solidarist distinction can be characterised as the conflict between the priorities of order and justice in international society. Bull in the past has illustrated this by highlighting the pluralist concern for the just conduct of wars versus the solidarist distinction between just and unjust wars (Bull 1962 in Alderson & Hurrell 2000, pp. 119–24). The sovereign rights of states (to acquire nuclear weapons) versus humanity's broader interests (in nuclear non-proliferation) is another way of expressing the pluralist/solidarist divide. But perhaps the clearest example of how the two 'factions' of international society diverge is their different attitudes to humanitarian intervention. According to Wheeler,

> pluralist international-society theory defines humanitarian interven-
> tion as a violation of the cardinal rules of sovereignty, non-intervention,
> and non-use of force. Pluralists focus on how the rules of inter-
> national society provide for an international order among states
> sharing different conceptions of justice. States and not individuals
> are the principal bearers of rights and duties in international law,
> and pluralists are sceptical that states can develop agreement beyond
> a minimum ethic of co-existence ...
>
> This view of the moral possibilities of international society is
> challenged by the more radical – or solidarist – voice that looks to
> strengthen the legitimacy of international society by deepening its
> commitment to justice. Rather than see order and justice locked in
> perennial tension, solidarism looks to the possibility of overcoming
> this conflict by developing practices that recognise the mutual
> interdependence between the two claims. ... the defining character
> of a solidarist is one in which states accept not only a moral respon-
> sibility to protect the security of their own citizens, but also the wider
> one of 'guardianship of human rights everywhere'. (Wheeler 2000,
> pp. 11–12)

Whether the solidarist conception of international society is still 'premature' as Bull claimed in 1966 or whether there is more evidence of an emerging cosmopolitan moral consciousness, remains a matter of much debate within the English-School tradition. Towards the end of his life Bull had shifted from his earlier position that order must come before considerations of justice to a more symbiotic, rather than antithetical view. In considering what he called the 'revolt against the West' and Third World demands for justice, Bull argued in the 1980s that 'the question of justice concerns what is due not only to states and nations but to all individual persons in an imagined community of mankind' and that 'order in international relations is best preserved by meeting demands for justice, and that justice is best realised in a context of order' (Bull 1984 in Alderson & Hurrell 2000, pp. 220 & 227).

From the point of view of the national interest, its definition broadens as the solidarist position is approached. Whereas a pluralist conception requires states to modify the way they conceive of their interests to take account of the basic need to co-exist with other states which define their interests in broadly similar ways, a solidarist conception requires states to surrender their national interests to the binding laws of international society. Pluralists do not want international order being upset by states redefining their interests in ways which will undermine or override the sovereign independence of others. They do not believe a common human community with shared values and a common notion of justice is imminent or even likely in the future. There are strict limits on the prospects for cultural and political homogeneity beyond the boundaries of states.

Solidarists, on the other hand, argue that moral obligations to the species, including their protection from avoidable harm, poverty and environmental degradation, supersede a narrow and parochial focus on the pursuit of the interests of individual political communities. The temporary division of the species into separate and estranged states should not blind us to both the possibilities of and necessity for species-wide solidarity. If this is to occur, states will need to stop thinking in traditional national interest terms and instead commit themselves to the broader interests of humanity as a whole.

National interests and obligations to humanity

In a series of lectures at the University of Waterloo in 1983, Hedley Bull claimed that the revolt against the West

is the struggle of those peoples who were subject to European and North American dominance of the international system late in the last century and early in this century, to bring this domination to an end. The people of Europe and North America, or at least the positions of privilege that they have inherited, are the targets against which the revolt has been directed. (Bull 1984 in Alderson & Hurrell 2000, p. 242)

According to Bull, the revolt against the West had already passed through two phases. The first was the campaign by non-Western states for recognition of their equal rights as independent sovereign states. This period effectively concluded with the withdrawal of the British from the Persian Gulf in 1971. The second was the anti-colonial revolution which intensified after the Second World War and culminated with the collapse of the Portuguese empire in 1975 (Bull 1984 in Alderson & Hurrell 2000, pp. 227–44). Despite lingering anomalies such as the Falklands/Malvinas, French Polynesia and Palestine, we now live in a post-colonial world.

Bull identified three additional components to the revolt against the West. The racial revolt, including the abolition of slavery and an end to all forms of white supremacism and state-sanctioned racial discrimination, was a prerequisite for the freedom and dignity of all states. The right to economic justice and the struggle against inequality and exploitation which was a consequence of Western global commerce and finance, was the fourth aspect of the revolt. Finally, a revolt against Western values and cultural imperialism centred on a rejection of the view that the rest of the world should live by Western standards such as liberal conceptions of political freedom (Bull 1984 in Alderson & Hurrell 2000, pp. 227–42).

Just how the next phase in the revolt against the West played itself out would, according to Bull, depend on how seriously the West took these Third-World claims for justice. The stakes – maintaining order in the international system via the spread of international society – could scarcely be higher for everyone. As we have seen, Bull thought that 'order in international relations is best preserved by meeting demands for justice, and that justice is best realised in a context of order' (Bull 1984 in Alderson & Hurrell 2000, p. 227). This did not mean adopting a position 'of supine concession of whatever is demanded' or abandoning legitimate interests and principles (Bull 1984 in Alderson & Hurrell 2000, p. 244).

However, the West would have to 'make adjustments that are unwelcome … abandon privileges' and make themselves 'more vulnerable than they are now to the decisions of others' (Bull 1984 in Alderson & Hurrell 2000, p. 244). They would have to break the habits of centuries because this would entail a radical redistribution of power and wealth from the North to the South (Bull 1984 in Alderson & Hurrell 2000, pp. 213–18). The prospects for a change of outlook by the West that would meaningfully respond to Third-World claims for justice had to be measured against the reality that 'particular states or groups of states that set themselves up as the authoritative judges of the world common good, in disregard of the views of others, are in fact a menace to international order ... [and] states are notoriously self-serving in their policies, and rightly suspected when they purport to act on behalf of the international community as a whole' (Bull 1984 in Alderson & Hurrell 2000, pp. 222–3).

According to Bull, addressing the revolt against the West will require Western states to reformulate the way they define their interests – to incorporate consideration for other states and devolve power and authority which would normally be jealously guarded, preserved and maximised. To the extent that the national interest must be seen as enlightened self-interest, the emphasis will need to be on 'enlightened'.

Obligations to humanity

Though states will vary in their commitment to 'good international citizenship' and their preparedness to modify the primacy of their strategic and economic concerns, it is important to acknowledge that this represents either a substantial departure from conventional national interest thinking or a thorough redefinition of it. Most adherents of the English School, concerned to retain many of the theoretical strengths of realism, would prefer to regard 'obligations to humanity' as a third category of national interests after the pursuit of strategic and economic security. It represents a substantial qualification of, and supplement to, the narrow strategic concerns of realism, though as with the pursuit of economic interests, there is less agreement amongst nation-states about the priority to be accorded 'purposes beyond ourselves' and what might specifically constitute the moral principles which are applicable to all.

Unsurprisingly, international compliance with the English-School concern for obligations to humanity is far from uniform. Importantly, however, the promotion of global moral and ethical considerations rests not only on an assumption of common national interests but also on a recognition that there are universal human interests, shared across cultures and boundaries by every individual in every nation-state. It would be impossible to produce international law which states appear to feel a strong obligation to comply with, unless there was a considerable amount of common ground of this kind.

One way to test the existence of international society and its concern for international humanitarian obligations has been to subject its examples to the realist test – i.e. how could realism explain this phenomenon? The key point here is whether important areas of international diplomatic behaviour can be properly explained in conventional national interest terms. Here are five obvious examples.

How could realists explain the fact that states frequently antagonise each other and even jeopardise their own commercial interests by raising concerns about human rights violations with their interlocutors? It would seem difficult to justify on conventional national interest grounds when strategic and commercial damage is a consequence and little if any gain is achieved.

How can the provision of safe asylum by refugees be explained in conventional national interests terms when refugees are initially a financial burden on the countries which provide resettlement? The acceptance of refugees is often politically controversial and rarely confers any advantages upon governments with an ethical outlook.

How is the allocation of a percentage of a state's GNP for development assistance (aid) to the 'South' consistent with a national interest argument when the recipient constituency cannot provide political support to the government of the donor state? Overseas Development Assistance is sometimes tied to export promotion, but governments do not always receive substantial equivalent benefits.

How can a realist national interest argument explain states limiting their industrial development to comply with multilateral environmental regulations (Kyoto) or the protection of regions from resource exploitation and wealth generation (Antarctica)? Why would a state voluntarily surrender power and the possibility of considerable resource wealth out of a commitment to environmental conservation?

If the primary national interest of states is survival and security through the accumulation of military power, how can arms control and disarmament agreements be explained when they either freeze or reduce a state's strategic power?

Realists will argue that states will only engage in behaviour that is consistent with the pursuit of their national interests, even if this may have a veneer of altruism or regard for others. The English School provides a more compelling argument and explanation. They do not see self-interest and altruism necessarily as antonyms. Instead they bridge this divide with their emphasis on the idea of enlightened self-interest which is cognisant of the needs, desires and interests of others. Enlightened self-interest assumes that there need not be any necessary conflict between self-regard and a concern for others.

The national interests of states, as far as the English School is concerned, need to be framed in a way that includes both a clear understanding of what the state wants internationally and an awareness of, and respect for, the impact of the pursuit of that want upon other states. The English School regards co-operation as a much more effective tool in the satisfaction of wants than coercion. They believe it is easier to get other states to comply with your wishes because they want to rather than because they have to under fear of coercion. The realist approach is more binary – one state against the rest with limited prospects for co-operation or permanent accommodation. The English School argue that states are not only aware of the impact of their behaviour on others and make adjustments accordingly, but are also aware of the impact of their behaviour on the preservation of international order.

So, for example, while arms control and disarmament agreements limit the strategic power of states, they regulate what can be a destabilising arms race between rival states and bring greater levels of order and stability to international society – a benefit, not just for the parties to the agreement but to the global community generally. Détente between the US and USSR in the 1970s stemmed from the reciprocal, if sometimes reluctant belief in the legitimate co-existence of both states. In this case there is no necessary contradiction between the self-interest of states and interests of global humanity.

Similarly in the case of environmental regulations, states have gradually recognised they have a common interest in addressing global challenges such as greenhouse gas emissions, global warming and ozone holes, but also understand that they cannot successfully solve these problems acting alone. A degraded or polluted environment does not respect the fluctuating and artificial political boundaries erected around communities. Shared life-support systems, whether they be river systems, climate patterns or sea levels, break down the political and cultural barriers between peoples. A collective response in this arena is the only meaningful way of acting selfishly.

The fact that states allocate, in some cases, significant funds for aid to the developing world suggests the North owes an important moral obligation to the South. But there are also practical benefits to the donor from this pattern of wealth transfer. States often use development assistance as a form of trade subsidy and understand that poverty alleviation and the creation of prosperous new trading markets and sites for foreign investment will, in the medium to long term, become a net economic benefit to the rich world. Again, there is no necessary contradiction between altruism and self-interest in this field, in fact some might argue that a self-interest tie-in will increase domestic support for development assistance in donor countries.

The moral obligation on states to provide a safe haven and resettlement for people fleeing their homeland out of a well-founded fear of persecution, has proved a significant challenge for governments around the world. Significantly, few have sought to shirk this responsibility, especially over the last five decades. How can this be explained? Refugees represent a heavy financial burden for recipient states, to say nothing about the cultural, social and political complexities that they also bring with them. In national interest terms, it would be much easier for states to simply reject refugees and send them back to their place of origin. That they frequently do not suggests states are acknowledging humanitarian obligations which take precedence over their more narrow political and economic interests. Realism fails to provide a convincing explanation of this development.

Human rights and humanitarian intervention

The subject of human rights advocacy is a significant challenge for conventional conceptions of the national interest, and is the most controversial and problematic aspect of the English-School idea of 'obligations to humanity'. It deserves a more detailed analysis.

References to essential human needs are implicit in some of the earliest written legal codes from ancient Babylon, as well as early Hindu, Buddhist and Confucian texts, though the first explicit mention of universal principles governing common standards of human behaviour can be found in the West.

The idea of universal human rights has its origins in the Natural Law tradition, debates in the West during the Enlightenment over the 'rights of man' and in the experience of individuals struggling against the arbitrary rule of the state. The Magna Carta in 1215, the development of English Common Law and the Bill of Rights in 1689 were significant, if evolutionary steps along the path to enshrining basic human rights in law, as were intellectual contributions from Grotius (the law of nations), Rousseau (the social contract) and Locke (popular consent, limits of sovereignty). An early legal articulation of human rights can be found in the American Declaration of Independence in 1776 ('we take these truths to be self-evident, that all men are created equal, and that they are endowed by their Creator with certain unalienable Rights, that amongst these are Life, Liberty and the pursuit of Happiness') and in France's Declaration of the Rights of Man and the Citizen in 1789 ('all men are born free and equal in their rights').

Human beings are said to be endowed – purely by reason of their humanity – with certain fundamental rights, benefits and protections. These rights are regarded as inherent in the sense they are the birthright of all, inalienable because they cannot be given up or taken away, and universal since they apply to all regardless of nationality, status, gender or race. They are not conferred by states, nor are they contingent on any particular form of political community.

The extension of these rights to all peoples has a particularly important place in liberal and English-School thinking about foreign policy and international relations for two reasons. First, these rights give a legal foundation to emancipation, justice and human freedom. Their denial by state authorities is an affront to the dignity of all and a stain on the human condition. Secondly, states which treat their own citizens ethically and allow them meaningful participation in the political process are thought to be less likely to behave aggressively internationally. The task for liberals and the English School has been to develop and promote moral standards which would command universal consent, knowing that in doing so states may be required to jeopardise or subordinate the pursuit of their own narrowly conceived national interests.

This has proven to be a difficult task, despite evident progress on labour rights, the abolition of slavery, the political emancipation of women in the West, the treatment of indigenous peoples and the end of white supremacism in South Africa. In the modern period, states are both the principal violators of universal human rights and an ultimate authority for their defence. This paradox is reflected in the often ambivalent status human rights enjoy, even in those Western states which claim to be their authors. States have struggled to find the appropriate location for human rights diplomacy in their national interest formulations because advocacy almost certainly entails some level of interference in the domestic sovereign affairs of others.

The creation of important legal codes, instruments and institutions in the post-Second World War period is a measure of modern achievement in the area. The most important instruments are the Universal Declaration of Human Rights (1948), the International Covenant on Civil and Political Rights (1966) and the International Covenant on Economic, Social and Cultural Rights (1966), while the International Labour Organisation and the International Court of Justice play a significant institutional and symbolic role in the protection of human rights.

In his seminal account, Vincent identified the right of the individual to be free from starvation as the only human right which is likely to enjoy the support of a global consensus. The world community, regardless of religious or ideological differences, agrees that a right to subsistence was essential to the dignity of humankind (Vincent 1986; see also Hoffmann 1981; Dunne & Wheeler 1999). Beyond this right, nation-states struggle to find agreement, not least because the developing world is suspicious that human rights advocacy from metropolitan centres is sometimes little more than a pretext for unwarranted interference in their domestic affairs. Most states are reluctant to give outsiders the power to compel them to improve their ethical performance, although there is a growing belief that interference in domestic affairs should no longer be used by governments as a credible excuse for avoiding legitimate international scrutiny.

This is the nub of the problem. Active human rights diplomacy is perfectly consistent with a state's wider obligations to humanity, but it conflicts with another English-School foundation stone of international society – the sovereign independence of states. If states are left to enforce, or at least advocate compliance with human rights benchmarks, this conflict appears inevitable and irreconcilable. Depending on their particular location on the English-School spectrum, pluralists will be reluctant to support any intervention which undermines sovereignty while solidarists will push for tighter compliance and enforcement measures consistent with international ethical instruments. Attitudes towards an emerging norm of humanitarian intervention are a good indication of the divide within the English School. Pluralists tend to be opposed on the grounds that it imperils the sovereign independence of states. Solidarists see it as a humanitarian obligation and regard some violations of human rights as so shocking that the suspension of the doctrine of non-intervention is justified. There is no consensus.

Many Marxists have dismissed human rights as mere bourgeois freedoms which fail to address the class-based nature of exploitation contained within capitalist relations of production. Realists would add that 'conditions of profound insecurity for states do not permit ethical and humane considerations to override their primary national considerations' (Linklater 1992, p. 27). After all it is interests which determine political action and in the global arena, politics is the amoral struggle for power to advance these interests. Even in cases where an appalling humanitarian crisis elicits calls for intervention by the world community, there is still no global consensus in favour of enforcing human rights standards because of the implications of this for state sovereignty and autonomy.

Liberals and the English School battle to avoid the charge that their conceptions of democracy and human rights are culturally specific, ethnocentric and therefore irrelevant to societies which were not Western in cultural orientation. To many societies, the claim to universality may merely conceal the means by which one dominant society imposes its culture upon another, while infringing on its sovereign independence. The promotion of human rights from the core to the periphery assumes a degree of moral superiority – that the West not only possesses moral truths which others are bound to observe, but that it can sit in judgement on other societies.

The issue is further complicated by the argument that economic, social and cultural rights should precede civil and political rights – one made earlier by Communist states and more recently by a number of East-Asian governments, and which is a direct challenge to the idea that human rights are indivisible and universal – a revolt against the West. It implies that the alleviation of poverty and economic development in these societies depends on the initial denial of political freedoms and human rights to the citizen. However, the claim that rights can be prioritised in this way or that procedural and substantive freedoms are incompatible is problematic and widely seen, with some justification, as a rationalisation by governments for authoritarian rule.

Conservative political leaders in the East-Asian region (sometimes called the Singapore School) have also argued that there is a superior Asian model of political and social organisation comprising the principles of harmony, hierarchy and consensus (Confucianism) in contrast to what they regard as the confrontation, individualism and moral decay which characterises Western liberalism. Regardless of how self-serving this argument is – and it is rarely offered by democratically elected rulers – it poses a fundamental challenge to Fukuyama's suggestion that in the post-Cold War period liberal democracy faces no serious universal challenge. It is clear that these states are not necessarily striving to imitate the Western route to political modernisation.

Even if universal rules and instruments could be agreed upon, how could compliance with these standards be enforced? Liberals and the English School are divided over this issue, between non-interventionists who defend state sovereignty, and those who feel that the promotion of ethical principles can justify intervention in the internal affairs of other states (Bull 1984). Recent examples of so called 'humanitarian intervention' in Somalia, Cambodia, Rwanda, Serbia and East Timor pose a growing challenge to the protection from outside interference traditionally afforded by sovereignty claims. As does the prosecution of those suspected of committing war crimes and crimes against humanity by international tribunals such as the International Court of Justice and, more recently, the International Criminal Court.

Modern forms of humanitarian intervention follow a pattern established in the middle of the eighteenth century when the British and Dutch successfully interceded on behalf of Prague's Jewish community, which was threatened with deportation by authorities in Bohemia. The protection of Christian minorities at risk in Europe and in the Orient in the eighteenth and nineteenth centuries by the Treaty of Kucuk-Kainardji (1774) and the Treaty of Berlin (1878) are also part of the same legal precedent, as is the advocacy of British Prime Minister Gladstone in the second half of the nineteenth century and US President Wilson early in the twentieth century.

Vietnam's invasion of Cambodia in 1978, when refracted through the ideological prism of the Cold War, highlighted both the underdeveloped and politically contingent nature of humanitarian intervention in the modern period. To the West, Vietnam was a pariah state which had violated Cambodia's sovereignty, to others it was a liberating force which had freed the population from the brutal repression of Pol Pot. Adherents of the English School who support both the sovereign rights of independent states and the right of external intervention in cases where there is an acute humanitarian crisis, find it difficult to reconcile both international norms.

Conclusion

Realists argue that the insecure and anarchical nature of the international environment does not allow states to consider ethical and humane issues above their primary national interests. States are said to be too pre-occupied with their own physical security to be bothered with broader humanitarian concerns. International and universal interests are not a priority for realists. They may be addressed but only after the primary concern for security is satisfied, and often not even then.

The English School, particularly the solidarist kind, claims that a nation-state's pursuit of its national interests should be supplemented by ethical and moral concerns, such as the promotion of global peace and respecting duties to humanity. The English School is convinced that the *international society of states* which nations form, where common rules, values and institutions are created, is recognition of the common interests states have in co-operation and co-existence. The development of international law, the proliferation of international organisations, and a growing framework of rules and conventions, comprise an expanding international diplomatic culture which the English School believes challenges realism's assertion that conflict and war are endemic and inevitable.

To restate the point, the English School believes international order rests on a balance of power in the world, a recognition of common functional or utilitarian interests where the mutual benefits of reducing instability and enhancing predictability are recognised, and common procedural (rather than substantive or cultural) values which establish rules and infrastructure for the mediation of conflict and the possibility of co-operation on broader fronts.

For the English School, the key to the viability of this 'international society' is the legitimacy of the international order. Unsurprisingly, for (Western) liberal-democratic societies from where adherents to the English School generally come, human rights, justice, economic development and international law are essential to the maintenance of a legitimate international order. This approach to international relations has often been described as 'international humanitarianism' and has been called 'good international citizenship'. The promotion of what Bull called 'purposes beyond ourselves' – the promotion of global moral and ethical considerations – rests on the assumption that there are universal human interests which are shared across cultures and boundaries by every individual in every nation-state. These interests are regarded as universal because they exist beyond individual, class, cultural or national interpretation.

The difficulty for policy makers who subscribe to aspects of both discourses is synthesising realism's concern with state security and the English School's wider regard for international order and justice. How do policy makers frame a coherent foreign policy which reflects these apparently irreconcilable goals? Or to put it another way, how do states reconceptualise their idea of the national interest without creating an inherently contradictory formula?

In practice the wider concerns of the English School tend to be faithfully pursued until they conflict directly with the primary needs of economic and strategic security. 'Purposes beyond ourselves', therefore, provides a broad moral direction or framework for contemporary foreign policy which can be followed providing these purposes are consistent with the strategic and economic interests of the nation-state. To put it another way, the motivating factor behind the foreign policy of some liberal-democratic states could generally be characterised as enlightened self-interest. Ethical humanitarian concerns are an important consideration for states, though for many they have not yet reached the status which strategic and economic security enjoy within policy formulation.

A cynical interpretation would dismiss 'good international citizenship' or enlightened self-interest as little more than image-building for liberal democratic states. It would claim that the only significance of 'good international citizenship' is that many governments feel obliged to cast their foreign policy in these terms, thereby indicating a rhetorical, if not actual commitment to the English-School agenda. But this may be too harsh. The diplomatic behaviour of many states – not exclusively Western – in the areas of development aid, human rights, refugees, the environment and disarmament would indicate that there is substance to the view that states have redefined the idea of the national interest to include broader obligations to global humanity. Global concerns and problems, such as environmental degradation and international terrorism, which cannot be successfully addressed at the level of the individual state will force states to broaden the way they conceive their interests – to become what Bull called local agents of 'the world common good' (Bull 1984 in Alderson & Hurrell 2000, p. 222).

Turning to the Frankel and Rosenau dichotomy, the English School avoids easy classification because it regards the interests of states as an expanding domain rather than a fixed set of knowable concerns. Striving to broaden the way states conceive of their interests to include the needs of others is clearly a slow process which takes place over many years. In that sense national interests for the English School are not objective, rather they are subjectively negotiated through dialogue and eventual consensus.

Because the English School argues that it is wrong for states to promote their national interests without regard for global human interests, this may mean the national interest is no longer 'national' in any obvious or exclusive sense. The English School seems to have effectively redefined it beyond its conventionally recognised form.

6
Progressive Perspectives: Constructivism

> I define the national interest as the objective interests of state-society complexes, consisting of four needs: physical survival, autonomy, economic well-being, and collective self-esteem.
>
> (Alexander Wendt, *A Social Theory of International Politics*)

> We do not know what we want if we do not know who we are. This insight holds for foreign policy as much as it does for personal preferences.
>
> (Glenn Chafetz et al., *The Origins of National Interests*)

In the last decade constructivist theories of International Relations (IR) have made a significant impact upon the discipline. Like Feminist, Postmodern and Green IR theory, there is no one constructivist position, but instead a variety of positions stretching across the theoretical spectrum from conventional-realist variants to more critical-postmodern perspectives (Hopf 1998 in Linklater 2000b; Reus-Smit 2001).

Although it is difficult to identify common threads throughout this particular theoretical cluster, according to Jackson

> constructivists accept that there is no external, objective reality as such when it comes to human relations. Their key idea is that the social world, including the international world, is a human construction. It is not something 'out there', as behaviouralists and positivists believe. Rather, it is an inter-subjective domain: it is meaningful to the people who made it and live in it and who therefore must be able to understand it. (Jackson 2000, p. 33)

The social and political world, according to constructivists, is not an external, objective reality beyond human consciousness. It does not exist in temporal isolation. It exists

> only as inter-subjective awareness among people. It is a human invention or creation not of a physical or material kind but of a purely intellectual and ideational kind. It is a set of ideas, a body of thought, a system of norms, which has been arranged by certain people at a particular time and place. If the thought and ideas that enter into the existence of international relations change, then the system itself will change as well. That is because the system consists in thought and ideas. (Jackson & Sorensen 2003, p. 253)

According to leading constructivists such as Alexander Wendt, there is no objective international domain which is independent of the conventions, practices and institutions that states create amongst themselves. Anarchy is not an external given or a natural reality, 'anarchy is what states make of it'. The importance of power in global politics and the self-help nature of the international system are the conscious products of state behaviour. The anarchical condition of the international system is not a gift of nature or an unavoidable given, but is instead something states have constructed between themselves. This construction, in turn, has tended to define their relations.

Wendt and other constructivists argue that human structures are determined more by shared ideas than material forces. Thus the identities and interests of human beings are a product of these shared ideas rather than being natural endowments. Constructivists believe that these shared ideas and normative practices are a key determinant of state behaviour, and have been a missing ingredient from previous accounts of international politics.

The focus of constructivism is on human volition and human agency, or more specifically those agents who act on behalf of states and international organisations. It is humans who have created the structures and conditions of the international world. Inter-subjective reality defines international social practice – common interests, rules, conventions and norms. Neo-realists, who start from the assumption that the external order is objectively given and difficult, if not impossible, to change, have missed a critical influence on state behaviour which is not simply axiomatic behaviour based on the absence of world government.

For most constructivists, the national interest is an important social construction which should be seen as a key indicator of state behaviour.

As will be shown, there are a variety of constructivist approaches to the national interest. Each of the key constructivist contributions will be examined in turn. However, what they all seem to have in common is an agreement with Hans Morgenthau's claim that national interests depend on the 'political and cultural context within which foreign policy is formulated' (Weldes 1999, p. 7). Constructivists believe that this aspect of Morgenthau's work was underdeveloped and has been largely neglected by scholars since. This chapter will examine the role of this political and cultural context in constructivist thinking, and assess the claim of constructivists that the national interest is again an important explanatory tool in international politics providing it is understood as a social construction.

Because it is both a recent entrant to the theoretical field and does not bring with it the same philosophical heritage of the other theories under examination, this chapter is shorter than its predecessors. This does not imply that constructivist views of the national interest are proportionally less important, but that the constructivist project in this area remains a work in progress.

Wendt

Constructivism is a broad church with both modern and post-modern wings, and within both these groups there is a further range of sub-groupings. One of the earliest and most important thinkers in the field is Alexander Wendt, whose work has been influential in shaping the application of constructivist thinking to the study of international relations. Although Wendt's more recent writings have been seen as somewhat idiosyncratic and atypical even within constructivist circles, few of his contemporaries have offered an analysis of national interests from a constructivist position which is as detailed as his (Reus-Smit 2001).

According to Wendt

> constructivism is a structural theory of the international system that makes the following claims: (1) states are the principal units of analysis for international political theory; (2) the key structures in the states system are inter-subjective, rather than material; and (3) state identities and interests are in important part constructed by these social structures, rather than given exogenously to the system by human nature or domestic politics. (Wendt 1994, p. 385)

Wendt's discussion of international politics rests on a heavily nuanced – some might say complex – definition of 'structure' which is normally conceived of as a material or organisational entity (e.g. an NGO), but for Wendt is a social construction. For constructivists, structures are 'relatively unchangeable constraints on the behaviour of states' (Hopf 1998 in Linklater 2000b, p. 1757). This definition of structure can sometimes obstruct a clear understanding of the meaning of Wendt's argument.

According to Wendt, 'self-help and power politics are institutions, not essential features of anarchy. Anarchy is what states make of it' (Wendt 1992 in Linklater 2000a, p. 617). This is an important insight because it challenges Kenneth Waltz's neo-realist assumption that anarchy is a pre-condition of the international system which the actor units – states – must live with and can do little if anything to alter. For Wendt, anarchy is the social construct of states, not an external objective given under which they must seek to survive. Thus the prospects for changing the international system – its order and structure – are much greater than neo-realists such as Waltz claim. This is a profound challenge to conventional thinking in the field, even if change doesn't seem as straightforward as Wendt implies. However, to claim that 'self-help and power politics are institutions' only seems to obfuscate this central argument about the origins of anarchy, especially when 'institutions' is already well understood in a very different sense in the study of international politics.

Wendt is concerned with the relationship between agents (states) and (social) structures in international politics. Neither can exist independently of the other. Up to a point, says Wendt, they constitute each other. States and their interests cannot therefore be assumed: they are not exogenously given, as neo-realists such as Waltz imply. Treating the identities and interests of agents as exogenously given, as he claims both neo-realism and neo-liberalism do, is a mistake because it reifies them, which begs the important question of how they evolved as a consequence of social and institutional interaction (Wendt 1992 in Linklater 2000a, p. 615.) Other questions follow. For example, are the interests of states always and only self-regarding? What is the connection between the identity of a state and the way it conceives of its interests?

Wendt investigates how states see the international system, their own role in it, the possibilities of alternative roles for them, what they believe is significant and not, and the nature of threats. None of these questions can be answered, he believes, without a theory of social construction. Conventional approaches such as neo-realism largely discount the possibilities for change within the international system because of the dominating conditional effects of anarchy. According to this approach, neither the structure of the system nor the way the units within it define their interests, are likely to alter. Wendt does not accept this argument because he believes it misunderstands the ways in which state interests are defined. 'State identities and interests can be collectively transformed within an anarchic context by many factors – individual, domestic, systemic, or transnational – and as such are an important dependent variable,' he says (Wendt 1992 in Linklater 2000a, p. 640). The prospects for change within an anarchical environment are therefore significantly greater than realists concede.

A key to understanding Wendt's approach is his reluctance to distinguish between human beings as agents of volition, and the structures they build, such as states, to perform certain specified functions. Both are regarded as intentional actors and therefore capable of having interests which are formed as much out of social interaction as from material need or perspective. Wendt claims that '1) human beings and their organisations are purposeful actors whose actions help reproduce or transform the society in which they live; and 2) society is made up of social relationships, which structure the interactions between these purposeful actors' (Wendt 1987 in Linklater 2000a, p. 501).

Wendt poses the question: how are national interests constituted? Conventionally, interests have been defined by realists in 'material' rather than 'social' terms. According to realists, they are rooted in human nature or anarchy, economic and military capabilities, and usually measured in terms of power. The distribution and constitution of these interests is crucial in understanding the actions of states in the international system because it is assumed by realists that state behaviour is largely explained by the pursuit of these objectives. Neo-liberals, on the other hand, emphasise norms, ideas and institutions as key explanatory factors in addition to power. In their discussion of regimes and regime theory, neo-liberals focus on how ideas can have causal effects which are independent of other inputs such as power and interests.

According to Wendt, however, 'ideas also have constitutive effects, on power and interest themselves' (Wendt 1999, p. 114). Some, though not all ideas, actually constitute interests. 'Only a small part of what constitutes interests is actually material. The material force constituting interests is human nature. The rest is ideational: schemas and deliberations that are in turn constituted by shared ideas or culture' (Wendt 1999, pp. 114–15). Overcoming the materialist bias in the understanding of interests is therefore one of Wendt's prime concerns. As far as he is concerned, interests can be material or ideational, but until now the latter has been almost totally ignored because of the dominance of realism and its conception of national interests in material terms.

The exploration of the ideational basis of interests by Wendt rests on a very specific notion of state agency which is not generally shared, either by other constructivists or more generally by theorists in the discipline. According to Wendt, 'the structures of human association are primarily cultural rather than material phenomena' (Wendt 1999, p. 193). This means that 'states are people too' because they are 'purposive actors with a sense of Self' (Wendt 1999, p. 194). States should therefore be considered agents with interests because they are intentional actors. According to Wendt, states can be anthropomorphised on the basis that they are purposive or act with intent. In the discussion and analysis of international politics, attributions of corporate actorhood are unavoidable and necessary to make proper sense of state behaviour in the international domain (Wendt 1999, p. 196).

This is the key point in Wendt's understanding of national interests. Those who want to distinguish between human agents and states have argued that the state is a useful fiction or a metaphor, and that human characteristics cannot be imputed to it because it is clearly not a moral agent. It should be seen as an organisational structure and not an organic entity with inherent moral attributes. This is true of both nominalist approaches which are sceptical of the idea of the separate existence of the state, and what Wendt calls the 'reifiers' or realists, who constantly raise the importance of the state without explaining its internal structure and constitution.

According to Wendt, 'states are real actors to which we can legitimately attribute anthropomorphic qualities like desires, beliefs, and intentionality' (Wendt 1999, p. 197). But how can we attribute human qualities such as interests, intentionality and identity to a corporate being? Wendt regards the corporate agent as 'actually a kind of structure: a structure of shared knowledge or discourse that enables individuals to engage in institutionalised collective action' (Wendt 1999, p. 215). Because this structure generates a pattern of observable effects, it should be considered a purposive actor with collective interests that cannot be reduced to the preferences of dominant individuals in government – a key difference from critical approaches to the national interest. If we can observe their behaviour and feel their effects, states must exist. States have a collective dimension. 'States are real and not reducible to the individuals who instantiate them,' argues Wendt (Wendt 1999, p. 218). This is a direct challenge to critical perspectives of the state, including

Marxist and anarchist approaches, which seek to unpack the state with an eye to identifying its principal functionaries and beneficiaries.

According to Wendt's notion of corporate agency, it is their internal structure which constitutes states as real, unitary actors or corporate persons which have collective interests which can be articulated (Wendt 1999, p. 197). It is possible to argue for 'justified ascriptions of agency by showing how states are constituted by internal structures that combine a collective Idea of the state with rules that institutionalise and authorise collective action by their members, and by arguing that these structures are real because they have real effects' (Wendt 1999, p. 243). It is important to note here that Wendt is not claiming that states are moral agents. For him it is the idea of corporate agency and a decision-making structure that both institutionalises and authorises collective action, which in turn justifies his argument that states have particular, unique and irreducible national interests (Wendt 1999, p. 218). By virtue of their corporate identity as intentional actors, states generate what Wendt describes as universal 'national interests' (Wendt 1999, p. 233).

In response to the claim made by critical approaches to the national interest that it is impossible to argue for common interests in complex, class-divided societies, Wendt claims that 'individuals accept the obligation to act jointly on behalf of collective beliefs, whether or not they subscribe to them personally' (Wendt 1999, p. 219). In other words, the citizens of a state agree to surrender to the common view even if they personally dissent from it because of their attachment to the idea of the purposive state. This is an interesting argument, if only because it is made without any invocation of the binding power of nationalism. In Wendt's somewhat idiosyncratic constructivist position, there appears to be no place for nationalism at all, even though some binding notion of a social contract allows the citizens of a state to speak with a common voice.

In Wendt's view, interests and identities are both linked and socially constructed. 'Identities refer to who or what actors *are*. They designate social kinds or states of being. Interests refer to what actors *want*. They designate motivations that help explain behaviour. Interests presuppose identities because an actor cannot know what it wants until it knows who it is, and since identities have varying degrees of cultural content so will interests' (Wendt 1999, p. 231). This argument moves Wendt away from the realist contention that the national interests of states vary only marginally because they are socialised into the game of power politics by the conditioning effects of anarchy. The logical extension of his argument is that national interests will vary in proportion to differences of state identity, which would seem to be vast. Wendt says little about the constraints – either social, cultural or structural – on variations of national interests. Curiously, he adumbrates four basic interests which he claims are common to all states, and says little about how differences of political identity affect them. Considering the amount of trouble he takes to highlight the ideational, non-material aspects to interest formation, his list is remarkably conventional.

'I define the national interest as the objective interests of state-society complexes, consisting of four needs: physical survival, autonomy, economic well-being, and collective self-esteem' (Wendt 1999, p. 199). According to Wendt, these needs must be met if states, or what he calls state-society complexes, are to sustain and reproduce themselves. There is very little here that mainstream conventional realists would take issue with. It is somewhat surprising that after such a long and complex deconstruction of identity and interest formation, he arrives at precisely the same position as 'materialist' thinkers who have traversed a much less circuitous route.

> Identities are the basis of interests. Actors do not have a 'portfolio' of interests that they carry around independent of social context; instead, they define their interests in the process of defining situations. As Nelson Foote puts it: 'Motivation ... refer[s] to the degree to which a human being, as a participant in the ongoing social process in which he necessarily finds himself, defines a problematic situation as calling for the performance of a particular act, with more or less anticipated consummations and consequences, and thereby his organism releases the energy appropriate to performing it.' Sometimes situations are unprecedented in our experience, and in these cases we have to construct their meaning, and thus our interests, by analogy or invent them de novo. More often they have routine qualities in which we assign meanings on the basis of institutionally defined roles. When we say that professors have an 'interest' in teaching, research, or going on leave, we are saying that to function in the role identity of 'professor,' they have to define certain situations as calling for certain actions. This does not mean that they will necessarily do so (expectations and competence do not equal performance), but if they do not, they will not get tenure. The absence or failure of roles makes defining situations and interests more difficult, and identity confusion may result. This seems to be happening today in the United States and the former Soviet Union: without the cold war's mutual attributions of threat and hostility to define their identities, these states seem

unsure of what their 'interests' should be. (Wendt 1992 in Linklater 2000a, p. 620)

Wendt's approach rests on what he calls a 'primitive anthropology' which directly analogises states with individuals – he anthropomorphises states. This is not just a deployment of the domestic analogy, but extends further to the view that states are actually organic in much the same way individuals are. According to Wendt there are two sources of identity formation for individuals, and therefore for states: the corporate and the social. The former derives from internal organic attributes, the latter from social interaction. Wendt believes that states not only acquire interests through learning (much as individuals do), but they also have intrinsic interests. In this regard Wendt sees few if any differences in the processes of identity formation and interest acquisition between biological and administrative entities. This contention raises a number of issues.

First, even if individuals construct their interests in this way – as an expression of their personal identity as they see it, can the interests of states be explained in the same way by extrapolating to the collective identity of a nation, if such a thing can be identified? This assertion cannot be separated from the claim that the state is a moral agent, a highly contested idea. In most other theoretical approaches to international politics, it is not the state which is a moral agent but rather the individuals who control the state apparatus. Wendt, and constructivists more generally, seem to be arguing that the state has a collective moral identity of its own, that it constitutes a moral agent in international politics and therefore has collective national interests based on this moral identity. Wendt doesn't say this explicitly, preferring to use the terms 'purposive' and 'intentional' actors. But he seems to treat states as if they were moral agents and many scholars would disagree, arguing that as moral agents, only humans can have interests.

There is no contesting the fact that state behaviour has moral implications and that governments enter into moral commitments with others which commit their populations as a whole: the community can be committed to moral or immoral acts which survive the governments that are specifically responsible for them. There is also no doubt that states make decisions that affect the lives of other people, and are often required to take responsibility for these decisions. But does this mean the state is a moral agent or merely a legal personality? Presumably, states – or the agents of states – can behave morally or immorally without being moral agents.

Although there are few firm foundations for constructing elementary moral principles, according to consequentialist approaches to ethics, people are responsible for the anticipated or predictable consequences of their behaviour, both their actions and inaction. According to Noam Chomsky, this responsibility mounts with greater opportunity and more clearly anticipated effects, and 'extends to the policy choices of one's own state to the extent that the political community allows a degree of influence over policy formation' (Chomsky 2000, p. 8). In other words, the citizens of democratically-accountable governments accept to varying degrees, shared responsibility for the actions their governments commit in their name. This does not endow the state with a separate moral existence. A moral agent is usually a being who is capable of acting with reference to right and wrong. How can a collective act in this way?

Secondly, are interests only defined in a social context? This seems to entirely discount the view that instinct, intuition and biological inheritance play a part in an individual's interest formation. If humans are born with a moral disposition – one that is genetically determined in some way – then the social construction of individual identity and interests is inextricably bound up with their biological endowment. There is a strong argument that the conditions of moral judgement are firmly rooted in a person's internal nature. This is uncontroversial in many fields. When confronted by unfamiliar or unprecedented circumstances, to the extent that there is evidence (and it has been shown in cognitive science and linguistics – theory of language acquisition), the environment is an impoverished guide to behaviour and instinct or internal nature tends to takes over. The social construction of identity and interests seems, at best, only part of the story of interest-based behaviour.

Assuming this to be true, to what extent does interest formation remain, for constructivists, solely defined in a social context? Are we not thrust back into the age-old, and largely intractable debate about which is the greater influence on human behaviour – biology or the environment – nature or nurture? Defining all organic behaviour in social terms does not necessarily confine convincing explanations of it to the social world (Pinker 2002).

Wendt's claim that without the other against which to define their roles, the former Soviet Union and the US struggled to determine their interests after the Cold War: they both required the Cold War's mutual attributions of threat and hostility to define their identities (Wendt 1999). This seems contestable on a number of levels. It exaggerates the extent to which the national interests of both were determined solely by the bilateral relationship. Both states had clearly defined interests before the Cold War and after it, including interests which have lasted through all three periods. In the aftermath of the end of ideological hostilities, both had to reassess their foreign policy priorities and the ways they would interact with each other and the rest of the world. In other words, their roles needed revising and their priorities required re-sorting. But were they really struggling to define their identities and were they suddenly unsure of their interests because they had only been formed in the context of their 'social' relationship? Beyond the predictable consequences of 'regime change' for one party, there is scant evidence of this.

In summary, to inhere or impute moral characteristics to large social groups, and then argue that this enables their collective interests to be defined in a socially constructed way, seems to be an approach fraught with dangers.

On the national interest

Whereas Marxists would argue that material structures are crucial in determining class interests and behaviour – interests are shaped by the location of people in the production process – and realists would emphasise the accumulation of relative power as key explanation of state behaviour, constructivists claim that normative and ideational structures are equally important in determining the identity and interests of people and states in the international environment. In fact constructivists such as Wendt argue that human interests are inter-subjective and ideationally based, rather than being primarily grounded in material reality as Marxists believe.

Constructivists argue that shared ideas, beliefs and values exert significant influence on social and political action. In fact they shape both the social identities of political actors and, in turn, the interests they express. Identities inform interests which, in turn, determine actions. Chafetz defines identity as 'the state of being similar to some actors and different from others in a particular circumstance. Identity involves the creation of boundaries that separate self and other' (Chafetz et al. 1999, p. viii). Identity, especially group identity, is crucial because it 'is the mechanism that provides individuals with a sense of self and the means for comprehending the relationship of the self to the external environment' (Chafetz et al. 1999, p. ix). Accordingly, interests and identities are constantly being moulded and remoulded through socialisation (Hobson 2000, p. 146). National identity, and therefore national interests, change over time.

If Wendt is correct in suggesting that identities are the basis of interests, constructivists are right to emphasise the importance of studying how the social and political identities of individuals and states are constructed, and therefore how interests are formed.

Constructivists argue that national interests are constructed by dominant groups in society in part to secure particular identities. They accuse neo-realists and neo-liberals of regarding interests and identities as pre-determined by external conditions, whereas they argue that interests and identities arise out of social interaction. As Reus-Smit explains,

> instead of treating actors' interests as exogenously determined, as given prior to social interaction, constructivists treat interests as endogenous to such interaction, as a consequence of identity acquisition, as learnt through processes of communication, reflection on experience, and role enactment. (Reus-Smit 2001, p. 219)

For constructivists there can be no a priori interests 'out there'. Interests are developed, learned and re-learned over time as a consequence of experience and reflection. Within the limits of the actor's imagination, the realms of realistic possibility, an acknowledgement of limitations and constraints, a knowledge of what is necessary and with an understanding of what is considered legitimate conduct, interests form, develop and change (Reus-Smit 2001, pp. 219–20). It is important here to emphasise that constructivists reject the idea of permanent and fixed interests, which is the basis of much realist thought on the subject. If interests are largely determined through social interaction, they must change as the experience of social interaction varies over time.

Wendt, for example, regards identities as fundamental and argues that interests give expression to identities. The national interest, therefore, tells us much about the particular identities of those articulating it. Conventional approaches 'that dominate the field of international relations usually assume interests and preferences, rather than try to explain these interests and preferences' (Chafetz et al. 1999, p. xiv).

For constructivists, the social world differs from the natural world in the sense that while the latter is a given which human beings must seek to understand, the social world – in this case the international domain – is a human construction which, by definition, must be explicable to those who built it and live in it. The international system is an historical creation and is therefore more open to reconstruction than those who stress immutable forces are prepared to concede.

Accordingly, national interests are inter-subjective beliefs that are shared among people – ideas, conceptions and assumptions. These shared beliefs compose and express the interests and identities of people – the way people conceive of themselves in their relations with others (Jackson & Sorensen 2003, p. 253). The key ingredients of the national interest therefore include questions such as: how do people express their interests and think these interests should be expressed by their representatives? What do they think they have in common with fellow nationals and conversely how do they think their interests diverge and separate from outsiders? How do people want their beliefs, prejudices, values, traditions and history to be translated into political institutions and diplomatic behaviour?

If interests are an expression of the identity of an agent, it is important to know just how that agent is viewed. For conventional approaches to international politics, the key agent is the state and its interests are largely assumed. For most constructivists, the state is more than the individuals who control it. It is an institution, a system of norms, rules and principles that organise power and authority in distinctive ways. When constructivists speak of the state's identity, they refer not to its 'sense of self', but rather to its role identity, its socially ascribed character. Thus, when they refer to a liberal democratic state, constructivists are not primarily referring to the institution's sense of self, but rather to its purposive character as an institution concerned with organising power and authority in a manner that expresses the interests, and protects the rights, of its citizens.

This is more obvious in discourses by political elites about the national interest. They seek to relate their conceptions of the national interest to established, socially ascribed ideals about the identity of the state: 'Australia has these interests because it is a liberal democracy, etc.' Of course elites always try to define their interests as the national interests, but for constructivists this is constrained by the norms that constitute the identity of the state. These norms can be formal and informal, international and domestic. They empower and dis-empower social and political agents in complex ways. Crucially, this relates to moral agency in a distinctive way: states, as they are not human actors, cannot be moral agents. However, individuals empowered by the state as an institution are. The crucial point for constructivists is that it is the identity of the state, and the norms that constitute that identity, which determines the nature and scope of the moral agency that those actors can express. In other words, the debate over moral agency and how it is constructed becomes, for constructivists, a debate over the norms which largely determine moral behaviour.

Finnemore

How do large complex societies have common interests? When constructivists speak of the state 'having interests', they are not speaking about 'society having interests'. They are speaking about the interests qua the socially ascribed purposes of an institution – the state.

Martha Finnemore has written extensively about how states define their national interests, from a broad constructivist perspective (Finnemore 1996). She defines constructivists as concerned 'with the impact of cultural practices, norms of behaviour, and social values on political life and reject the notion that these can be derived from calculations of interest. They emphasise the importance of inter-subjective understandings in structuring the ways in which actors understand what kinds of actions are valuable, appropriate and necessary' (Finnemore 1996, p. 15).

Finnemore believes that the end of the Cold War raised doubts about the utility of 'obvious' security interests for states which had been taken for granted for five decades. Approaches which stressed 'rational choice' and 'strategic interaction' were no longer adequate to deal with the new uncertainties of a post-bipolar world.

According to Finnemore – and she is generally representative of constructivists on this point – the explanatory power of the dominant theories of neo-realism and liberalism are limited by their a priori assumptions about how states conceive of their interests. A different approach is required, one which is based on

> understanding state interests and state behaviour by investigating an international structure, not of power, but of meaning and social value. We cannot understand what states want without understanding the international social structure of which they are a part. States are embedded in dense networks of transnational and international social relations that shape their perceptions of the world and their role in that world. States are socialised to want certain things by the international society in which they and people in them live. (Finnemore 1996, p. 2)

Finnemore rejects the view that the interests of states are defined by objective criteria such as power in the context of immutable forces such as anarchy. Instead, states should be regarded as social agents whose interests and identity are formed, developed and changed as a result of the environment – the 'normative context' – in which they operate.

State interests are defined in the context of internationally held norms and understandings about what is good and appropriate. That normative context influences the behaviour of decision-makers and of the mass publics who may choose and constrain those decision-makers. The normative context also changes over time, and as internationally held norms and values change, they create co-ordinated shifts in state interests and behaviour across the system. [State interests] are shaped by internationally shared norms and values that structure and give meaning to international political life. (Finnemore 1996, pp. 2–3)

It would appear that some version of a domestic analogy is being applied here. States are like individuals in a domestic social context. They define their interests as actors within the social milieu they find themselves. They are not especially conscious of bringing pre-determined interests to this setting, but rather define their interests through social interaction, which varies over time. Thus 'states are socialised to accept new norms, values and perceptions of interest by international organisations . . . ' and through their own direct experiences with others (Finnemore 1996, p. 5).

This is a crucial point made by constructivists. Their approach to national interest formation is a theory of how state preferences change. They are rejecting the argument made by neo-realists in particular – but also Marxists, liberals and others – that the interests, and therefore the behaviour of states, can be explained by unproblematic inherent qualities which are a reflection of material or functional needs. When Finnemore argues that if we focus on what goes on within a state we can miss the international societal and systemic factors, she would find herself in general agreement with neo-realists until she leaves systemic constraints behind and focuses instead on social norms (Finnemore 1996, pp. 6–7).

Finnemore asks whether state preferences can 'be readily deduced from the objective conditions and material characteristics of a state', as neo-realists and liberals believe, or whether in fact they are much more 'malleable' (Finnemore 1996, pp. 8 & 11). Clearly she believes that through interaction, actors such as states shape and are shaped by the social structure they form a part of:

Socially constructed rules, principles, norms of behaviour, and shared beliefs may provide states, individuals and other actors with understandings of what is important or valuable and what are effective and/or legitimate means of obtaining those valued goods. These social structures may supply states with both preferences and strategies for pursuing those preferences. (Finnemore 1996, p. 15)

It is important here to note that for Finnemore, states are unproblematic agents, meaning she assumes them to be unified actors which can speak with one voice on the question of national interests. She makes little, if any distinction between the way in which an individual is socialised by domestic society and the way a state is socialised in international society. Norms, which she defines as 'shared expectations about appropriate behaviour held by a community of actors' are equally held by individuals and political communities. They are 'collectively held ideas about behaviour' which are internalised, and which in turn produce common interests (Finnemore 1996, pp. 22–3). Norms – which can be seen in patterns of behaviour and official public discourse – establish what the community regards as appropriate behaviour, both domestically and internationally. It is the test of appropriateness versus the emphasis on consequences, which separates constructivist approaches to national interest formation from more conventional perspectives. As cultural mores change over time, so do norms and so too do the interests which further these norms.

For Finnemore, principles, norms, shared discourses and identities are causal variables which shape preferences and behaviour (Finnemore 1996, p. 15). The fact that they are 'variables' means that a nation's interests which reflect them will also vary. She employs three case studies to demonstrate that states are not necessarily motivated by an interest in maximising their power through their diplomatic conduct. These are: (1) Norms and State Structure: UNESCO and the Creation of State Science Bureaucracies; (2) Norms and War: The International Red Cross and the Geneva Conventions; and (3) Norms and Development: The World Bank and Poverty.

In the first case study, Finnemore examines the role of an International Organisation (UNESCO) in socialising states into developing science policy bureaucracies after 1955. In the second, she looks at the rules and norms which govern the conduct of war by highlighting the extent to which states forgo sovereignty and subject themselves to the Geneva Conventions which relate to the treatment of prisoners of war. In the third case study, Finnemore notes the emergence of a redistributive norm in Third-World states in the 1970s, when community welfare came to rival capital accumulation as a policy objective.

In each case 'power-maximisation' and naked self-interest directed towards relative gains, are insufficient explanations of state behaviour.

In other words, whereas neo-realism cannot explain the way states have behaved in these circumstances, a constructivist approach which stresses the importance of normative socialisation can. This is a generally convincing argument, even if the case studies selected are somewhat marginal to the key debates in the discipline. The argument Finnemore seems to be making is not exclusive of realist concerns with power but rather a supplement to them. The strength of her position is her exposure of the inadequacy of neo-realist and neo-liberal approaches, which place too much emphasis on materialism and agency, in explaining more nuanced state behaviour. Constructivists such as Finnemore, who argue that states are constrained by social norms (structures) as much as they are by anarchy, are concerned with the normative processes which define the national interest. This is an important contribution to a wider debate.

One question which arises about Finnemore's account is whether she is actually describing how national interests are perceived and change over time or whether she is explaining how states have altered the means they employ to pursue interests which have not changed very much. Neo-realists might claim that she has overlooked the fact that national interests are a small core of fixed concerns (e.g. security) and that what she is actually explaining is how states redefine the means to secure those interests in a changing world – something they would have few concerns about because it is merely a reflection of new realities – new means to the same ends.

Weldes

In a 1996 article, and later in an extended monograph, Jutta Weldes has mounted a constructivist re-examination of the Cuban missile crisis by redefining the way in which national interests are constructed (Weldes 1996; 1999).

According to Weldes, the national interest is important to the discourse of international politics for two reasons;

> First it is through the concept of the national interest that policy-makers understand the goals to be pursued by a state's foreign policy. It thus in practice forms the basis of state action. Second, it functions as a rhetorical device through which the legitimacy of and political support for state action are generated. 'The national interest' thus has considerable power in that it helps to constitute as important and to legitimise the actions taken by states. (Weldes 1996, p. 276)

The continuing salience of the national interest is obvious to Weldes, but its analytical usefulness is limited until it is understood as a social construction. What this means is that because state officials and representatives are charged with acting on behalf of the state, they can only discharge this duty by engaging in a process of 'interpretation' which should be properly understood as a product of social construction (Weldes 1996, p. 276). According to Weldes,

> This process of interpretation, in turn, presupposes a language shared, at least, by those state officials involved in determining state action and by the audience for whom state action must be legitimate. This shared language is that of 'the national interest'. The content of 'the national interest', I then argue, is produced in, or emerges out of, a process of representation through which state officials (among others) make sense of their international context. 'The national interest', that is, is constructed, is created as a meaningful object, out of shared meanings through which the world, particularly the international system and the place of the state in it, is understood. (Weldes 1996, p. 277)

In contrast to realist conceptions of the national interest which are inferred from the anarchic character of the international system, Weldes argues that the national interest is in fact a process of interpretation and communication by those with diplomatic responsibilities. Realism can define the national interest as an objective and independent reality with fixed terms because of its confidence in the immutable qualities of the international system. Weldes' constructivism allows for subjective variation in how the national interest is defined, according to changing circumstances, personalities and available diplomatic choices. Thus while realism assumes that threats to the survival of the state are self-evident, it cannot explain 'why particular situations are understood to constitute threats to the state' (Weldes 1999, p. 7). Weldes' constructivism seeks to accomplish this task.

For Weldes, the behaviour of state representatives largely determines what the national interest actually is at any point in time. For realists the national interest is obvious and barely requires a defence. For Weldes it is a matter of interpretation, hence her case study of the Cuban missile crisis where the interpretation of momentous and rapidly unfolding events by key state officials was crucial to the ultimate peaceful resolution of the conflict. Focusing on a range of key players from a variety of different perspectives helps Weldes to demonstrate the importance of interpretation, communication and a common dialogue during diplomatic crises.

How do state officials interpret events, and thus constitute the national interest? Weldes cites Wendt 'that people act towards objects, including other actors, on the basis of the meanings that the objects have for them', meanings that are inter-subjectively constituted (Weldes 1996, pp. 279–80). Adopting a constructivist approach allows Weldes 'to examine the inter-subjectively constituted identities and interests of states and the inter-subjective meanings out of which they are produced' (Weldes 1996, p. 280). Only then will the true national interest be revealed.

However, this process is not always clearly explained. For example, here is Weldes' description of inter-subjectivity in international politics:

> My argument is that national interests are social constructions created as meaningful objects out of the inter-subjective and culturally established meanings with which the world, particularly the international system and the place of the state in it, is understood. More specifically, national interests emerge out of the representations – or, to use more customary terminology, out of situation descriptions and problem definitions – through which state officials and others make sense of the world around them. (Weldes 1996, p. 280)

This seems somewhat obfuscatory, unnecessarily abstract, complex and vague, especially the reference to national interests emerging out of representations, as if they have a life and agency of their own. The impression that is left is of a process more complex than the actors themselves might recognise.

Weldes rejects Wendt's analytical assumption that states are unitary actors and that inter-state interaction is the basis of this inter-subjectivity, preferring to concentrate on the individuals involved in the process. However, in a clever sleight of hand, Weldes effectively redefines the state – the 'pre-eminent site for the construction of the national interest' – as the 'institution or bundle of practices that we know as the state', within which there are individuals who 'play a special role in constructing the meaning of "the national interest"'. Whereas Finnemore stresses normative structures over agency, Weldes places the emphasis squarely back on the individual agents. The key actors are therefore the 'foreign-policy decision-makers', the statesmen whose thoughts and deeds Morgenthau spent so much time trying to anticipate (Weldes 1996, pp. 280–1). 'In representing for themselves and others the situation in which the state finds itself, state officials have *already* constructed the national interest,' Weldes claims (Weldes 1996, p. 283).

It is a mistake, however, to simply reduce the national interest to the blank slate preferences of decision makers. The process is more complex. According to Weldes,

> To speak of state officials as producing, reproducing, or transforming national interests is not to imply that national interests are wholly reducible to the conscious intentions of these state officials, Rather ... the security imaginary preexists these state officials and is, in part, the condition of possibility for state actors, their practices, and their authority and, in part and conversely, the unintended outcomes of state actors' representational practices. When state officials (and others) construct the national interest, they do so out of extant resources – including linguistic, cultural, and institutional resources – provided by the security imaginary and, in so doing, reproduce their own positions and those responsible for the national interest. State officials, then, are subjects in both senses of that term: They are, on the one hand, intentional actors actively engaged in the construction of meaning, and they are, on the other hand, always already subject to the repertoire of meanings offered by the security imaginary that produces them. (Weldes 1999, pp. 11–12)

Decision-making and the construction of the national interest, according to Weldes, is a product of the interaction of individual preferences and representations from a pre-socialised environment with a range of constrained cultural choices in a new and rapidly changing environment. In retrospect this seems rather obvious, though the key issue is how much weight is given to a socialisation process which is independent of conventional material needs and perspectives.

Clearly, visions of the international system, interpretations of values and priorities, assumptions of intent and behaviour, 'interpretation and interpellation', give identity to a range of state and non-state actors, weak and strong, friend and foe. Interests are always going to be in part a function of state identity, as familiar terms such as East, West, North, South, Occident, Orient, etc. suggest. But to argue that these identities and interests are inter-subjective rather than rooted in material and historical reality, remains a contestable issue.

Conclusion

Constructivist conceptions of the national interest are a timely reminder of the importance of inter-subjectivity in the conduct and expression of diplomatic behaviour. By emphasising the political and cultural context in which national interests are forged, they draw attention to how national interests are constructed rather than assuming them to be the axiomatic products of elite material interests or externally given structures. The importance of shared ideas and meanings, interpretation, and normative practice is highlighted in explanations of recent diplomatic events.

It is clear, using Frankel and Rosenau's dichotomy, that constructivists regard national interests as essentially subjective. In fact, despite Wendt's conventional list of factors, they largely discount objective and material criteria for defining the national interest. For them, questions of interpretation, identity formation and shared meanings – all subjective factors – are central to their concerns.

It is not clear, however, what constructivists generally regard as the actual relationship between ideational accounts of the national interest and more conventional materialist-based conceptions. For example, Wendt seems to reject materialist-based accounts of interest formation completely, whereas Finnemore wants her constructivist approach to be a supplement to materialist accounts such as neo-realism, without explaining how both approaches connect.

The linear progression from identity formation to interest recognition is important but generally presented in somewhat simplistic terms. Whilst constructivists sensibly point out that anarchy is a product of conscious state rejection of world government and not an external given or gift of God, they are divided over the issue of moral agency. Some regard the state as a moral agent with specific interests (Wendt), others choose to focus on the actions and words of individuals who control the levers of state power (Weldes). This is a crucial point, as yet unresolved within constructivist circles. Added to this confusion is the charge that what is actually being discussed here is the different ways in which state officials pursue national interests – new means to achieve old ends – rather than an innovative understanding of how the ends of policy are defined. The resuscitation of the national interest by constructivists would therefore seem to have some way to proceed before it is brought fully back to life.

Conclusion

The book has argued that despite its ongoing usage in modern political discourse, especially in the practice of diplomacy, 'the national interest' is now a term largely, though not totally, devoid of substantive meaning and content.

Although 'the national interest' has normally been considered in the disciplines of diplomatic history and political science as both a defence of and explanation for policy-making and decisions, the term has not been comprehensively assessed across the range of major theories within the discipline which is specifically charged with the explication of international politics – International Relations. This book attempts to fill this gap by providing a theoretical appraisal of the concept.

International Relations as a formal discrete discipline has only existed since the end of World War One. However, since then a rich theoretical literature has developed which examines and seeks to explain key issues, actors and problems in international politics from a range of theoretical perspectives. The methodology of this book has been to examine what the most prominent theoretical traditions in the field – realism, Marxism and anarchism, liberalism, the English School and constructivism – understand by the term 'the national interest'. In each case this involves an historical analysis, however the common focus is whether from the perspective of each theory, the national interest has contemporary meaning and force.

Before this could be done, however, the origins and antecedents of the term needed to be explained. It was shown how the national interest evolved out of Rousseau's notion of 'the general will', Machiavelli's idea of *'raison d'état'*, and how the rise of nationalism and the democratisation of the state gave it modern form. The marriage of the nation as a social group with the state as a political community forged the national interest as the ultimate rationalisation for diplomacy – especially, though not exclusively, in liberal democracies. In other words, in its subjective form it became an important feature of diplomatic discourse.

The contemporary world, however, presents many different conditions to those which prevailed when the Treaty of Westphalia was signed in the seventeenth century. In the twenty-first century, the human race is becoming increasingly unified in two unprecedented ways. It has a universal economic system – capitalism – and a common form of political community – the state in a system of states. It is against the backdrop of these important modern processes that each theory is considered for how it understands the idea of 'the national interest'.

The influential tradition of realism, comprising both classical and neo-realism, has been the principal progenitor and promoter of the term. Early realists such as Hans Morgenthau regarded the national interest as both a guiding maxim for statesmen and the ultimate measure of foreign policy legitimacy. For neo-realists such as Kenneth Waltz, the national interest is a systemic given, the pursuit of state survival in an anarchical world.

According to the realist tradition, diplomacy must only aim at furthering the interests of a particular state, whose citizens are assumed to have common interests. There is no similar duty to promote the interests of people in other states or to advance internationalist ideals. The realist horizon does not stretch far beyond the territorial concerns of the state, and certainly falls well short of universal concerns. Going it alone seems safer and more defensible than a reliance on co-operation.

Realism assumes that the state can act autonomously from dominant sectional interests. The population's common interest in security and state survival is said to be evidence of this claim. While this is a strong argument, it is not impervious to criticism. Persecuted minorities and secessionist groups do not necessarily share an interest in the ongoing territorial integrity of the state, in fact they are often the primary victims of attempts to prevent state fragmentation. The military-industrial sector within each society has a disproportionate rather than a common interest in defence and security policy. And pursuing common national interests may occlude or discourage individuals from embracing new forms of political community such as regional groupings, which might better meet their needs, including their security concerns.

Although the state continues to play an important role in an era of economic globalisation and in the latest confrontation between the secular West and its religious enemies, the traditional realist definition of national interests does not retain either the same resonance or relevance that it once did in international politics. The national interest will enjoy a revival during the so-called 'war against terror' as the power and reach of the state is enhanced, but it is no longer especially national.

There are cosmopolitan influences in modern political life. Many individuals increasingly see themselves as part of a broader human community than simply the nation or the state. The English School, therefore, argues that it is wrong for the national interest to be promoted without regard for the impact of policy on others and on international morality generally. After all, global concerns and problems such as terrorism and ecological threats cannot be meaningfully addressed at the level of the individual nation and will require states to substantially broaden the way they conceive their interests. States now need a sense of 'world common good'.

Strong national ties remain, however local or provincial attachments must, on occasion, surrender to a higher ethical conviction which emphasises global humanitarian obligations. From an English-School perspective which stresses the importance of world order, for example, the well-being of individuals must sometimes come before the territorial integrity of states. Humanitarian intervention, despite its often dubious motives, is an indication that the broader international community will sometimes place the alleviation of humanitarian crises above the protection of the sovereign rights of states and the pursuit of exclusive national interests.

States should consider the predictable consequences of their actions for humanity as a whole, and relinquish national affiliations and cultural attachments when they pose a threat to world order. According to the English School, this ultimately provides the most propitious environment for the security of justice.

They believe the national interest of a state must be enlightened self-interest. This is not the same as selflessness or altruism. The English School argues that 'good international citizenship' profits all peoples and all nations. It does mean, however, that the national interest must be redefined away from its realist egoistic conception, effectively transcending its traditional meaning altogether.

Marxists, and to a lesser extent anarchists, have thought in terms of cosmopolitanism and internationalism rather than national interests. Nationalism and state ideology, they believe, have falsely promoted the idea of common national interests which has concealed the particular interests of the working class in its struggle against the bourgeoisie to overthrow capitalism.

These two traditions pose major challenges to conventional claims that the nation-state remains an active agent in international affairs with collective, common interests, and instead expose the particular interests of special groups within it. According to Marxists, only the principal beneficiaries of capitalism – the middle classes – speak in national interest terms. A distaste for repressive exclusive political communities and the dynamic effects of the spread of capitalism would bring nationalism and the states system to an end.

This vision has not come to pass. Human beings have not submerged their parochial differences in one world society regardless of their opposition to the repressive apparatus of the state. Class identity has not superseded nationalism. Marxists have also grossly neglected the issue of war and the level of state autonomy which exists within the strategic interaction of states.

Nonetheless, by disputing the existence of common economic interests in class-divided societies and in emphasising the domestic structure of the state as a key determinant of foreign policy, Marxist and anarchist perspectives remain powerful critiques of the idea that the citizens of nation-states have national interests in international relations.

The idea of the cohesive, unified and integral nation underpins concepts of the national interest. However, the nation itself is under challenge from the forces of globalisation and its flipside – fragmentation. Minorities, the marginalised, the persecuted and disaffected, as well as outsiders, frequently argue that 'the nation does not speak for us'. Regional groupings, moral communities and global activist groupings which span territorial frontiers all pose a serious challenge to the contemporary relevance of nation-states speaking with a common voice.

For classical liberals, the apparent demise of the state and national interests is cause for celebration. The impact of globalisation at the end of the twentieth and the start of the twenty-first century promises to usher in a single global economy and a united world community. There is some division and ambivalence about the role of the state in the global market place, with economic liberals stressing the corrupting influence of the state and its vulnerability to capture by special interest groups masquerading as champions of the national interest. On the other hand, state liberals are more cautious about the supremacy of market forces and advocate the retention of a minimal state with necessary powers to provide the economic and legal infrastructure in which markets can flourish.

Liberals are united, however, on the promotion of capitalism and liberal democracy as antidotes to endemic violence in the international system. Like Marxists, they are genuinely convinced that human beings are on a linear trajectory towards a better future. Whilst they are vulnerable to questions about the unequal benefits of globalisation and why its victims would share a common interest in the pursuit of free trade and unfettered foreign investment, an important and welcome stage in human progress will come when individuals stop thinking nationally.

Liberals doubt that the national interest has much in the way of a residual meaning, and think states should be promoting internationalist ends. They believe that the national interests of states will eventually be replaced by global perspectives because the idea of national interests is ultimately incompatible with the preference for unrestricted and unregulated commercial ties across territorial frontiers, and the long-held liberal promise of a united human community.

Constructivists have sought to resuscitate the national interest as an explanatory tool for foreign policy analysis by arguing that it should be seen as a social construction rather than a material reality. Although there are significant differences within the broad constructivist school, they generally agree that the national interest is a product of shared ideas, national identity, inter-subjectivity and normative practices. Far from being a set of permanent, objective conditions, the national interests of states are formed within a cultural context and are the outcome of social interaction. This should be the focus of those inquiring into the subject. They are not determined in response to an external given, nor are they fixed. Rather they vary as social conditions and national identities change.

Whilst constructivists may explain the means employed to pursue national interests, it is not clear that their ideas about the ends of policy significantly varies from more conventional accounts. Ultimately the national interest appears to be defined, even by scholars such as Alexander Wendt, in standard materialist terms – the desire for territorial security. Constructivists have provided a window into the way diplomatic practice interprets the interests of states, but not necessarily a new way of conceiving interests in the first place. Some of this is because there is an uncertainty over the question of agency within constructivism. Is the state a moral agent, as Wendt seems to imply? Or should the focus be on those representatives of states who are charged with translating the national interest into foreign policy? These important questions need to be clearly resolved before constructivism can confidently claim to be proposing a convincing non-materialist account of the national interest.

The national interest will continue to feature in the political discourse of states because it has important subjective utility. However, by examining the concept as it is understood across the spectrum of International Relations theory, it is clear that while it may retain rhetorical and lexical functions in the modern age, the national interest lacks substantive objective content.

Appendix: Tables 1 and 2

Table 1 What theories of International Relations understand by the concept of national interests

Theoretical approach	Realism	English School	Marxism critical	Liberalism	Constructivism
Conception of the national interest	The nation has a common interest in its survival & security in an anarchical world	Enlightened self-interest Obligations to humanity may override national interests	Cosmopolitan & Internationalist National interest conceals class divisions in capitalist societies	Anti-statist & ambiguous about role of national interests	Identity & interests are symbiotic – social construction Inter-subjective (ideational) rather than material
Means & purpose	Military power & alliances Interests are permanent & unaffected by ideology or changes in government	Wrong to set policy without regard for its impact on others & international morality Broader definition of interests	Bourgeoisie seeks to pass off its interests as national interests No common economic interests in class-divided societies	State can be captive to special interests National interest leads to protectionism & corruption of markets (foreign investment)	Shared ideas & normative practice changes as do interests – not permanent Political & cultural context of policy & interpretation
Obligations	No duty to aliens or to advance internationalist ideals	Universal interests mean parochial attachments may need to be relinquished	State is ruled by ruling class National interests will surrender to class interests	Globalisation: free trade & unrestricted commerce take priority	States have corporate interests not reducible to individuals

Table 2 Examples and problems with theoretical approaches to the national interest

Theoretical approach	Realism	English School	Marxism critical	Liberalism	Constructivism
Examples	Common interest in territorial integrity & deterring invasion; East Timor (Jakarta lobby)	Refugees; Human rights & Aid; Arms control & disarmament; Environmental challenges; Humanitarian intervention	Disparities of wealth & income under market capitalism – winners & losers from free trade	Globalisation is eroding state sovereignty & relevance of national interests	Physical survival, autonomy, economic well-being, collective self-esteem (Wendt); Norms of appropriate behaviour
Problems	Persecuted minorities; Secessionists; Shifting boundaries; Military-industrial sector; Global challenges? Nations without states (Kurds)	Challenges to international society & universality (Asian values, Islamist terror, religion & culture)	What about the persistence of nationalism? Divisions within ruling class (trade policy)	Nation-states remain preferred political community despite economic globalisation; Politics engenders nationalist thinking	States as moral agents too? Relationship between material & ideational interests? Role of nationalism?

Bibliography

Alderson, K. & Hurrell, A. (eds) (2000) *Hedley Bull on International Society* (Basingstoke).

Anderson, B. (1991) *Imagined Communities* (London).

Anderson, B. (2001) 'Democratic Fatalism in South-East Asia' in ABC (ed.), *The Alfred Deakin Lectures* (Sydney).

Arblaster, A. (1984) *The Rise and Decline of Western Liberalism* (Oxford).

Australian Financial Review (Editorial), 2 September 1997.

Australian Financial Review (Editorial), 16 September 1997.

Australian Financial Review (Editorial), 15/16 November 1997.

Bairoch, P. (1993) *Economics and World History* (New York).

Barnet, R.J. & Cavanagh, J. (1994) *Global Dreams* (New York).

Beard, C.A. (1934; 1966) *The Idea of National Interest* (Chicago).

Beard, C.A. (1935) *The Open Door At Home* (New York).

Blake, W. (1977) *The Complete Poems* (London).

Block, F. (1990) *Postindustrial Possibilities* (Berkeley).

Block, F. & Somers, M. (1984) 'Beyond Economistic Fallacy: The Holistic Social Science of Karl Polanyi' in Skocpol, T. (ed.), *Vision and Method in Historical Sociology* (Cambridge).

Bottomore, T. (ed.) (1991) *A Dictionary of Marxist Thought* (2nd edn., Cambridge).

Brady, R. (1943) *Business As A System Of Power* (New York).

Bromley, S. (1999) 'Marxism and Globalisation', in Gamble, A., Marsh, D. & Tant, T. (eds), *Marxism and Social Science* (London).

Bull, H. (1966) 'International Theory: The Case for a Classical Approach', in *World Politics*, 18, pp. 361–77.

Bull, H. (1977) *The Anarchical Society: A Study of Order in World Politics* (London).

Bull, H. (ed.) (1984) *Intervention in World Politics* (Oxford).

Bull, H. & Watson, A. (eds) (1984) *The Expansion of International Society* (Oxford).

Bull, H. (2000) 'The State's Positive Role in World Politics', 1977; 1979 in Alderson, Kai & Hurrell, Andrew (eds), *Hedley Bull on International Society* (Basingstoke).

Burchill, S. & Devetak, R., et al. (2001) *Theories of International Relations* (2nd edn., London).

Buzan, B. (2003) 'Implications for the Study of Internationl Relations' in Buckley, M. & Fawn, R. (eds), *Global Responses to Terrorism* (London).

Calleo, D.P. & Rowland, B.M. (1973) *America and the World Political Economy* (Bloomington).

Campbell, D. (1992) *Writing Security: United States Foreign Policy and the Politics of Identity* (Minneapolis).

Carey, A. (1995) *Taking the Risk Out of Democracy* (Sydney).

Carr, E.H. (1939; 1981) *The Twenty Years' Crisis* (London).

Carr, E.H. (1945) *Nationalism and After* (London).

Carr, E.H. (1951) *The New Society* (London).

Chafetz, G., Spirtas, M. & Frankel, B. (eds) (1999) *The Origins of National Interests* (London).

Chandler, A.D. (1977) *The Visible Hand: The Managerial Revolution in American Business* (Cambridge, MA).

Chase-Dunn, C. (1981) 'Interstate System and Capitalist World Economy: One Logic or Two?', *International Studies Quarterly*, 25, pp. 19–42.

Chomsky, N. (1969) *American Power and the New Mandarins* (Harmondsworth).

Chomsky, N. (1973) *For Reasons of State* (Suffolk).

Chomsky, N. (1982) *Towards A New Cold War* (New York).

Chomsky, N. (1988) *Language and Politics* (Montreal).

Chomsky, N. (1989) *Necessary Illusions* (Boston).

Chomsky, N. (1993/1994) *Year 501* (Boston).

Chomsky, N. (1993a) 'The Clinton Vision', *Z Magazine*, October.

Chomsky, N. (1994) *World Orders, Old and New* (London).

Chomsky, N. (1999) *Profit Over People: Neoliberalism and the Global Order* (New York).

Chomsky, N. (2000) *A New Generation Draws the Line: Kosovo, East Timor and the Standards of the West* (London).

Clark, I. (1989) *The Hierarchy of States: Reform and Resistance in the International Order* (Cambridge).

Clinton, W.D. (1986) 'The National Interest: Normative Foundations', *Review of Politics*, 48 (4), pp. 495–519.

Clinton, W.D. (1994) *The Two Faces of National Interest* (Baton Rouge).

Connolly, W.E. (1974) *The Terms of Political Discourse* (Lexington).

Craig, G.A. & George, A.L. (1983) *Force and Statecraft: Diplomatic Problems of Our Time* (New York).

Dalby, S. (1990) *Creating the Second Cold War* (London).

Dalton, G. (ed.) (1968) *Primitive, Archaic and Modern Economics* (New York).

Daly, H.E. & Cobb, J.B. (1989; 1994) *For the Common Good* (rev. edn., Boston).

Deane, P. (1979) *The First Industrial Revolution* (Cambridge).

DFAT (Department of Foreign Affairs and Trade – Economic Analytical Unit) (2003) *Globalisation: Keeping the Gains* (Canberra).

Dolgoff, S. (ed.) (2002) *Bakunin on Anarchism* (Montreal).

Donnelly, J. (2000) *Realism and International Relations* (Cambridge).

Doyle, M. (1986) 'Liberalism and World Politics', *American Political Science Review*, 80 (4).

Doyle, M.W. (1997) *Ways of War and Peace* (New York).

Dunkley, G. (1997) *The Free Trade Adventure* (Melbourne).

Dunne, T. (1998) *Inventing International Society* (Basingstoke).

Dunne, T. & Wheeler, N.J. (eds) (1999) *Human Rights in Global Politics* (Cambridge).

Emy, H.V. (1993) *Remaking Australia* (Melbourne).

Evans, G. (1989) *Making Australian Foreign Policy* (Melbourne).

Evans, G. & Grant, B. (1995) *Australia's Foreign Relations* (2nd edn., Melbourne).

Finnemore, M. (1996) *National Interests in International Society* (New York).

Frankel, J. (1970) *National Interest* (London).

Friedman, T. (2000) *The Lexus and the Olive Tree* (London).

Fukuyama, F. (1992) *The End of History and the Last Man* (London).

Gaillie, W.B. (1978) *Philosophers of Peace and War* (Cambridge).

Gallagher, J. & Robinson, R. (1953) 'The Imperialism of Free Trade', *Economic History Review*, 6 (1).

Gamble, A. (1981) *An Introduction to Modern Social and Political Thought* (London).

Gardner, R.N. (1990) 'The Comeback of Liberal Internationalism', *The Washington Quarterly*, 13 (3) (Summer).

Gellner, E. (1983) *Nations and Nationalism* (Oxford).

Gellner, E. (1997) *Nationalism* (London).

George, A.L. (1980) *Presidential Decisionmaking in Foreign Policy: The Effective Use of Information and Advice* (Boulder).

George, A.L. & Keohane, R.O. (1980) 'The Concept of National Interests: Uses and Limitations', in George, A.L., *Presidential Decisionmaking in Foreign Policy: The Effective Use of Information and Advice* (Boulder).

George, J. (1997) 'Australia's Global Perspectives in the 1990s: a Case of Old Realist Wine in New (Neo-liberal) Bottles?' in Cox, D. & Leaver, R. (eds), *Middling, Meddling and Muddling: Issues in Australian Foreign Policy* (St Leonards).

Gerschenkron, A. (1962) *Economic Backwardness in Historical Perspective* (Harvard).

Giddens, A. (1985) *The Nation-State and Violence* (Cambridge).

Gilpin, R. (1981) *War and Change in World Politics* (New York).

Gilpin, R. (1987) *The Political Economy of International Relations* (Princeton).

Gilpin, R.G. (1996) 'No One Loves A Political Realist', in *Security Studies*, 5, pp. 4–26.

Gilpin, R. (2000) *The Challenge of Global Capitalism* (Princeton).

Gilpin, R. (2001) *Global Political Economy* (Princeton).

Goodman, J. & Ranald, P. (2000) *Stopping the Juggernaut* (Annandale).

Gramsci, A. (1971) *Selections From Prison Notebooks* (New York).

Haas, E.B. (1953) *Dynamics of International Relations* (New York).

Habermas, J. (1971) *Knowledge and Human Interests* (Boston).

Hall, P.A. & Soskice, D. (eds) (2001) *Varieties of Capitalism* (Oxford).

Halliday, F. (1994) *Rethinking International Relations* (Basingstoke).

Harvey, D. (2003) *The New Imperialism* (Oxford).

Held, D. (ed.) (1983) *States and Societies* (New York).

Held, D. (1989) *Political Theory and the Modern State* (Cambridge).

Held, D., McGrew, A., Goldblatt, D. & Perraton, J. (1999) *Global Transformations* (Cambridge).

Held, D. & McGrew, A. (eds) (2000) *The Global Transformations Reader* (Cambridge).

Hill, C. (2003) *The Changing Politics of Foreign Policy* (London).

Hirschman, A.O. (1986) *Rival Views of Market Society and Other Recent Essays* (New York).

Hirst, P. & Thompson, G. (1999) *Globalization in Question* (2nd edn., Cambridge).

Hobsbawm, E.J. (1969) *Industry and Empire* (Harmondsworth).

Hobsbawm, E. (1975) *The Age of Capital 1848–1875* (London).

Hobsbawm, E.J. (1990) *Nations and Nationalism Since 1780* (Cambridge).

Hobsbawm, E.J. (2000) *The New Century* (London).

Hobson, John M. (2000) *The State and International Relations* (Cambridge).

Hodgson, G. (1984) *The Democratic Economy* (Harmondsworth).

Hoffmann, S. (1981) *Duties Beyond Borders* (Syracuse).

Hoffmann, S. (1995) 'The Crisis of Liberal Internationalism', *Foreign Policy*, 98.

Hopf, T. (1998; 2002b) 'The Promise of Constructivism in International Relations Theory' in Linklater, A. (ed.), *International Relations: Critical Concepts in Political Science: Volume IV* (London).

Horsman, M. & Marshall, A. (1994) *After the Nation-State* (London).

Howard, M. (1978) *War and the Liberal Conscience* (Oxford).

Howard, M. (1983) *The Causes of War and Other Essays* (London).

Jackson, R. (2000) *The Global Covenant* (Oxford).
Jackson, R. & Sorensen, G. (2003) *Introduction to International Relations: Theories and Approaches* (2nd edn., Oxford).
Kant, I. (1970) *Kant's Political Writings* (ed. Reiss, H., Cambridge).
Kauppi, M.V. & Viotti, P.R. (eds) (1992) *The Global Philosophers* (New York).
Kemp, R. (1998) *Assistant Treasurer Press Release* No. AT/005 (http://www. treasurer.gov.au/default.asp?main=/assistanttreasurer/pressreleases/1998/1998_005. asp sighted 2 April, 2001).
Keohane, R.O. & Nye, J.S. (1977) *Power and Interdependence: World Politics in Transition* (Boston).
Kerr, D. (2001) *Elect the Ambassador!* (Annandale).
Kofsky, F. (1993) *Harry Truman and the War Scare of 1948* (New York).
Kolko, G. (1969) *The Roots of American Foreign Policy* (Boston).
Kolko, G. & Kolko, J. (1972) *The Limits of Power: The World and United States Foreign Policy 1945–1954* (New York).
Krasner, S.D. (1978) *Defending the National Interest: Raw Materials Investments and US Foreign Policy* (Princeton).
Krasner, S.D. (1999) *Sovereignty: Organized Hypocrisy* (Princeton).
Kratochwil, F. (1982) 'On the Notion of "Interest" in International Relations', *International Organisation*, 36 (1), Winter, pp. 1–30.
Krippendorff, E. (1982) *International Relations as a Social Science* (Brighton).
Kropotkin, P.A. (1970) *Selected Writings on Anarchism and Revolution* (Cambridge, MA).
Kubalkova, V. & Cruickshank, A.A. (1980) *Marxism-Leninism and the Theory of International Relations* (London).
Kubalkova, V. & Cruickshank, A.A. (1985; 1989) *Marxism and International Relations* (Oxford).
Lazonick, William (1991) *Business Organization and the Myth of the Market Economy* (Cambridge).
Leffler, M. (1992) *A Preponderance of Power* (Stanford).
Linklater, A. (1986) 'Realism, Marxism and Critical International Theory', *Review of International Studies*, 12, pp. 301–12.
Linklater, A. (1990) *Beyond Realism and Marxism* (London).
Linklater, A. (1991) *Competing Perspectives on the State, the National Interest and Internationalism* (Melbourne).
Linklater, A. (1992) 'What is a Good International Citizen?', in Keal, P. (ed.), *Ethics and Foreign Policy* (Canberra).
Linklater, A. (1993) 'Liberal Democracy, Constitutionalism and the New World Order' in Leaver, R. & Richardson, J. (eds), *The Post-Cold War Order: Diagnoses and Prognoses* (St Leonards).
Linklater, A. (1998) *The Transformation of Political Community* (Cambridge).
Linklater, A. (ed.) (2000) *International Relations: Critical Concepts in Political Science: Volume I* (London).
Linklater, A. (ed.) (2000a) *International Relations: Critical Concepts in Political Science: Volume II* (London).
Linklater, A. (ed.) (2000b) *International Relations: Critical Concepts in Political Science: Volume IV* (London).
Linklater, A. (2001) 'Rationalism' in Burchill, S., Devetak, R., et al., *Theories of International Relations* (2nd edn., London).

Linklater, A. (2001a) 'Citizenship, Humanity and Cosmopolitan Harm Conventions', *International Political Science Review*, (Special issue) 22 (3), pp. 261–77.

Luttwak, Edward (1999) *Turbo-Capitalism: Winners and Losers in the Global Economy* (New York).

Machiavelli, Ni. (1961; 1999) *The Prince* (London).

Macpherson, C.B. (1973) *Democratic Theory* (Oxford).

Macpherson, C.B. (1977) *The Life and Times of Liberal Democracy* (Oxford).

Magdoff, H. (1978) *Imperialism* (New York).

Marx, K. (1964) *The German Ideology* (Moscow).

Marx, K. (1959; 1977) *Economic and Philosophic Manuscripts of 1844* (Moscow).

Marx, K. (1970/1973) *Grundrisse* (Harmondsworth).

Marx, K. (1974) *The German Ideology* (2nd edn., London).

Marx, K. & Engels, F. (1967) *The Communist Manifesto* (Harmondsworth).

Marx, K. & Engels, F. (1998) *The Communist Manifesto* (London).

Marx, K. & Engels, F. (n.d.) *Essential Classics in Politics* (on CD-Rom) (ElecBook 0002, London).

Mayall. J. (2000) *World Politics: Progress and its Limits* (Cambridge).

Mearsheimer, J.J. (1990) 'Back to the Future: Instability in Europe After the Cold War', *International Security*, 15 (1) (Summer).

Mearsheimer, J.J. (2001) *The Tragedy of Great Powers* (New York).

Meinecke, F. (1998) *Machiavellism* (New Brunswick).

Micklewait, J. & Wooldridge, A. (2000) *A Future Perfect: The Challenge and Hidden Promise of Globalization* (New York).

Millar, T.B. (1978) *Australia in Peace and War* (Canberra).

Mitrany, D. (1948) 'The Functional Approach to World Organization', *International Affairs*, 24.

Morgenthau, H.J. (1946) *Scientific Man vs Power Politics* (Chicago).

Morgenthau, H.J. (1948; 1985) *Politics Among Nations* (New York).

Morgenthau, H.J. (1951) *In Defence of the National Interest: A Critical Examination of American Foreign Policy* (New York).

Morgenthau, H.J. (1962) 'Negotiations or War?', *The New Republic*, 3 November.

Morgenthau, H.J. (1952; 2000) 'Another "Great Debate": The National Interest of the United States', in *American Political Science Review*, 46 (4), 1952 reproduced in Linklater, A. (ed.), *International Relations: Critical Concepts in Political Science: Volume I* (London) pp. 279–303.

Morgenthau, H.J. (1977) 'Comment', *The New Republic*, 22 January.

Mueller, J. (1989) *Retreat From Doomsday* (New York).

Nathan, G.J. & Mencken, H.L. (1997) *The Smart Set* (reprinted New York).

Nuechterlein, D. (1976) 'National Interests and Foreign Policy: a Conceptual Framework for Analysis and Decision-making', *British Journal of International Studies*, 2 (3), pp. 246–66.

Nye, J.S. (1988) 'Neorealism and Neoliberalism', *World Politics*, 40.

Offe, C. (1975) 'The Theory of the Capitalist State and the Problem of Policy Formation' in Lindberg, L., Alford, R.R., Crouch, C. & Offe, C. (eds), *Stress and Contradiction in Modern Capitalism* (Lexington).

Offe, C. (1975; 1984) *Contradictions of the Welfare State* (Cambridge).

Ohmae, K. (1995) *The End of the Nation State* (New York).

Otero, C.P. (eds) (1981) *Radical Priorities* (Montreal).

Pinker, S. (2002) *The Blank Slate* (London).

Polanyi, K. (1944; 1957) *The Great Transformation* (Boston).
Polanyi, K. (1968) 'Our Obsolete Market Mentality' in Dalton, G. (ed.), *Primitive, Archaic and Modern Economics* (New York).
Poulantzas, N. (1972) 'The Problem of the Capitalist State', in Blackburn, R. (ed.), *Ideology and Social Science: Readings in Critical Social Theory* (Glasgow).
Powell, R. (1994) 'Anarchy in International Relations Theory: the Neorealist-Neoliberal Debate', *International Organization*, 48.
Pusey, M. (2003) *The Experience of Middle Australia* (Cambridge).
Rawls, J. (1999) *The Law of Peoples* (Harvard).
Ray, Dennis M. (1972) 'Corporations and American Foreign Relations', in *Annals of the American Academy of Political and Social Science* (AAPSS, Philadelphia), pp. 80–92.
Renton, D. (2001) (ed.), *Marx on Globalisation* (London).
Reus-Smit, C. (2001) 'Constructivism' in Burchill, S., Devetak, R., et al., *Theories of International Relations* (2nd edn., London).
Ricardo, D. (1911) *The Principles of Political Economy and Taxation* (London).
Richardson, J.L. (1997) 'Contending Liberalisms – Past and Present', *European Journal of International Relations*, 3 (1) March.
Robinson, J. (1966) *The New Mercantilism* (Cambridge).
Rocker, Rudolph (1937; 1998) *Nationalism and Culture* (Montreal).
Rosenau, J.N. (1964) 'National Interest', in Sills, D.L. (ed.), *International Encyclopaedia of Social Sciences, Vol. II*, (New York), pp. 34–40.
Rosenau, J.N. (1969) 'Intervention as a Scientific Concept' in *The Journal of Conflict Resolution*, 13 (2).
Rosenau, J.N. (1980) *The Scientific Study of Foreign Policy* (rev. edn. London).
Rosecrance, R. (1986) *The Rise of the Trading State* (New York).
Rousseau, J.J., 'The Social Contract' in Barker, E. (ed.), *Social Contract: Essays by Locke, Hume, Rousseau* (New York).
Russett, B. (1993) *Grasping the Democratic Peace* (Princeton).
Scholte, J. Aart (2000) *Globalization* (London).
Smith, A. (1976) *An Inquiry Into The Nature And Causes Of The Wealth Of Nations* (Chicago).
Stern, G. (2000) *The Structure of International Society* (2nd edn. London).
Stiglitz, J. (2002) *Globalization and its Discontents* (London).
Strange, S. (1985) 'Protectionism and World Politics', *International Organisation*, 39 (2).
Strange, S. (1988) *States and Markets* (London).
Strange, S. (1991) 'New World Order: Conflict and Co-operation', *Marxism Today*, January.
Strange, S. (1996) *The Retreat of the State: the Diffusion of Power in the World Economy* (Cambridge).
Strange, S. (1998) *Mad Money: When Markets Outgrow Governments* (Michigan).
Swift, J. (2001) *Gulliver's Travels* (London).
The Age (Editorial), 17 September 1997.
The Australian (Comment), 25 June 1994.
Thucydides (1954; 1972) *History of the Peloponnesian War* (London).
Thurow, L. (1992) *Head to Head* (New York).
Tilly, C. (1992) *Coercion, Capital, and European States, AD 990–1992* (Cambridge, MA).
Treitschke, H. von B. (1916) *Politics* (London).

Tucker, R.W. (1952) 'Professor Morgenthau's Theory of Political *Realism*', *American Political Science Review*, 46 (4), March, pp. 214–24.

Tucker, R.W. (1971) *The Radical Left and American Foreign Policy* (Baltimore).

Vagts, A. (1934; 1966) 'Introduction', in Beard, C.A., *The Idea of National Interest* (Chicago).

Vincent, J. (1986) *Human Rights and International Relations* (Cambridge).

Viotti, P.R. & Kauppi, M.V. (1992) *International Relations Theory* (2nd edn. New York).

Vogler, C.N. (1985) *The Nation State: The Neglected Dimension Of Class* (Aldershot).

Walker, S.G. & McGowan, P. (1982) 'U.S. Foreign Economic Policy Formation: Neo-Marxist and Neo-Pluralist Perspectives', in Avery, W.P. & Rapkin, D.P. (eds), *America in a Changing World Economy* (New York).

Walter, A. (1996) 'Adam Smith and the Liberal Tradition in International Relations' in Clark, I. & Neumann, I.B. (eds), *Classical Theories of International Relations* (Basingstoke).

Waltz, K.N. (1959) *Man, the State and War* (Columbia).

Waltz, K.N. (1979) *Theory of International Politics* (New York).

Waltz, K.N. (1990) 'Realist Thought and NeoRealist Theory', *Journal of International Affairs*, 44, pp. 21–37.

Waltz, K. (1991) 'America as a Model for the World?', *PS: Political Science and Politics*, 24 (4).

Waltz, K.N. (2000) 'Globalization and American Power' in *The National Interest*, Spring.

Weiss, L. (1998) *The Myth of the Powerless State* (New York).

Weldes, J. (1996) 'Constructing National Interests', in *European Journal of International Relations*, 2/3, September, pp. 275–318.

Weldes, J. (1999) *Constructing National Interests: The United States and the Cuban Missile Crisis* (Minneapolis).

Wendt, A. (1994) 'Collective Identity Formation and the International State', *American Political Science Review*, 88 (2), pp. 384–95.

Wendt, A. (1999) *Social Theory of International Politics* (Cambridge).

Wendt, A.E. (2000) 'The Agent-Structure Problem in International Relations Theory' in Linklater, A. (ed.), *International Relations: Critical Concepts in Political Science: Volume II* (London).

Wendt, A.E. (2000a) 'Anarchy is what States make of it: the Social Construction of Power Politics' in Linklater, A. (ed.), *International Relations: Critical Concepts in Political Science: Volume II* (London).

Wheeler, N.J. (2000) *Saving Strangers* (Oxford).

Wheeler, N.J. & Dunne, T. (1996) 'Hedley Bull's Pluralism of the Intellect and Solidarism of the Will', *International Affairs*, 72, pp. 91–108.

Wheelwright, E. (1993) 'Free Trade?', in *Arena*, February/March.

Wight, M. (1996) 'Western Values in International Relations', in Butterfield, H. & Wight, M. (eds), *Diplomatic Investigations* (London).

Wight, M. (1986) *Power Politics* (Harmondsworth).

Wight, G. & Porter, B. (eds) (1991) *International Theory: The Three Traditions – Martin Wight* (London).

Williams, R. (1983) *Keywords* (London).

Wolff, J. (2002) *Why Read Marx Today?* (Oxford).

Zacher, M.W. & Matthew, R.A., 'Liberal International Theory: Common Threads, Divergent Strands', in Kegley Jr, C.W. (ed.), *Controversies in International Relations Theories* (New York).

Zinn, H. (1997) *The Zinn Reader* (New York).

Zinn, H. (1998) *The Twentieth Century: A People's History* (rev. edn., New York).

Index